The Long Road to Rwanda
Nigel Clayton

Copyright © Nigel Clayton t/as Meni Publishing and Binding/ Zuytdorp Press, 2006, 2008, 2020: Nigel Clayton asserts the moral right to be identified as the author and owner of this work.

All rights reserved. No part of this publication may be reproduced, stored in a retrieval system, or transmitted, in any form by any means, electronic, mechanical, photocopying, recording or otherwise; nor shall it be resold, hired out or otherwise circulated, without the prior permission of the copyright owner of this book/eBook.

The National Library of Australia [Original] Cataloguing-in-Publication:
Kelly, Simon. [pseudonym for Nigel Clayton]
The Long Road to Rwanda.
ISBN 978-0-9757409-7-2 (Book)
ISBN 978-0-9873913-3-9 (eBook)
1. Kelly, Simon, 1963- . 2. Australia. Army. Royal Australian Infantry Corps - History. 3. United Nations - Peacekeeping forces - Rwanda. 4. United Nations - Peacekeeping forces - Papua New Guinea. 5. Soldiers - Australia - Biography. I. Australia. Army. Royal Australian Infantry Corps. II. United Nations. III. Title.
355.0092

BISAC Codes:
HIS037030 HISTORY / Modern / General
POL061000 POLITICAL SCIENCE / Genocide & War Crimes
HIS004000 HISTORY / Australia & New Zealand

The Role of Infantry

To seek out and close with the enemy;
To kill or capture him;
To seize and hold ground;
To repel attack by day and night;
Regardless of season, weather, or terrain.

Citation

Do you know what death is?
Do you know what it smells like?

Epic Poems:
Kibeho: An Epic Poem
Afghan - Song of the Desert
Orcinus Orca - Song of the Ocean
Hollandia Nova - Song of the Coast
Song of the Templar

Novels:
Dreamtime: An Aboriginal Odyssey
Templar, Assassination, Trial & Torture

About the Author

Nigel joined the Australian Army in 1980 at age 17yrs and two months, and on completion of training at Kapooka was whisked away to the School of Infantry, Singleton, New South Wales, Australia.

He served in the Infantry until injury forced a medical discharge upon him in 1996, after having served in Southeast Asia, 1982; PNG (with the AATPT), in 1990: during the Bougainville Crisis; and in Rwanda, 1995: known world-wide for the Kibeho Massacre which occurred on April 22nd of that year.

Serving in PNG was a major highlight within his career, more so than the service in Rwanda. He hopes that reading this book will indicate to you why that is.

He was married in 1999 and has two children.

Prologue

December 1980

I joined the Australian Army on 10th December, 1980, just 9½ weeks after celebrating my 17th birthday; still wet behind the ears, but out of diapers. From the recruitment office in Melbourne around thirty of us 'raw recruits' stepped onto a coach and headed for Kapooka in New South Wales. It was here that three months of basic training was to be endured.

Although the training was a shock to some who'd just signed their name to that dreaded, dotted line, nothing much can be reported upon in regards to our stay. Oh; there was this one guy who bumped his head and couldn't get up in the morning: He was medically discharged after just three day's service, suffering headaches. But Kapooka in general was the same, day in and day out; day after day of lectures and evenings filled with 'homework'.

It doesn't leave much for the imagination to reflect upon, in any real measure, when compared to this story as a whole. Training at Kapooka is 'basic training', not infantry training, and that is the premise of this book.

At the conclusion of training at Kapooka we were all classified as being 'basic-trained', and carried with us, to our new postings, the newly-earned rank of Private: being trained at the basic level for acceptance into the Infantry Corps. It can be truly said that each and every one of us had a 'basic' understanding of Infantry skills [skills which could be easily forgotten if pursuing a career as a cook, storeman, or one of the other, many careers made available to you] where the general 'Role of the Infantry' was heard, but never came into full fruition.

Both, best shot, and 'A' grade shot, were awarded to me for shooting ability at Kapooka, my only real, substantial achievement whilst there.

And so, to cut the long story short, and being of no real importance to me, from a platoon of 35 at Kapooka, 13 of us were assigned a posting to the RAINF; our 'call to duty', if you'd like to call it that. For me it was a matter of not being accepted into the corps of my

Nigel B.J. Clayton

preference [catering], so what choice did I have? I ended up requesting the transfer to 'grunts' simply so I wouldn't have to go and work out of a Q-store for the next 20 years. Oh; if you're wondering why I initially chose catering then the answer is simple enough; I wanted my 20 year service to end with my being able to enter the civilian workforce with good standing and maybe the option of opening a restaurant of my own.

So grateful I am for the way the future turned out.

I can still recall our arrival at the School of Infantry, located on the outskirts of Singleton, NSW. The obstacle course was the first thing we saw as we approached the rear gate, and entered into what appeared to be nothing less than hostile territory; we could all feel the dreaded fear of the place creeping up our backs. I think the guy next to me shat his pants when he saw the length of the obstacle course: either that or he forgot to clean his teeth that morning.

I won't give any details as to my stay in Singleton as I was eventually posted there as an instructor in 1990 for a period of three years, and I have plenty to say on that a little later on, so hang in there, you'll not miss out on anything. But you can get a real feel for army life at Singleton, more so than Kapooka; or so was my learned appreciation of the whole. But it's not until you arrive at your first major posting that your career can be truly considered as having 'taken off'. I was also an instructor in PNG for a period of six months, where I go into the training of civilian into 'basic trained' private, and private into a reasonably, well-trained infantryman. There is more here, over the coming pages, to provide sufficient light on this subject matter, in particular for those interested in the basic training itself.

And so, here you have it. This is my story; my 15-year career in the Australian Infantry, after having experienced Kapooka and Singleton.

There is also a full glossary at the end of this book for those who may require it.

First Impressions

August 1981

The wooden buildings were growing mouldy, the odour of mouse droppings and rot rising to slap men in the face as the heat from the Brisbane sun gave willingly to a rising humidity. Boards and rafters creaked under the glimmering waves of heat that had now formed over the contours of the ground around. Two flies were then seen out of the corner of my eye, seemingly scrambling up the wall, sharing their opinions on the new soldier that was now walking back from the urinal. It was me; sure as sure can be; and even with the feeling of wetness in my pants, from not having performed the appropriate three shakes, I still felt content within. I was young but genuine, a boy of seventeen, many years short of manhood and maturity; and I was simply marvelled by all of these new experiences so far.

There was also a lot of experience around me, men who'd endured many years of military life; and to think that I was just beginning my long road towards professional service to my country.

Enoggera Barracks was always under the hammer of perpetual change, in particular when it concerned the conditions of accommodation. Accommodation was constantly being updated and changed for the better, and the army was always seen to be trying to maintain a step in the right direction – seemingly concerned with 'keeping in stride' with the growing standards of society. It was also very true that the conditions changed vastly from one barracks to the next; the Bronx of Townsville, to the swag style of living-in-quarters at Campbell Barracks, WA.

Although most living-in members of the company were quite comfortable with their new accommodation, living-out members of the platoon had to be satisfied with what they could be provided in regards to 'private space' whilst on duty: a place to store their gear, somewhere to rest during lunch, an area in which to change after PT, or to prepare for weeklong trips into the bush. In fact, there was little facility available to persons that decided to live out-of-barracks, whether they were single or married. In most cases the latter were situated next door to the platoon and company offices; steel lockers in the shower block, nowhere to run and hide when the platoon sergeant came a-hunting for soldiers, placing individuals caught onto a never-ending list of work parties and other meaningless tasks or duties.

It was here that I, the newest of soldiers, was to meet with my platoon commander for the very first time, the steps creaking beneath me as I commenced the short march to the 'fresh-out-of-Duntroon' officer's office.

Here I waited, outside of the platoon commander's door, standing at attention, waiting patiently for my march into position, to the front of the Boss' desk.

This was to be my first meeting with the officer and my eyes didn't stray for a moment as I was marched into place, just three feet from the edge of his desk.

The platoon sergeant gave the orders: 'Quiiiiick march! Right wheel; left wheel; halt! Lefffft tah!' each of the executive commands given with that crisp, slap of precision, except where they were drawn out – it was all done for good reason, I suppose. When I was at Kapooka I thought that all sergeants had a lisp, and that having a speech impediment was a prerequisite for promotion. I guess the other soldiers at Kapooka felt the same as me, too, because they always looked so defeated and sad with these types of prospects facing us in the future.

The desk must have been a Boer War antique, many years separating the young blood of the platoon commander and the face of the office furniture. Its surface was riddle, the officer's workspace giving off a look of 'I-need-my-retirement-now'. It was a silent cry for retirement that was never heard, not even by the flies that walked the wall.

I now stood face-to-face with my new platoon commander; he was sitting confidently and silently behind his desk, his refuge, his place of work and hiding. I peered down at the reports that had been written on me, the new march-in. There was a mixture of remarks from my instructors at Kapooka and Singleton, a complete repertoire of my training results, training that I had endured during my struggle to become an infantryman.

I looked down, my name being spoken with a slather of bitterness: 'Private Clayton.'

'Yes, sir.' I was nervous, but steady; who wouldn't be nervous. I wasn't yet 18 years of age, being told that I could go and drink myself stupid at the bar on barracks and in town, but still not old enough to be deployed into active service – this was my understanding, and very little effort was placed on trying to steer young men away from drinking: to abstain from alcohol, something the army should be more interested in, but not, to the detriment of many men.

My eyes quickly found a mark on the wall above and behind the officer's head; I concentrated my stare on this, but the pressure to look down was too much. I tempted fate then and looked down into the seated man's eyes, his hands playing hypnotically with a pen.

My career in the infantry had now well and truly commenced, with the jotting down of notes – either that or the officer was simply trying to look as though he knew what he was doing for the sake of gaining respect from his peers and subordinates.

'I've read through your reports and it appears that you've met with all of your test results to an average degree of competence, not excelling in any particular infantry skill; oh, except that you can run reasonably well.' This must have been his way of breaking-the-ice.

'Believe me, skills are extremely important here. We class this platoon as one of the best....' isn't that what they all say? I mean... come on... was this platoon really that good? I wanted to look down at my legs to see if one of them was being pulled.

He paused then, for just a second, seemingly thinking out his strategy with this newest young soldier (an old boy, not quite a man – and I would have put my hand up too, but for the fear that he'd think I was asking permission to go to the toilet). He was thinking of what to say next; his next comment; to save himself the embarrassment of saying the wrong thing, and at the wrong time; or maybe he had some breakfast still stuck in his tooth which he was concentrating on.

It seemed to preoccupy an officer's mind, this saving-of-face, no matter what its form. They always seemed to want to blame someone else for their mistakes, if able to get away with it – soldiers were good for that, if nothing else. But maybe this was also a show of discipline, his wish, and need, to make things clear, as well as precise. An officer wanted all those subordinate to him, to look up to him with respect, and this had to be earned. He was a hero to his mother, but a chimp in the eyes of most of his men; and to his girlfriend... a sex toy with rank. But I must be fair in admitting that 40% of all of the officers encountered during my military career were extremely good soldiers; and in all respects; though the gene difference between man and ape –

so I am led to believe – was quite miniscule in real terms. But maybe I was being unjustly harsh, for it was hard, even for an NCO, to give commands to his men, and at the same time be their mate. I would remember this; always savour command over friendship, for lives had been lost at the pittance of familiarity.

And what of the reports; surely they couldn't be that bad. Expectations were always high, and had to be, in order to maintain professionalism. But this was my first day in the battalion, home of all manner of man; the drinker, gambler, profiteer, and lawbreaker; the mechanic, butcher, builder, and miner; professional shooter, rehabilitated drug addict, and many-a-score more. All of society's troubles and aspirations thrown together, each uniting for a common purpose and goal: To train for war, or war-like operations... how naive I was; but such naivety would become reality.

Some of the platoon sergeant's, and a few of the section commanders throughout the battalion, had seen service in Vietnam; and some private soldiers, too. This was the 8/9th Battalion, of the Royal Australian Regiment, Brisbane's burden and pride; but lest we forget our sisters, those in dresses; 6RAR: I was always advised that politics in the military were important, and the name calling was by way of the competitive spirit within us all; I can only hope that such an explanation will satisfy the cronies in the buildings across from us. They thought they were so good, just because they jumped out of aeroplanes. I jumped once, when I saw an old lady outside her house dressed in a nightie, but I didn't think it was worth bragging about.

The platoon commander continued: 'I won't put up with anything but a one-hundred percent effort, one-hundred-percent of the time. I'll get you to fill out some forms later on today, just your personal particulars – for my records. Do you have a will-and-testament lodged?'

'Yes, sir,' short and sweet. I think I saw him smile; he must have been impressed with my answer.

'Good.' The conversation continued for a short time before I was marched out of the office and sent on my merry way to mingle with other members of the platoon. It was here that a story rose out of the ashes in direct answer to a question asked by me. Small holes in the rear wall of the living-out member's quarters, the outside sunlight easily penetrating the thin shell of the wall; what were they; how did they get there?

Private Robert Crisp released a short muffled laugh. 'A few years back... a section commander was giving a lesson on the set-up and firing of the claymore mine. He thought it was inert so set it up for demonstration in firing. When he hit the tit, it blew up. Caused a few injuries, too. It apparently blew his legs off,' and he laughed again.

If you've seen the effects of an M18A1 being detonated then it would be easy to dismiss the claim, but at the time there was no one around to assume that the story was anything else but matter-of-fact, and it was told many times over the years. Was this to mean we were all fools, and easily misled? Nowadays it's simply one of those stories that gets you thinking; something that someone has told someone else in the hope of seeming more important than they actually are, like an officer walking around with a smile on his face, as though he's just received a compliment from the CO, when the truth of the matter is, he's just figured out how to undo the fly in his pants. Nevertheless, their sense of humour was indescribable, but seeing the hundreds of holes in the wall certainly put an eerie truth to the story.

I could only wonder: If I were in such a situation and blown up by a claymore; would I procure a laugh, or a first-aid dressing?

Bully-at-Large

September 1981

You beauty... work parties and duties week; what more could one ask for from the Australian Army... any army for that matter? Bashing dixies, washing cups, and scrubbing those thick-skinned pots and pans... the ones with inch thick crud burnt on the inside, courtesy of the cook: that was catering for you; cooking meals fit for a king, and then coming into work and burning everything in sight to feed the soldiers' appetites. There's nothing better than early mornings, late nights, and that fresh smell of leftovers from the bins full of trough food; fit for pigs at the local hobby farm and the Officers Mess. But I never met a cook I never liked, until he cooked a meal. So glad I never became one.

A 15-hour shift in the kitchen, cleaning up after two battalions of pig-eating grunts wasn't without its enjoyment and friendly chatter... except where the uninvited came sneaking around.

How was it that a large-framed man (the term used with much restraint) of 25 years, could sneak up behind a boy of 17 and slash – quite heavily, mind you – the blade of a knife across the back of his neck? I considered myself rather fortunate that the knife was blunt, but the fact that the knife had been held under a tap of hot-running water didn't do much for the shock of the incident; it felt as though I had indeed been slashed with a sharp-edged knife – and this incident was repeated three times during the course of the day. I guess he didn't like the food much and was trying for something with more flesh upon it.

Shame on me; shame, shame, shame. Was I to put up with this for the few hours I was in the mess hall, or stick up for myself and then be clobbered and bashed on my way back from the toilet block when the lights were out and the big thug was running loose around the barracks at night? In all truth the guy concerned for the immature behaviour had probably missed out on some casual sex and had decided to take out his aggravations on... me. Could I be summoned to court for saying his name? Pte Mason: If I knew then, what I know now, you'd be crying yourself to sleep with your thumb in your mouth; as it is you're probably bald, divorced, and have a bad case of... actually,

The Long Road to Rwanda

you're probably dead already.

It's hard to admit, and even disappointing to say, that I wasn't yet man enough to stand on my own two feet, and that the army had recruited this dim-witted individual. Yes, shameful I know; I was supposedly a professional soldier yet unable to defend myself. But the bully... it's hard to fathom the intellect of such a person, and even harder to accept that he'd managed to pass the army's psychological testing, in particular when his only comment was; 'tell anyone I did this and I'll kill you'. Maybe he'd been in the infantry too long. It wasn't like being at high school where I was known to turn around and clobber a guy back. Here on barracks you never knew what was lurking around the corners at night: At least after school, after returning a bully's anger, you could retreat to the safety of home; here on barracks all you had was a room to share with three other men, and the naked picture of a blonde taped on the ceiling above where you slept.

Yes indeed, there was a strange assortment of men that had signed the dotted line and most of them seemed to be living in the same building as me. Maybe it was time I changed from being a half-decent and respectable student to a rough-n-tough infantry soldier, and if any changes did take place then they weren't going to happen overnight; not unless I started concentrating on my situation and stopped looking at that damn picture on the ceiling above my bed.

Duties week, a fine collection of tasks that needed to be competed for, sold, bought, and auctioned off; and where there was a weekend's worth of duties to be gained from the guy in the room next door, there was money to be made; besides, what was I going to do on weekends. A few days in the kitchen, dodging knives, could have been turned into a hobby with me, except for the fact that the incident only occurred once. It's honest to say, and quite understandable too, that individuals would sell their weekend duties in order for them to get away to the Gold Coast for a few days and nights of uninterrupted, horizontal pleasure with the neighbourhood cat; and some of the guys even went out with ladies.

Guard duty was, I considered, one of the best duties to be gained: A few hours of rove-n-picket would be followed by rest and relaxation on the bunk bed, and in front of a small television; or for some, sitting on the dunny with a porno magazine... gee whiz; what about those sick bastards who stuck the pages together. But whoa, what's that I

Nigel B.J. Clayton

see; the bully walking from the toilet block with a grin on his face and a magazine in his hand, and on seeing me his grin was dislodged for quite some time. It seems that my intuition was correct and he had been missing out on sharing something special with the opposite sex.

Water Discipline

October 1981

I soon found myself on my first ever exercise, amongst the drying contours of the Shoalwater Bay Training Area. The bush trip was similar to most but with the added privilege of paying homage to the northern battalions; 1RAR and 2/4RAR. We were to act as the infiltrating enemy force, known quite simplistically as the Musorians, a fictitious enemy to the northern regions of Australia, an enemy that was forever invading this great country of ours. And for all of the high-school drop-outs out there, the name Musorian can be more readily translated into any of the following: Indonesians, Asians, Russian, Koreans... you get the picture. An American marine amphibious unit was also present during the four-week long exercise. This unit was withdrawn early on in the tactical exercise of 'engaging the enemy at time of war' for deployment on a much more realistic scale; in order for them to clash in arms with some very real and far away foreign and very hostile enemy. It didn't really matter much to the Yanks where it was in the world; so long as the enemy wore a turban on their head they were happy to shoot them.

    The evacuation process certainly gave way to a lot of daydreaming as Australian diggers delved upon the move, feeling a little bit left out of the picture. The natural instinct was for an individual to prove himself in front of a live enemy, rather than employ himself in the shooting of blank ammunition at friendly troops; some of whom wore familiar faces. We had all enlisted by employing our freedom-of-choice; I was here because I wanted to be here, not because mummy told me to get a job. And it might seem like a strange thing to say, but most of us could see how fulfilment might be received by being committed into the arena of conflict.

    These northern battalions were known as the ODF, a force to supposedly reckon with, but on closer inspection seemed no different than members of the 8/9th Battalion. I considered the roles of each of the battalions, Townsville compared to Brisbane. 8/9RAR was apparently trained in all aspects of desert warfare, beach assaults, urban warfare, and brandished with the responsibility of 'training battalion'; the ODF were jungle fighters, patrolling through the scrub with their knuckles scraping across the ground, and at the same time scratching at their heads and armpits looking for ticks.

Not a single one of these aspects of warfare ever appeared to be taken into our framework of training to any great degree, but the future would bear some fruit and produce experiences in regards to one of them in particular.

But how true was the role of those in the ODF?

I heard a story once that mentioned that the jungle of Tully was visited no more than once a year by any individual company of soldiers from Townsville. Of course, there were always individuals that escaped its clutches – or was it laziness on part of the soldier's lack in spirit, where an over-zest effort was made, on that individual's part, to keep from exercises within that area of Australia? It was always raining up there. Maybe some guys didn't like taking long showers, and Tully was like one big shower head following you around wherever you went; it just couldn't be turned off.

Training must be conducted in order to maintain discipline and the ever-changing circle of knowledge. Call me crazy if you will, but I rather liked it in Tully, though a few bitches of complaint did escape me on the odd occasion – I even once went out of my way and volunteered myself for a trip in order to get a posting to another rifle company in 1994: A little more on that, much later on.

I compared the operations as they stood, all of the cross training and obvious broad skills that were to be learnt; but I had a different task to undertake at present. The enemy force was approaching our Musorian company position. Here the northern battalions advanced, set out in assault formation, ready to inflict as many casualties as possible upon us, a superimposed firing of shells from artillery and mortar creating a dent in our defences. DS moved around the perimeter throwing grenade simulators on the ground. They made a big BANG, but I wasn't scared; not until one idiot accidentally tossed a grenade in my pit.

The soldiers from 1RAR then came into view.

We watched in all eagerness, the will to win overspilling all of our senses, so that nothing really mattered, so long as we performed our job to the best of our ability; or was I speaking for the minority? We carried out fire control orders as they were flung in all directions, a verbal assault of commands from section commanders and platoon sergeants alike, whilst platoon commanders sat back in their pits with that crazy smile painted on their faces.

We fired our French-made blank ammunition as indicated, into the closing ranks of the approaching foe. I paid more attention now – what a rabble; but what did I know? This was my first ever exercise – of a real definition – for those exercises conducted in singleton were lucky to be a week in duration; this four-week stint in the bush however, was to be my first of many.

I heard the section commander give another fire control order and as I turned around for confirmation I saw the head of the platoon commander, the whites of his teeth seen through his lips as he smiled. I turned again and commenced firing.

I paid more attention now at what was going on to my front as several soldiers closed in on my position, almost close enough to see the white of their eyes. Closer still, unshaven. And then they were upon me, fighting through on their guts, gasping at the air as they fought from fighting bay to fighting bay. They were crawling forward on their guts, throwing themselves from shell scrape to shell scrape in semblance to what you'd see in any war movie; but this was no game, this was 'training for war'. I saw another soldier and thought that he was doing very well with his 'running-about', and then I realized that he'd landed on an ant nest and had one biting him on the scrotum. They went through all the actions as taught, bayoneting the enemy as they pushed on through to the depth pits of our Musorian defensive position.

Finally it was over, the assault had finally come to an end and now a reorganisation of troops on the ground was taken into hand, and the poor soldier that had been bitten on the scrotum had his pants around his ankles, and the platoon sergeant felt a little awkward as he knelt there before the private's private.

Platoon commanders, and section commanders alike then blast out orders over broken gasps and wind-cracked lips.

The force from the north was soon secure on the ground and were told by the platoon commander to form a harbour (a defensive position of troops set up in a circular pattern), set up similar to that of the face of a clock. Some officers even looked at their watches when they did this, so that they wouldn't get it wrong, looking at their watches and then at the ground, telling section commanders to 'put your machine gun over there, Corporal,' and then smile at him as his order was being carried out.

The centre of the clock was the HQ element, and the hours of the clock were the two man pits, weapons pointing outwards in all round defence. The section commander along with his scout acted as the depth for each individual section. There were three sections to a platoon, three platoons to a company, and so on and so forth: it was fortunate that the highest ranking soldiers in this man's army could count to three, or we'd all be in strife. The harbour position looked vastly like a cordon designed with one simple task in mind, to provide all round defence in respect to the ground you were currently occupying at the time. It was now that I turned my head to look at the soldier beside me. His uniform stank and it was stained beyond belief. His shirt and trousers were torn in some places, fraying here and there. The man from 1RAR turned his head slowly to face me, relieving his observation from possible enemy counter attack for just a moment, the four days of growth upon his face choking under the layers of camouflage cream.

He looked into my eyes as though to ponder something with a half-smile cascading across his face, seemingly content with the job he was doing, capable of continuing on forever and a day. His mouth opened and spittle ran down his chin. He wiped it away with embarrassment, 'G'day mate, how ya gowen?'

'Good, thanks mate, yourself?'

'Ah yeah, not bad. Hey, ya aint got any spare wata on ya, have ya? Just a mouthful, while me CSM aint watchen.'

I pulled my water bottle from its cover, 'Sure.' I could only hope that he wouldn't get any spit in it.

'We aint aloud ta touch ours unless we get told we can. Prob'ly get charged if we did. Bloody wata dis'pline. Sux it does; bloody sux.'

Now, he was more-than-likely telling the truth, and then again, he could have been a compulsive liar and just after my water, but character of body can usually be determined. I'd heard of this so-called 'water discipline,' just hadn't yet experienced it - maybe due to the fact that I always tried to carry plenty. I guess it was simply another way of saying that the resupply situation sucked big-time and due to the inability of the supporting units to provide an adequate water supply, the troops on the ground could not be sufficiently supplied with their daily ration. It was far easier to call it 'water discipline' and be done with it.

It might be interesting to note that within a few years 'water discipline' was scrounged upon by the medical fraternity within the military; it would seem that the army was crumbling under the pressures of society and its standards, much the same as the change in accommodation back in barracks was now becoming fit to live in and quite tolerable. It looked like the resupply of grunts on the ground had to be improved upon, and there was no choice in the matter. There was, of course, only one thing wrong with that. We now had to carry more water in order to maintain a good supply. The overall weight of my back pack now ranged anything from 30 to 40 kilograms in weight – all the bloody time: which was truly amazing considering how small the 1980's Aust pack was.

Orders

October 1981

Bush; I loved being in the bush.

I was lying down with my rifle extended, the barrel pointing outwards and away from the perimeter. I was maintaining watch from a sentry post which had been positioned by the section commander under direction of the boss – I wanted to call the boss Smiley behind his back but didn't know how the others would take it.

I couldn't see the remainder of the platoon that sat in the perimeter of security just 30 metres to my rear and had no friendly covering fire to speak of – if I was to withdraw from my post due to being in contact with the enemy. What I did have was a short covered route that took me back to the section machine gun and a smoke grenade which I needed to throw in order to help conceal my move from enemy view. I knew, too, that the smoke grenade – by all realistic terms – only offered concealment from view and not from hostile fire, but the smoke grenades did come in a lot of pretty colours. Many other thoughts travelled my mind as I slipped into a daydream.

I was only going to be here 30 minutes, after which I'd be relieved and afforded the time for something to eat, prior to the platoon fighting patrol being resumed. It had been a hard morning so far and we still had a long way to go. This was the part where we had to 'seek out and close with the enemy': That was my favourite bit.

Orders for the patrol the day before, as given by the platoon commander, had been quite precise and covered all aspects for the smooth running of our fighting patrol; although breaking-wind and nose-picking was genuinely considered as a free-for-all and not covered in orders: Unless moving into an ambush site; when that happened you had to do silent farts, just like the Queen of England does in her palace.

Sitting through orders was a constant recurrence in the army, either in barracks or in the field, especially during IET at the School of Infantry. Here in the field we received at least two sets of orders a day, but whilst in camp little more than an update to keep us informed of up and coming events. This however, wasn't the problem, the sheer length of orders was, especially if you were on barracks and it was nearly time for morning tea. It usually came down to what was referred to as 'time and space', and rarely was enough time ever provided for decent orders to be given, especially when the canteen was selling hot pies with sauce.

Now, I didn't realise it, but I was slipping further into a world of my own, thinking of all the things I wanted to do on returning to camp. I commenced to play with the trigger guard of my rifle and watched an ant as it made its way across the barrel and down towards the dust cover of the SLR I held in my hands. I then commenced to do some house cleaning and removed some dust from my nose.

Suddenly a sound caught my ear. I looked up. There to my front were two motorbikes as they made their approach from the T-junction and down to the closed gate just 20 metres to my slight right.

I pulled myself down for better cover but maintained good visual on the pair. Who were they? Were they the enemy? What should I do? I pulled my finger from my nose.

Five metres separated the two men who sat upon revving engines, the visors to their helmets pulled down over their faces. The front man came to a stop, side-on to the gate. He reached out to lift the latch. The man to the rear, what was he doing? Looking around, searching the ground around him and covering his mate. No weapons were visible. Maybe they were special soldiers and carried guns in their pockets.

Another sound was then heard, this time to my rear. I turned to see what it was, and that was all it took. The man on the second bike had seen movement. As though linked by an intercom they both turned in synchronisation, speeding off from whence they came, nothing more than a cloud of dust left to billow out from beneath their tires.

'Shoot! Shoot!' The platoon commander had arrived to see for himself what the noise was, and being obviously too scared to dirty his own rifle by shooting at those on the bikes, wanted me to act on his behalf.

'What, sir?'

'Shoot them, now! Quickly, before they get away!' I could see that he was anxious and excited because he wasn't smiling any more.

I looked up; my weapon finally lifted into my shoulder in readiness to fire. Too late, they'd vanished. Nothing but dust could be seen.

'What the hell do you think you're doing, Private Clayton?' he yelled sarcastically. And what are you doing, sir, trying to see if you can break the record for weapons cleanliness in the field? 'I didn't know they were the enemy, sir,' was all I could say.

'You're a bloody idiot! You were told earlier.'

I felt like saying, 'I wasn't really picking my nose,' but thought the comment would clarify his accusation against me as being a 'bloody idiot'.

'Sentry orders said I should shoot on seeing the enemy, sir, but nothing was said about bikes.'

'You're a bloody fool. They were probably SAS.' Wow; they were special soldiers: I was right. They must have had deep pockets to keep their weapons in.

My Platoon Commander turned to depart. 'I told you this morning, no friendly forces exist within our area of operations.... Blah, blah, blah, blah, blah.'

So he was right and I was wrong. I'd have to learn to pay more attention to orders and not pick dust from my nose during picket, but it was no good crying over spilt milk. What if I'd shot and killed a friendly? But what if the enemy I didn't shoot at, later on, shot another member of the platoon? What if the platoon commander was to vanish in a puff of smoke; not that pretty smoke from the smoke grenades, but any old smoke? Maybe next time I'd have better sense, and better luck.

And as for the officer in question not firing his weapon, I must admit that his experience did out-weigh mine, and I was a private soldier of extremely little experience. Orders were an intricate part of the 'rules of engagement', and always would be, whether they were right or wrong.

Gun Picket

October 1981

I was growing keener – slowly but surely – and most of that which we carried out during the exercise was more-or-less considered as 'on-the-job-training'. Many of my previous mistakes had paved the way to a fuller understanding on how peacetime operations were carried out – or so I thought.

The older soldiers – meaning those with vaster experience than me; and weren't hard to find – had pointed out that 'you always learnt', and this was regardless of how many years of experience you had gained through bush trips, simple tasks on barracks, and training exercises in general. One soldier once said to me, 'it's not until you've had as many morning teas as me that you realise you've got a few years under your belt.' I'd take that on board; I never knew if it would come in handy, but you never know about these things... and I did like having morning tea, so I guess I was halfway there already.

Sleep in the bush was a wondrous thing to have but it was so often very hard to get, especially when you were sexually aroused and lying there with your eyes wide open. I recall one night in particular. The night was pleasantly warm due to the vastly overcast skies above. A light breeze was blowing and visibility was none existent. I'd just crawled into my sleeping bag and my sense of being slowly drifted away and I fell asleep, quite content in my sleeping bag and oblivious to the world around me. It was some time later, whilst lost in a blissful dream, where a belly-dancer was performing tricks before me, stroking my leg sexually with a feather duster, that I suddenly found myself rudely woken up. It was time for picket, being brought evident by the invisible man that stood over me, giving out a little kick to my leg, 'Get up, it's your picket.' My eyes opened to nothing but the black of night. All I could manage at the time was a short, 'Huh, what?' My whisper was heard and accompanied by a hungry yawn. 'It's your bloody picket. Get up.'

I fumbled for my watch and found the button for the little light within, a pixie at my beck and call – at least, that was what it was until I woke properly. The time was confirmed. I squinted again at the face of the watch, and then scratched my head as though searching for a clearer understanding as to what was going on. What the hell happened to the belly dancer? My sweet dream had been interrupted precisely at the wrong instant. Damn it! Experiences with feather dusters didn't come along very often.

It was 2330hrs. 'Huh, yeah. Okay. I'm coming.' I got to my feet and searched for my webbing.

It didn't take long before I heard: 'Come on, mate, what the hell you doing? I want to hit the farter.'

'I'm looking for my… ah, found it.' I fondled around, fighting to gain access to the harness of my webbing.

Time passed slowly for the waiting man, each second assuming the role of ten; 'What the hell are you doing?'

'I can't get my webbing on.'

'Shit. Give it here.' It was twisted awkwardly but logically, it always was. 'Here, get up and put the bloody thing on will ya? I want to get some shut-eye.'

I was finally ready. I picked up my rifle and followed the guy towards the machine gun by holding on tight to his harness, following carefully, staggering with a yawn. I still had no idea who this guy was, the cranky son-of-a-bitch. Some bloody mate, waking me up for a stupid picket.

But how much further from the truth could I be. Not one man in existence, within the ranks of the infantry, enjoyed doing picket. Not one man enjoyed doing 10 seconds more picket then he had to, let alone several minutes. Maybe, if luck were with us, an insomniac would be inducted into the section; better still, two.

I was soon at the gun pit; the man – now to my rear – positioned me safely and silently. Then came his whispered brief: 'Sit there. The guns in front of your right knee.'

'Thanks, mate.'

'Yeah; right,' and then he mumbled something to himself and disappeared back to his sleeping bag.

The surrounding blackness was as dark as I ever thought possible. I thrust my hand up in front of my face and waved it spastically. Nope; I couldn't see it. I then turned my head to the right. 'Hey; pssssst. You there?' The other section member on the gun. He was here – somewhere. 'Pssssst, you there?'

'Yeah.'

The Long Road to Rwanda

'Who is it?'
'It's Bob.'
'Where's the gun?' My hand was grabbed by the invisible individual and placed onto the butt of the machine gun. 'Ah, right.'
'The picket list and torch are on the left of the butt.' I was extremely glad that he said 'the butt' and not 'my butt'; I didn't fancy reaching over in his direction and touching his backside.
'Got it.' I placed my hand back into my lap, sitting; thinking. Only two hours and fifty minutes to go. A short picket compared to the night before. I could only wonder if that belly dancer would be waiting for me when I returned to my sleeping bag.

Bob then said to me: 'It's your turn to sleep.' The dead man on the gun, a style of picket used by 'very' few, and only experienced three times by myself during my entire 16- year career. One man slept at the gun whilst the other remained awake, and the following episode illustrates exactly why 'dead man on the gun' should never be used.

I had a smile on my face. The dancer was closer than I thought. 'Thanks, Bob.' How nice of him. He was a true friend; even if I couldn't remember what he looked like.

'I'll wake you when it's time.' I wish he wouldn't, but that's the way the cookie crumbles I suppose.

I slipped into slumber, oblivious to the passing minutes.

I awoke suddenly, a shudder flying through me, pins and needles attacking my arm. I quickly established the time by pressing the light on my watch – yes; the pixie was still there.

I was an hour overdue for the waking of my relief. I searched for the picket list and torch, and after getting low onto my stomach I scoured the paper for the name of the man I was supposed to have woken an hour before. The smallest bead of red light was emitted between my fingers. 'Hey, where's Banks sleep?' I asked Bob. There was no answer. The man to my right, was he awake, or asleep? 'Pssssst. You there?' But it wouldn't have been Bob; would it? Not on a staggered picket.

'What?'
'I'm supposed to wake Banks; an hour ago. How come you didn't wake me up?'
'Don't worry about it,' came the muffled voice.
He must have been asleep, too; 'I don't know where he sleeps.' This was confusion at its best, for this night's picket had been split into two,

25

the platoon manning just two guns as opposed to manning three. There were men in this platoon I simply didn't know; the other 25 were crazy bastards.

'Rifle pit, twenty metres over that way.'

Great help. Not only couldn't I see my hand in front of my face, but I didn't know where 'over that way' was. 'I don't know where his pit is,' I said.

I then realised that the man to my side wasn't Bob at all. He stood up and grabbed me by the harness, lifting me to my feet. I was turned into the general direction. 'Go that way for twenty metres. If you can't find him... come back and I'll fetch him for you.' Now that sounded fair enough. Twenty metres – twenty-four paces. 'If you hit the fence then you've gone too far.'

Hmm; sounded like good advice to me. 'Thanks mate.' I stepped off slowly, counting each step carefully as I maintained my direction. I knew how to count to twenty-four, and it didn't take long. Within less than half a minute I'd gone the distance.

I searched around on my knees. No one was found. I searched and searched again. No; nothing.

Several minutes passed before a thought entered my mind. I'd not gone far enough. A further twenty paces in the dark should compensate me for the short strides I was obviously taking. I counted again, accurate and sure. Coming to a stop I searched again. No relief was found.

I stood there, bewildered. What should I do? Go back to the gun, that's it. The other bloke can go look for the relief. I set off again after pivoting myself 180 degrees, wandering off towards the machine gun.

I counted carefully, but how many paces should I go? 'Pssssst, you there?' No answer. Around 30-odd guys lying in the bush around me, and not only couldn't I find any of them, but none heard my pleas for help – I found that somewhat hard to believe. I bet if I pulled out my penis and had a piss I'd hit someone square on the head. 'Hey mate. You there?' My whispers for aid continued to go unanswered. I'd obviously gone off in the wrong direction. I'd have to go back towards the rifle pit and keep going till I hit the fence, then I'd be right, I'd be safe, I'd know where I was: I'd be at the fence.

I continued searching, and wouldn't you know it; a full two hours had passed and the sun had commenced its climb above the horizon, and still I couldn't find anyone. I sat motionless; defeated. As soon as it was light enough I'd find my way back. It couldn't be far to the platoon position.

Eight hundred metres later and I found the perimeter. The platoon sergeant was going to go ballistic over this. He didn't like losing soldiers, unless they had crabs crawling around inside their crotch or something like that. Never again would I make the same mistake. Next time I'd be right on the ball.

Lost Yanks

October 1981

During the American soldiers' withdrawal of the Kangaroo exercise a few stories arose to dominate the conversations during lax periods of defensive routine. One such conversation was in the case of our standing patrol which was brought from its stand-down status to 100% stand-to, due to what was initially deemed to have been enemy movement to our front; but in actual fact it wasn't the enemy at all; it was one of those guys who didn't like people that wore turbans on their head.

I was on picket at the machine gun, lying with my ever-watchful eye searching for any possible sign of enemy incursion or movement, ears trying to listen to what lie beyond the range of the songs given off by the owls of the night. In the distance an APC engine could be heard to thunder to life, and experience so far had taught me that any other APC in the vicinity (of the same call sign) would also have turned over their engine; a simultaneous action. This was done to help conceal the true numbers from enemy ears, a practice of tactics that always seemed to be observed.

The night was still young when I caught a glimpse of something to my front, and as I stared I realised that it was a small hand-held torch flickering in the distance. Every soldier of the section was quick to jump into the comfort of his pit when woken, each with his rifle held steadily in his hand. The light at present was advancing slowly, definitely a torch and about 40 metres off down the spur to our direct front. One guy thought it might be the 'min min light', but he was wrong. Everyone watched in bewilderment, and until the voices reached our ears we had no idea who it was.

The accents were unmistakable. Three yanks were to our front and gabbling on to their heart's desire; something about boon-twangs and cod-wallops, high-fives and weeding the garden; or something like that. They were slightly muffled due to the distance, but became ever more distinct as the ground between them and our standing patrol diminished.

Our section commander jumped from his pit and approached the

The Long Road to Rwanda

three men once they were just ten metres to the front of the standing patrol position. It scared the shit out of them. 'Hey, man; you scared the shit out of us,' said one of the yanks.

The night wasn't as dark as previous nights and so the basic shape of the Americans were seen reasonably clearly by us all, and I think one of them had dark glasses on, but I couldn't see properly. 'Damn, man; I can't see shit out here.'

All of them had their weapons slung and the commander of the group just stood there, blazing his torch over the contours of the map that he carried, 'Shit man, where'd you come from?' He was definitely more surprised to see our section commander than we were to see them.

'I'm Corporal Roberts. What's up?' asked the section commander of the man with the torch.

'Hell, man. We haven't got a clue where we are. This goddamn map's all stuffed up.'

Roberts went to his aid, eyeing the map and placing a steady finger to the map's surface. 'Just there, mate; right on that spur which slopes down to the North.'

'Ah shit. We're not supposed to be there. Goddamn.' He pondered the map for a brief second. 'We've got to get to this place right here,' he pointed, 'the road junction.'

Roberts held back his laughter. 'Just go back down this way and you can't go wrong.'

'Yeah, right. Thanks, man.' He turned and the group of three proceeded back down the way they'd come, map thrust up to his face every now and again until they disappeared out of sight and sound, the owls once again dominating the night after the fading of the last 'goddamn-this-map-man'.

Maybe he should have taken his dark glasses off.

Some stories were ludicrous, to say the least; like this next one:

The moon could be seen in its first quarter before becoming shrouded in a sheet of black menacing cloud. The soldier had just come from his stint on the machine gun and he was looking forward to a good night's sleep.

The cloud opened up and the rain started to fall, steadily at first. Lightning could be seen in the distance, followed shortly by thunder that out-weighed the option of remaining where he was. He didn't like sitting under trees in a lightning storm, and we were in the bush, surrounded by them.

Another yawn escaped his lips as he crawled from his sleeping bag, rolling it up quickly and placing it under his arm. The armoured personnel carrier to his rear looked so inviting right then. He thrust his pack under the closest tree and headed for the vehicle with his rifle in hand, looking around as he moved, ensuring he wouldn't be seen. He was a sly little bastard. No one was going to wake him up until the sun came up the next morning; he was set on that point; for the cloud was opening to a downpour that he wanted to avoid at all costs.

He crawled under the small clearance between the ground and the metal hulk of the APC, thinking solemnly how smart he was; after all, his hutchie had holes in it and a wet night just wouldn't do.

He was soon sound asleep, and the rain fell faster and harder, no relent in the storms growing fury to be seen over the coming hours. The widening pools grew and the ground drank as fast as it could, the soil around growing wet, becoming softer and softer as the minutes ticked by. The grounds finally gave slowly, the APC sinking with gradual motion.

The soldier woke, feeling the crushing pain, unable to scream out. He tried desperately to thrash and dig his way clear, like he was a windmill, or doing calisthenics. The rain fell and fell, the APC's tracks sank, the bottom of the vehicles monstrous hulk now met with that of the sodden ground; the yank was now entombed in a casket of mud and on the sun rising his body was discovered.

The nights were always dangerous, and this brings to mind another story of an American victim.

Night patrolling was no man's favourite, unless you were a stalker and liked wearing women's clothing.

Moving slowly and cautiously was the key to success in reconnaissance by night, but it was raining. Larry felt that he could afford to lift the pace slightly. It didn't matter any longer how much noise he made because the downpour hid the sound of his movement.

He maintained his vigil, patrolling his arcs as best he could; after all, he was the lead scout and he had the best eyes in the section: I bet he wasn't wearing dark glasses. Raindrops dripped from the brim of his hat, cold liquid ran the length of his back, and his feet began to feel the slosh of his soaked socks. He wasn't a happy-Larry. He continued though, paying little heed to the discomfort he suffered.

Some heavy scrub presented itself to his direct front. He fought with it, pushing through with regret as he tripped over a protruding root and fell to his death, down a 30- metre cliff face. And that's not funny, because it's true and really happened, and you should never poke fun at the dead; that's what my mum says.

And the stories just keep on coming, like a jack-in-the-box.

Stand-down had been passed from pit to pit. It was time for sleep. The rifleman moved towards his erected hutchie, and the sleeping bag which he had laid out before the sun had set. He was a smart man, smarter than the rest.

His webbing was removed and the rifle placed onto this. His bush hat was also placed down, over the body of his weapon; this would help keep moisture from attacking its metal skin. He knew about rust and was a good soldier.

He grinned to himself – no, he wasn't an officer – he was looking forward to a bit of shut-eye before he had to take his turn on picket at the machine gun. He placed the first of his legs deep into the instantly warming sleeping bag, followed shortly by the next, squeezing down deep and grabbing the zip between his finger and thumb.

All of a sudden a shocking pain hit his leg, again and again. He tried to scramble from the confines of his bag, the zipper reached for; the kicking of his legs, bit again and again, the pain, the zipper, the kicking. It was as if he was dancing, but with lots of pain involved.

He managed to get free, 14 snakebites to his legs. He peered down, just making out the scaly menace. He kicked out at it and was bit again. He gave chase after the escaping snake, heading off into the bush, shouts echoing around him: 'What was it? What's going on, man?' Deeper into the unknown he went, into the dying night, the escaping peril. The pain was unbearable now, attacking the heart and bringing a horrific contortion to his face. He was found later, dead, the terrible pain scribed over his facial expression; but you've got to ask yourself: Would dancing lessons have helped?

And the motto is: Mother Nature was neutral; kind one day and murderous the next.

Single Picket

October 1981

Kangaroo 81 was reaching its final stages when an order for a surveillance operation was passed on to our section 2IC and three other private soldiers of the section – including yours truly. I was looking forward to it because Surveillance usually meant that you had time to rest, and all this walking through the bush was making me tired.

Intelligence reports from previous patrols had been gathered and it was proposed that 2/4RAR were going to take advantage of the road that sat just five kilometres to our north. This was a possible route that could quite easily lead the enemy into a suspected FUP, in final preparation for the decimation of 8/9RAR's Musorian Defensive Position. Regardless of the facts that lead to this highly valued information, the CO at the time felt that all boundaries around the area of operations, especially those cut or paralleled by road, or dirt track surface, should be secured by way of eyes and ears – a combined series of listening and watching posts. He must have been a smart officer to think up all of that.

We set upon our task, clear in mind as to the mission parameters. Patrolling to a secure observation post took a little under two hours, by which time the sun had commenced its decline to a beautiful hue, before the final blackness of night took stage. It was almost like being on holiday.

It had been decided to conduct a single picket, 2.5 hours in duration for each individual. All four of our section lay down beside each other in preparation for the night's duty, in order of relief. I was first on picket.

The 2IC said to me: 'Nigel; when you wake me for picket, make sure I'm sitting up and wide-awake. I talk in my sleep sometimes, so just be sure I'm right before you go to sleep. Ask me a few questions or something, but make sure I'm sitting up; ok?'

'Yeah, sure. No problem.' Night routine had now commenced.

The minutes ticked by, all 150 of them, one by one, boring and solemn, and in particular, repetitious. What thoughts travel a soldier's

The Long Road to Rwanda

mind during such periods of solitude? I'll tell you: All thoughts; the more thoughts the better, for the more thoughts you experienced the faster time would pass you by; but also, the more thoughts, the less concentration on the task at hand. But I can't tell you every thought I had because some weren't very clean.

Only repeated sessions of picket could quench the ability for anyone to wander off into a deep sleep, a self-discipline that could never be thought of as being hard by anyone who didn't understand the job of the Infantryman. It was also a good idea to sometimes sit on a sharp rock.

The more pickets you did and the more the mind won into self-control, blocking out that which was unimportant, but remaining weary of any possible threat around. It was like driving a car down the road and suddenly realising that the car to your front was braking fast, so you do the same, saving yourself from smashing into its rear, though you're quite unaware as to the past three kilometres of journey which was now behind you; unless you're a pathetic bastard, and then you just crash. To be aware of all around you without realising it, in particular the sounds which require immediate attention; like a mortar bomb exploding deep in the distance of the night; what was the bearing to the sound? Several bearings, taken from several OPs could determine the approximate position of the possible mortar base plate position, by way of intersection. Was that a vehicle moving along the road six kilometres to the North? Which direction was it travelling? What type of vehicle was it? How many? Ah... most of the time we didn't give-a-shit. But tonight, all my senses were alert: Only the slack individuals are incapable of paying heed to his personal responsibilities; besides, I was starting to really like my job.

Some would laugh at the last paragraph; those who couldn't understand; those who were slack in discipline, morale and equity; but everyone had a job to do, even the grunt who spent weeks on end in the field. No shower, no compromise, no comforts of life or amenities; just the will power and patience to live like a pig in filth, and to do well at it. This was a personal devotion; to live like crap.

The picket was soon over for me. I leant over and shook the foot of the 2IC, LCPL Smyte. Shaking the foot, a tactic employed so that the waking man wouldn't jerk up, thrashing out with a clenched fist – which occurred on several occasions. 'Hey, your turn for picket,' I whispered.

'Huh. What?'
'Sshhh. Time for picket. Sit up.'
Smyte sat, eyes gradually opening to the night. 'What?'
'It's your picket.' I was somewhat concerned and looked hard at the waking man. He was an ugly bastard but I didn't care. All I wanted to do was go to sleep. 'You awake or what?'
'Yeah, yeah; I'm awake.'
'You sure?' his nose was huge.
'Yeah.' He turned and looked at me with the rubbing of his eyes. 'I'm fine. Go to sleep.' No further words were necessary. I lay down and drifted off to be met by a wonderful dream filled with naked women.

The morning broke; singing birds and the bright rays of the sun bringing all to consciousness. Smyte reached over and shook me by the foot. 'Hey, you fell asleep on picket, didn't you? You're a butt-ugly, idiot; you stupid stinking turd. You're a useless bastard.'

'You what? You're joking, right?' was my defensive response. How dare he say I fell asleep on picket or that I was useless.

'Shit.' Smyte brought his watch up to his face. 'Great, we're late. We've got to be back at the defensive position in less than an hour. You just couldn't stay awake, could you?'

'I woke you up, Corporal; just like you said.' Maybe I should have made him sing a song or recite a poem when I woke him up.

'Yeah, sure.'

I took the brunt of the accusation, and became concerned with the fact that I'd done what was asked, and missed out on 150 minutes of sleep, by doing a picket which had died in the hands of the more senior soldier, a senior soldier with rank on his shoulder and a head full of nothing but a cold word.

Oh well, what can you do? Everyone, regardless of rank, was exposed to making mistakes.

In New Zealand

March 1982

Robert Studd and I stood shivering in the fighting bay, the plummeting cold of New Zealand affecting us both.
    It was the comfort of the two-man tents erected within the perimeter behind us that was present in our minds, not the job of security. Comfort was a luxury beyond belief in the field and those simple pieces of fabric behind us were everything at the moment. The two man tents acted as a windbreak more than anything else, a shield against the petrifying wind chill factor.
    It was midnight in a landscape that consisted mostly of rolling plains and little else. If there was a tree in the area then it was marked on the map; and that was fair dinkum, no boasting about it. We were in the Lake Tekapo training area and in the past 24 hours had seen but a single tree. We missed seeing trees out bush. It puts mans' mind to rest knowing that he has a tree to piss against.
    I climbed from the confines of the gun pit to fetch my relief for picket, saying nothing to Robert. He was awake and knew the routine well.
    I headed off towards the low silhouette of a two-man tent; hard to see even from my present distance of just twenty metres, arms held in tight against my body for warmth, misty vapours of breath escaping the confines of my mouth as I breathed in and out like a choo choo train.
    I was soon at the entrance to the tent and kneeling down. I hobbled forward, under the flap and to the foot of my replacement. I grabbed his foot and shook it. 'Pssssst. Get up. Your picket.' The relief woke with a moan and I reversed out to sit and wait, holding my hands across my chest. I knew he was awake because I could hear him cussing and carrying on. He didn't like the army very much, and didn't like taking orders from officers, but what can you do? Officers love giving orders, even if they were stupid ones like, 'sit there, Private,' and you were already sitting; or, 'come here, soldier,' and you were already walking towards him. It made them feel superior. I guess that's why they invented saluting, so that they felt recognised.

Several minutes of waiting had passed when a shot suddenly rang out through the night, a contact on the perimeter had occurred.

The platoon reacted immediately, standing-to, and the section commander could be heard bellowing out for information, an echoing authority for those concerned to break the silence and give a target indication. And then Robert Studd suddenly found himself under verbal reprimand.

I ran over to the gun pit and knelt down beside it.

'But I thought it was Nigel coming back with the relief,' Robert explained to no avail. I think he was lying because he had that dumb-schmuck look on his face: I could see it quite clearly, because I was real close, and from the light given off by the moon; but I didn't want to get too close in case the section commander started swinging punches.

'You've got to be joking, Studd.' Corporal Matthews brought the weapon down from his shoulder and crouched on one knee beside the gun pit, a voice in the darkness giving indication as to the enemy's location. The enemy was indeed nearby. Suddenly a figure could be seen running off into the night. Corporal Matthews engaged the target with several rounds. 'What the bloody hell happened, Studd?'

Robert looked up from within the pit, to the crouched form of his section commander, no machine gun present. 'Well; Nigel went to get Greg for picket when I heard a noise to my front. I thought that Greg had got lost and was on his way back into the perimeter. I asked who it was. All he said was that I should give him the gun. I thought that he'd seen something.'

'So you gave him the machine gun?'

'Yeah.'

'You're an idiot, Studd! What ever happened to the challenging procedure and password?'

'I thought it was Greg.'

'Shut up! Here.' He thrust his weapon out for Robert. 'And watch your bloody front. The platoon commanders going to be real happy with this, I can tell you that for nothing.' He probably would be, too. We didn't have Smiley anymore and this new officer was always laughing, just like when you first lose your virginity.

The incident with the machine gun was never lived down. The section machine gun was returned five days later with the inscription 'First Blood' still scribed on the feed cover, a motto that the machine gunner had placed there four months earlier. It's too bad that the gun never lived up to its name.

Leopard Tanks

August 1982

Diamond Dollar was an exercise involving direct work with APCs and tanks, most of which was conducted using live ammunition. Numerous lessons were given to the battalion during the first six days of the exercise, lessons to familiarise us with tanks, familiarisation that was essential for the understanding of all fundamentals.

Much was learnt. Harbour drills, clearing defiles, giving target indications by tank telephone and radio, fire control orders, types of ammunition available to the 'beasts of war' and much, much more. We even had a safety brief and were told not to carry our weapons onto the tanks. One of our guys didn't listen properly and must have thought they said that you had to carry your weapons onto the tanks because when the tank commander turned the turret during a demonstration his SLR got crunched up and mangled. Gee, it was so funny. I'd never seen a corporal lose his boot up a soldier's arsehole before, but on that day we were all in for a real treat.

Safety officers made themselves easily recognisable by way of wearing white armbands and remaining 'clean skin' (not wearing any webbing). They were always present during the live fire serials of the exercise, the dawn assaults upon wooden figure-eleven targets being numerous in number and undertaking. They used to walk around with big sticks, white bandages attached to them, as though trying to look more important than the officers. I recall one assault in particular that was endured time and time again, until the CO was happy with its result.

The leopard tanks crept forward with the forward most assaulting troops of the battalion in line with the second road wheel – a purely safety aspect for the conduct of fire and movement with the vehicles. I could see safety officers hitting soldiers with their sticks, telling them to pull back a little. And then, as soon as we closed into 'effective firing' range of enemy bunkers and fighting bays – a position set up by the battalion only days before – a mass of fire was produced, tanks and soldiers letting rip.

The ground vibrated in tune with the thundering engines, the noise was incredible. Lying on the ground was like lying down on top of a vibrating mobile phone – not that I knew what it felt like, I'd just heard stories – and the less said on that, the better. Control of the sections by voice became a real problem. All section commanders then reverted to the use of field-signals for the moving forward of their groups within the sections.

Another deafening blast from a tank sent a shock wave of admiration and perpetual relief through the soldiers as a round of HE ammunition shattered a target to smithereens, an enemy simulated gun pit which was there one minute and gone the next. Two hundred metres from the enemy pits and an arsenal of all calibre of ammunition streaked through the air, air that in turn could be heard cracking into the vacuums created by the path of the projectiles. This was the part of the 'role of infantry' where we were to 'kill or capture him,': I liked that bit, too. Noise upon noise, an adrenalin rush of satisfaction, satisfaction in the belief that no real foe could withstand the devastation that was now being created, filled us with cheer. It felt like Christmas but without the presents. As with normal though an appreciation that this was only a one-way firing range was taken into mind (there was no enemy shooting back at us; no defensive 'live' fire).

Slowly but surely the assaulting troops closed the gap towards the staked targets and machine-prepared pits in which they stood. We received the order to fix bayonets and the man next to me smiled, his eyes bulging out of his head. Some soldiers were real happy in the infantry, I could tell.

It was time again for another fire control order that was to align the massive barrel of the tank up with another enemy bunker.

'Nigel!' The section commander turned towards me, thrusting out with a pointed finger towards the tank to the left flank, 'Give a Fire Control Order!'

'WHAT?'

The tank fired another shot, with an inherent explosion, followed by the expulsion of gases from the muzzle break, which made it impossible to hear a thing. And out to its flank an APC with its .30 and .50 calibre guns was blazing a trail of dust that lead from the front of the vehicle to the sandbag wall of its target, the APC lying down its barrage of covering fire. All gave its accumulative gift of deafness freely.

Again the section commander gave the pointing finger, an over exaggerated thrust to counteract his frustration; frustration built up by the difficulties now showing on his face. 'Fire! Control! Order!' He was starting to look agitated; I could see he was getting red around the collar: Maybe the platoon commander was watching him.

I turned to the tank and back again. The commander held his left hand up towards his ear to signal the use of a telephone. I understood that signal. I nodded in acknowledgment, picked myself up, and raced to the rear of the tank, keeping low as I moved, maintaining a reasonable distance from the rear of the tank so as not to be inadvertently crushed if it should be put into reverse – an unlikely but scary thought.

Three metres behind the covering metal hulk of the tank, and with handset in hand, I looked out for confirmation of a target. There was still a lot of dust flying around. Little was seen as the tank crawled forward a little more and I followed up the rear until a target presented itself.

The commander at the turret waited patiently, loaded and ready to fire. I then saw an opportunity. 'One hundred and fifty metres, reference barrel, right, one O'clock, enemy bunker at base of large ghost gum!' There were about a hundred or more ghost gums in the area but the tank commander pretended to know what I was talking about.

'Seen!' The commander pushed the tank forward as I secured the phone back into its metal pillbox. The barrel exploded with deafening noise and the target was obliterated from existence. My section commander looked relieved. I guess this meant that the platoon commander was going to be happy with the results. The platoon sergeant and corporal were good mates; the sergeant was always patting the corporal on the shoulder and saying things like, 'well done, Corporal; good job,' just loud enough for the platoon commander to hear. It was times like that that we all wanted to be corporals.

The assault continued until we were within effective small arms firing range but without tank fire support due to safety restrictions and closeness of targets. The DS continued to move around and hitting soldiers on the backs with their sticks, saying, 'you're dead, you little shit,' and then moving on to find someone else to pester.

As Infantry we now had to fight through on our guts, crawling and fighting the whole distance that remained between us and the objective. Then, after quite some time, we were finally done and the objective was won. We could now go into our harbour drill and sit there, watching the DS standing around with their arms folded in front of them, as though they were God; but playing God was the RSM's job.

Much was learnt during the morning's activities with the monstrous metal coffins, and a bond of knowledge was tied to the mind forever and a day, an unforgettable experience for sure.

Rum Courage

August 1982

We found ourselves sitting silently, faces full of muck, clothing smelling like that of a sewer - To anyone except those that had been wearing them for the past sixteen days. We were watching the living beauty, the transformation of day into night, hatches to all APCs gaping to the cooling air that surrounded us as the sun made its journey to the far side of the world, to be seen by the world's populace, from all of the planet's trouble spots. It was really relaxing to be able to sit there with your hand in your pants and watch nature at its best.

As we sat waiting our turn to play out our roles in the mock assault ahead many of the other countries of the world were carrying out morning routine and preparing themselves for a real conflict, [or maybe night routine] to cause nothing but devastation, carnage and casualties upon their own species. Man; a creature of the world bent upon killing for the sake of killing, to leave decaying corpses to litter the surface of their land; quite unlike other animals of the world who killed for food, to sustain the essence of life itself – was that a fair comparison?

The platoon sergeant visited each of the sections as they rest in the metal hulls of the APCs, taking with him a bottle of rum, to be shared equally amongst the section commanders and then these portions amongst the men – but he always slipped our corporal more than the others. Suddenly I didn't care anymore about the stupid bastards on the other side of the world, for the sergeant was now my friend, too.

Section commanders took their quota and began the equal distribution, not a drop wasted to the dry and dusty grounds of Shoalwater Bay.

Each soldier held his cup canteen out patiently for his share of the rum, and those that didn't drink gave their portion readily to the man beside them. Morsels were swallowed, followed by widening grins that were brought on by the pleasurable warming of the rum.

Cups were folded away and placed back into the water bottle covers. It wouldn't be long now and the assault would commence.

Orders for the night attack finally came over the speakers, breaking the silence in the rear of all APCs in the area. All listened intently, or so it seemed. Some soldiers simply sat there with their bush hats tipped forward, hiding their eyes, trying to catch up on a little sleep.

Solid compressed-aluminium doors were then closed and secured on the raised ramps, machine gunners and section commanders stood in the open hatches of the APCs and the vehicle engines were turned over simultaneously. The guys that were sleeping now woke up and could only wonder as to where the smell of rum was coming from, but I didn't tell them; I just told them to 'go back to sleep'.

The APCs pressed on towards the line of departure, bodies vibrating heavily inside, with some men being thrown around like rag dolls in the confines of the personnel carriers. All section members, of all sections, would break from the safety of their vehicles in two minutes and the assault into the night would commence – by foot and without the comfort of fire support from our APC .30 and .50 calibre friends.

All faces appeared serious now, serious and tired, some with eyes closed and others looking precariously over their weapons in final preparation for the coming assault, and one man learned back and stole some of the rations that belonged to the APC driver, shoving a tin of corned beef into his basic pouch.

We were all so very tired. Another night move, another enemy position, more human shaped targets; and yet another night move was to follow this assault. If we kept on going like this then the driver wasn't going to have many rations left.

One man looked over to another, 'I hate this shit.' Eight years on and he was still saying the same, and a few years after that he was in Somalia. And when in Africa he found himself amongst the same type of characteristically built individuals that were doing exactly the same thing some ten years before, when they were all drinking rum, thinking of a warm and comfortable bed, and stealing rations from the driver of the APC.

Lost Cause

August 1982

Thirteen APCs raced out of the creek-line some fourteen hundred metres short of the objective, a huge objective which now stood to our direct front; three monstrous features; the enemy position. Three distinct knolls of interest existed here and each was heavily defended.

Our 'friendly' company assault was aided by a superimposed small arms fire, and simulated artillery and mortar fire support. Sustain fire machine guns sat at right angles to the main axis of assault, and DS threw whiz-bangs around the objective to portray the friendly onset of bombs and shells striking the ground. They always did a good job. Throwing whiz-bangs upon the ground was like chicken-feed to them.

Foliage in the area offered little concealment but the soft waves of undulating ground gave to periodic sanctuary of cover from fire; a rock here, an indent in the ground there; wherever it was possible to gain an advantage it was sought. If it had been raining it would have been a different kettle of fish, because none of the soldiers like sticking his head in the mud.

Although the assaulting vehicles were outside of Musorian small arms fire, they weren't out of reach of the enemy company 60mm mortars. Commanders and drivers alike were soon forced to secure the hatches to the main cavity of APC's, drivers and commander's cupolas also being secured, a protection from shrapnel hence gained. This gave the soldiers in the back greater opportunity to have a quick rest and to steal more rations.

Visibility was now drastically reduced and ground was slowly gained on the enemy objective, for drivers were forced to peer out of glass ports which were literally inches thick, each a rectangle the size of two fists placed side by side. This had forced the reduction in speed. This adjustment in speed however was given praise by many of the soldiers as they were now receiving less bumps and bruises from being tossed around within the confines of the death traps, and those with light fingers continued to concentrate more on their task at hand.

DS in the backs of HQ vehicles assured the degree of protection to each of the vehicles was carried out. A death penalty would more than likely be the outcome to any vehicle load of troops whom disobeyed the command and the DS were always happy to award wounded.

A minefield was haphazardly entered, unmarked and unknown until the DS gave a command for one of the vehicles of the platoon to halt and for its occupants to debus. I guess he would have been disappointed because he wasn't able to use his big stick to whack the soldiers, instead he just waved his hand over them, as though he was Moses, and told them to stay where they were: 'Stay where you are, you're all dead.' They were now out of the exercise, just for the duration of the assault. They had supposedly run over an anti-tank mine and were, for all intents and purposes, considered dead.

The platoon commander would now have to take his particular objective with no depth section, which was a reliable source of reserve during any assault, and so we pushed on with two sections and entered into enemy small arms firing range. And then the word was passed around; the platoon was going to exit the vehicles shortly.

APC .30 and .50 calibre weapons opened up to help with the covering of infantry on the ground as they left the confines of the APCs behind them. Ramps folded down to reveal the outside world and we sprang into action, leaping from the vehicles, taking a sharp left hand turn, to hit the dirt and push out into assault formation.

Our platoon was now linked with the neighbouring platoon. Private Kurtts was to the far right of the flank and used as the linkman for our joining. He wasn't a very good soldier. He was looking in the wrong direction until his corporal threw a big rock at his head. It was pretty funny too, the way in which it bounced off his skull and Kurtts then turned around to face the enemy.

The sloping ground to the front was so ominous; it was enough to put the fear of God into an atheist. But we had little choice but to go up it: It wasn't like working as a QANTAS baggage handler and going on strike because you felt like taking a day off due to the work being too hard.

A fight through method of assault was adopted immediately and the enemy-held ground taken inch by precious inch, men working in pairs as they moved forward, providing each other with covering fire, but maintaining the line of assault throughout. Every time I hit the ground, after taking a bound forward, the radio I carried hit me in the back of the head. I had to keep looking around to make sure it wasn't a DS with his stick in his hand, but it wasn't.

Nigel B.J. Clayton

As we ascended the hill the two platoons arrived at the base of their objective as laid down in orders, two distinct knolls rising from the rocky hill that we were now fighting up. The saddle between each of the platoon's objectives played with the minds of the soldiers and as per normal each individual began to converge upon the targets on the knolls to his front. Everyone wanted a piece of the action, to be the one to jump into an enemy pit and be seen to clear it of enemy. These first two features had to be won and secured quickly, before the flanking third platoon, to our left, swung around to the remaining objective to the rear. Although this segregated platoon was in close small arms fire with the enemy, they couldn't begin their assault until friendly fire was in a position to pin down their particular objective [friendly covering fire]. Every round mattered in real life, each square inch of ground was as sacred as the next, and the only secure piece of turf was the stuff on which you were standing.

A DS strode up behind the man with the machine gun, a stick held tight in his hand. He stretched out and tagged the man on the shoulder. The gunner turned, sweat pouring from his face.

'You're dead,' the DS ordered.
'No I'm not.'
'You're dead. Stay put, and no more firing.'
'Bullshit, I'm not dead.' He got up and took another bound forward, two more metres. An enemy pit sat to his front and the enemy opened fire. If only he'd remained crawling along on his guts like everyone else and he wouldn't have endangered his life – or that of his mates.
'You're bloody dead!'
'Bullshit.'
'Another word from you, sunshine, and you're on a charge. You're dead, now stay put.' The DS pushed on past the cursing soldier and towards another – they loved their job. 'You're dead, get down and stay down.' The DS continued on and on.

By the time the objective was secured only five men of our platoon remained alive; the remainder of the company wasn't much better off. A good 80% of the company now lie dead and spread out along the extended trail, from the low ground to the peak of the three objectives.

Not a good result by anyone's terms. But how realistic was the assault? No one really ever wanted to die for his or her country; it was far better to make the other guy die for his – after all, we weren't fanatics: That's left to the terrorists who think they have 72 virgins waiting for them in heaven.

Bunghole

August 1982

We were well into the exercise and the time had arrived to lose all of the APC support; the remainder of the exercise was to be conducted on foot, an advance to contact, prior to a further three days spent conducting activities revolving around that of a battalion in defence. Even at this point in time all of the soldiers had their minds focussed on the city lights and nightclubs of Brisbane.

I looked over towards the section commander for confirmation, 'What?'

'Go over and get some spare food. Just tell the commander that we've got no stuff left and are starving to death:' hmmmm, ransack the APCs of everything we can before they depart; good idea.

'What do you want?'

The 2IC spoke up: 'Get some bunghole.' He then received a cold stare from some within the section.

'No way. I'm not eating that shit,' another voice from somewhere behind. The platoon was harboured up in a non-tactical environment prior to the advance to contact; H hour – after that there would be little time to rest.

The section commander: 'Good idea; bunghole it is. Go get it, Nigel. And quickly, before they take off.'

I picked myself up and raced over towards the crew member atop the APC. The NCO was checking his two weapons and cupola; playing with his headset and eyeballing the map that he held in his left hand. He was chewing on a ration pack biscuit and looking down upon me as I made my approach, his mind awash with tasks.

'Hey mate; you haven't got any bunghole to spare have you; or maybe something else?'

'Bunghole? sure. I hate the shit myself.' He peered down into the APC interior, his driver handing him two cans of the finest vintage, a Christmas style cake rich with fruit, and as dry as... 'Here, catch.'

'Thanks mate.' I returned to the section commander and handed it over. The can was soon opened and the smell simply wafted out.... mmm; delicious.

The Long Road to Rwanda

It was somewhat of an advantage in advance to contact exercises, preventing the need to go to the shitter each day as part of a normal daily routine – or so it seemed. It was said by many to be better than the diarrhoea powder in the army med-kits, which each section 2IC carried, and it wasn't uncommon to see guys taking this in aid to induce constipation for a week, a benefit that secured peace of mind in some individuals. No one enjoyed going to the crapper during a tactical exercise, wiping your arse with a piece of flimsy paper, with the possibility of getting shit over your finger and under your nails. Section members advanced like a swarm of flies around the cans as they were opened with a metallic click, each and every one looking on as though a naked woman was about to be revealed.

The fruity rolls were cut into equal portions and all stuffed their faces on returning to their packs, sitting there, chewing, swallowing, fingernails full of dirt and uniforms stinking, crumbs being picked from trouser legs as they were dropped and quickly placed into mouths.

Smile upon smile burnt at the muscles of faces, a burp here and there giving that indication of gratification. Another was heard, a pig type burp with corners of the mouth pulled back willingly to extenuate the sound. All were trying effortlessly to achieve the loudest call of satisfaction, a burp that would have received a hit around the back of the head from any wife or girlfriend with the words 'you pig' accompanying the slap.

I lay back on my pack, sighing with pleasure and closed my eyelids, trying for another 30 minutes of shut-eye before the deadline for the battalion to move was finally upon us all.

It would be a long time between trips to the dunny from this day forth.

Smell This

August 1982

On return to the barracks the mind was awash with thoughts; beers, sex, food, and for some sleep. From the time that the final words 'Company dismissed' reaches your ears only two things stand between you and the pub; the clothes you have had on your back for the past four weeks, and the jam between your toes.

March in step as fast as you can back to the barracks, for there are only four showers on each floor of our accommodation, and approximately 16 soldiers to each floor waiting to use them – the others of the platoon of 30 having headed for home, wife, and warmth of bed.

You wrestle with the key around your neck and get it into the door; you push it open and commence to strip the clothes away; first the boots, then the socks, and the uniform in general. Grab your towel, soup and shaving kit, get hold of the shampoo and step into the shower block as quick as can be.

The camouflage cream was literally caked upon your face; shaving will fix the worst of the gunk. Into the shower and start scrubbing away, and 15 minutes later you are still covered in filth; cam in the ears, on backs of hand, and in every wrinkle of your weary face.

After some considerable time, and much anxiety stressed from other members of the platoon waiting for a shower, you finally emerge from the shower cubicle and head back to your room to get dressed. You get hold of the doorknob, turn it quickly and step through the doorway (the one you share with four other men). You step into the room, your first beer in a month not that far away, and you suddenly find yourself choking on the fumes, for its only now that you realise how badly you needed a shower; you wouldn't touch your clothes with a ten-foot pole, let alone attempt to pick up your crystallized socks. The stench was always wicked.

Orchid, Orchid; Where Art Thou

August 1982

Robert Crisp and I – along with the remainder of the platoon – ventured down to Holsworthy in the latter part of the month, for a short three-day exercise with a logistic support group. A scenario had been painted for the platoon to indicate that we were operating out of the north, near Darwin. It was too bad that the same scenario couldn't govern the weather conditions; it was atrocious.

For the logistics exercise to be a success, the campsite required that poles be made for the erection of camouflage nets over vehicles. It was quite usual for the poles to be made from lightweight material, similar to bamboo, but the 'system' was not always effective and initiative was often required.

The platoon sergeant attended a briefing from those appointed to the security group (the infantry element on the ground), so even before the exercise had commenced we were well swamped with work parties of wide variety.

It came to pass that a short trip, by truck, was required into the field in order to obtain, via fowl means or fair, wooden poles for the purpose mentioned above. It was cold and wet, but to hell with that, we were infantry soldiers and a part of our motto was 'regardless of season, weather, or terrain'.

We arrived in the forest ready to do our deed upon this haven for trees; protected by law... No wonder the platoon sergeant was looking over his shoulder every few minutes, lifting his head at the slightest sound that was NOT vibration from the chainsaws as they were throttled into action.

The platoon sergeant pointed here and pointed there; this tree will do, and so will that one too... but the trees in question; weren't they too thick... too large to be employed as they were supposed to be employed. And a cold stare was met by the man in authority, for the platoon sergeant himself had other ideas on his mind, not the exercise in general.

'There; over there, Private Andrews."
'Okay, Sarge, I see it.'

Nigel B.J. Clayton

And what was it, you ask; why, another orchid high up in a tree, for his collection back home, broad leaves which would one day spring beautiful colour to adorn his home; the entire forest was at the sergeants beck-and-call, to do with as he pleased; and the soldiers, we were but another tool for him to unleash upon the State Forest.

What a despicable character, and although he held a soft spot for the beautiful orchid, he clearly held no regard for nature itself.

Exercise LSG

August 1982

Enemies on this exercise were also a figment of the imagination, and this 'lack of enemy' only tempted to lower the platoon's morale further than what it was, all brought on by the stresses of the current situation. To maintain a security picket on any of the platoon gun positions was seemingly foolhardy, but carried out regardless. After all, what was the point in conducting a picket, when no enemy incursion was possible? This was another time when 'dead man on the gun' was employed by me.

Work parties were a common thing, and a heavy burden to the platoon from the start, so not only were pickets and sentry positions manned as per normal, but a heavy workload and burden of additional duties was now set upon us all. We had to suffer this humiliation because we were 'dumb grunts' and being such meant that we'd be happy doing work parties. Maybe the 'support group' thought we'd go jumping for joy about the whole set up, smiles on our faces as though we were puppies trying to hump the leg of our masters.

Setting up tents took up a majority of the work parties and then of course came the laying of the electrical cable, which had to be laid throughout the campsite, from the strategically placed generators, to – and through – all of the tents in the area.

Light bulbs were then attached to specific points along this cable so that when the generators were turned over and running, the tents would become illuminated – work in the dead of night could now be pursued. Most of the pogo bastards probably needed the light to see what they were doing when blowing up their blow-up dolls prior to bedtime, so they had something to lie upon at night, in the same way that grunts laid on top of women: And all grunts know that it's more fun to lie on top of a woman than a pneumatic: so who's the more stupid?

It wasn't until the day after the cable had been erected that it was passed down to the platoon members that the cable now had to be painted a different colour. They probably needed something nicer to look upon. It must have been horrible for them to see that white cable stretched out above them whilst wrestling with their blow-up dolls.

Everyone appreciated this pogo-officer's brilliant scheme. All we had to do now was to go around and paint the white cable, olive drab. Wonderful initiative from another officer of a depreciating and somewhat, estranged corps. I didn't like those officers very much; they always had a small sparkle in their eyes and lips pursed, as though they wanted to bend you over the nearest fallen log. It was enough to make you shudder, unless you liked being stuffed like a turkey.

The reason of course was explained to all. To manufacture the cable in the colour that the army required cost too much, so it was marvellously cheaper to purchase white cable and then add a splash of 'logistical support group' initiative. Yeah, right; I think they just did it on purpose so as to make themselves feel more superior than us; to make themselves feel special. Well, that's okay, because we might not have been special soldiers with deep pockets but we were smart enough to conduct 'dead man on the gun'. But why paint it whilst it was up? 'Because the tents had to have light as soon as possible,' said one of their officers with a grin on his mouth, 'the cables receive priority', the same as everything else in the bloody army. One thing you had to learn in the army was to prioritise your priorities. Light was far more important than green cable and tents had to be erected in case it rained. Wouldn't want a pogo to get wet now, would we?

The idea behind the entire scheme was so that any low flying aircraft – so was the logic – wouldn't be able to see the white cable showing through the foliage provided by the trees. What aircraft? But what about the tents and their silhouettes?

Crisp and I were soon given orders and we in turn gathered our resources. Six-foot broom handles were issued and to the end of these a paintbrush was attached. A formidable plan was then formulated and executed with pride.

Dip the brush into the can of paint and paint the cable whilst it was still erected. A sound conclusion to the most idiotic of ideas, but we all realised from the start that we were there for this very reason, to do work parties, to carry out tasks that the pogo fools themselves couldn't be bothered with. Once again we were to be used as a resource instead of as a platoon of infantry. No wonder there wasn't any enemy around; that would have taken us from the precious tasks offered by the pogo officer.

Thirty-six hours of painting saw to the end of the task and the exercise. All members of the platoon were more than overwhelmed to see an end to the biggest ever 'rock show' on earth.

PS: It wasn't mentioned, but whilst being painted, some tents were moved. Yes; about 20% of all tents erected were moved no more than ten metres, picked up by groups of men and moved with cable in place... like that of a cable car. Three metre lengths of white cable now dominated the area.

But who was the bigger fool; really? The officer who couldn't correctly position his tents on the ground in some form of proper organisation, or the poor old grunt on the ground who had to go around with more olive drab paint?

Commonwealth Games

September-October 1982

The Commonwealth Games of Brisbane was something special to look forward to for a majority of the 8/9th battalion. Some were used as drivers for the different teams of the commonwealth, and others like me took pride in distinguishing themselves as a member of the Guard of Honour, and some just stayed on barracks with their fingers in their butt and being employed on work parties as required. The guard was used primarily for the opening and closing ceremonies of the commonwealth games and took part in honouring the Queen at the time of her arrival in Australia. I was honoured too, because I liked being a guard. Once, a long time ago, I wondered what it would be like to be a guard, guarding another guard, but I never found out.

In the four weeks leading up to the 105-man guard for the opening ceremony, well in excess of 117 hours of drill was performed in rehearsals; all of which was taken out on the parade ground at 8/9RAR, Enoggera Barracks. The RSM liked marching us up and down the parade ground – I guess he was bored and didn't have anything else to do, and I was always happy to help him out. Several full dress rehearsals were also encountered during the lead up training, but less the low flying aircraft. But nothing could prepare us for the noise as we marched into the arena of the games themselves, it was unbelievable; the crowd, the low flying aircraft, and the commentator's voice as it echoed throughout the auditorium, but it was exciting too, because the girl in the front row of seats was performing like Sharon Stone from Basic Instinct.

The commands that had been rehearsed in the build-up of anticipation were barely heard over the combined decibels; even the wind seemed to be against us as it lashed out a sudden gush that blew off five slouch hats in front of 350 million viewers. It was nice to see someone from the crowd pick up one of the hats which was in direct danger of being driven over by a vehicle as it came passing the front of the guard.

Without boast there was a story printed in a London paper which stated that the first gold medal should have been given to the Guard of

Honour for their efforts. It gave a nice feeling to receive public recognition, even if it was from across the sea.

But the misfortunes were not over with by a long shot, for the next step was to greet the Queen at the airport with a hearty welcome of precision drill. This was unfortunately let down, for as the Queen stepped out from the door of the plane, an order for present arms was given, at exactly the same time that the artillery commenced with its twenty-one gun salute. Nothing could be heard over this.

Half the guard paid compliment by thrusting their rifles out central to their bodies, and the others remained steady with rifles tucked in close under their armpits, steady as a rock. But seeing the Queen's head bobbing up and down as she walked past during her inspection of the guard must have been some consolation for all of the drill rehearsals endured; surely. I wanted to ask her if she really did silent farts, or if it was just a furphy, but I didn't think she'd know what furphy meant, so didn't bother asking.

The closing ceremony was of little concern, nothing more could possibly go wrong, and didn't. It went like clockwork and all were glad to see the end of the drill rehearsals, but the RSM seemed disappointed that he had to go back to being bored: It must have been a horrible job, baby-sitting officers in BHQ.

A surprise did come through the mail though, for all of those who performed as part of the Guard of Honour. All 105 men received a commemorative medallion, but it wasn't made of gold, so I guess the article in the London paper didn't have the effect that we'd all hoped for.

The only downfall of the guard was the fact that most of the guys on that parade never got to see the fruits of their labour on TV or video. Such was life I suppose.

Close Call

November 1982

Exercise Aries Pride was the final exercise for the year.

On the morning of a starlit night, A Coy was formed up in an FUP awaiting the order to move forward in an extended line – to close with the enemy. I was smiling because I was thinking of Brisbane, and then I turned around and saw the pearly whites of the platoon commander, which quickly tore my smile away; I didn't want him getting the wrong impression. There was sufficient cover from view in the re-entrant, and it was our firm belief that the trees that were in the vicinity had been planted by the hand of God – why?

Illumination from 81mm mortars came in thick and fast over the objective so that fire support could be brought to bear on the enemy position. With the illumination the commanders could adjust the friendly fire to better break up the enemy defences and to hopefully force the enemy to cower in the bottom of their pits during the A Coy advance – saving on friendly casualties.

The line of fire for the mortars placed a high trajectory over the heads of troops on the ground and as each round burst into illumination, hundreds of metres above these contours, the canister in which each was originally contained would drop to Earth, its task of delivery having been met. The approach of these canisters could quite easily be identified as they whistled through the air and thumped into the ground. In some cases they sounded like that of the tempo created by a drummer, each spinning out of control through the cold night air, tumbling to earth faster than a speeding locomotive. One might daydream and consider that the drumming was actually the drummer of a band and that he might have fallen out of an aeroplane from overhead on his way to the Tamworth music festival; but I waved the stupid dream from my head; but a drummer, drumming away, is exactly how it sounded. Anyway; a good dozen or so of these fast-falling objects literally crashed through the canopy of the trees to the depression – re-entrant – in which the friendly Coy waited; into the very midst of our confines.

One hit a branch and was deflected to miss a man by no more than two centimetres. Many were blessed with lucky escapes that night, and within a year a ban was placed on all firing of illumination over the heads of troops. I was surprised it took a year to have the ban put into place, but the army was always surprising me with its slow reaction to circumstance in getting things done. Our Platoon Sergeant said it was the stupid officers fault and when I asked him which one he said, 'all of them', and I was surprised that it took so many officers to make such a slow decision because I'd heard that 'two heads were better than one'. Then the Platoon Sergeant said that 'too many cooks spoilt the broth' and I suddenly realised why the food in the mess hall always tasted like shit.

The second close call came two days later during a battalion advance to contact along three separate ridges. Each Coy of the Battalion had its own ridge, which consisted of numerous live-fire target positions: Numerous, figure-eleven targets, being deployed as Coy, PL and SECT stands – a live fire contact lane. As each objective was taken, the information was passed back to BHQ; a coordinated BN – Coy by Coy – advance to contact. I was reassured by the exercise because there were only three ridges and I knew that this was in the capabilities of the officers in charge, because they were all good counters when the number was no more than three.

One of these companies came upon an enemy position, and one of the platoon commanders, not fond of taking advice offered by subordinates (in particular section commanders), decided that he knew where he was on the ground, and that all others were geographically embarrassed – that was to say, they were hopelessly lost. He then proceeded with his call to bring sustained machine gun fire support to bear upon the objective – remembering that this was a live fire exercise.

The gun line quickly prepared the ammunition and was about to bring fire to bear upon the enemy position some 1,200 metres away when one of the commanders of that group lifted a pair of binoculars to his eyes. That was strange. One of the figure-eleven targets was moving, and he'd not been smoking a joint because drugs weren't allowed in the army, so the movement was not part of his imagination.

He gave the command to check fire and the men on the firing line moved back from their firing positions.

Incorrect grid coordinates had been sent to the SFMG firing line. What was thought to be an enemy position was in fact the position to

Nigel B.J.Clayton

which A Coy was holding. I then realised why there were always so many officers, because a six-figure grid reference was in fact 'two sets of three numbers'. It was no wonder the RSM had grey hair; it was from working in BHQ.

This type of mistake was seen more than once during my career in the army, due to incompetent individuals who didn't care to ride on advice as given by others. Maybe the officers should have been made to work in pairs all the time. There happens to be a few around whose promotion has become directly affected by such mistakes. Let's hope that a lesson was learnt in each of the circumstances. The accidental calling in of mortars, adjacent to a friendly position, was to be the worst I heard of that year, but hearsay was nowhere near as reliable as being there on the ground, at the time of the incident. Some of the officers were good for saluting, and... well... that's about it, really.

Tully

March 1983

The Field Force Battle School was to be the first treat for A Coy, and Tully in March was a place you didn't want to be in if you didn't like the rain, but then again, nearly every month in Tully was the same, wet and miserable. It was one of the heaviest rainfall areas in Australia, and the monsoon season was in full swing.

The big adventure started like many, with an innocent flight in a C130. This took the clan to Townsville where we stayed the night prior to being loaded onto trucks for the two hour trip into the mouth of the jungle, the last night of innocence for several weeks. Something had to be done and fun had to be sought.

Orders were passed down to stay away from town, namely a disco christened Scums, a favourite hide for many of the Infantry soldiers of Townsville. But rules were made to be broken and so Scums was visited by many.

It came as quite a surprise to wake in the morning and find that the Coy had spent an entire night in Townsville without causing any trouble, and none being marked as AWOL during the morning parade, which was held at O-dark-hundred. There were however a lot of sore heads that morning and it was obvious that some had finished drinking just moments before loading themselves onto trucks.

The boys from Brisbane clambered aboard the trucks and pulled the tarps down tight before arranging their gear in such a manner that some shut-eye could be attained during the short trip to Tully. It wasn't until we reached the halfway point in the journey that the rain started to fall, the end to any sobering thought of 'an easy trip' fleeing from mind.

Very few of the soldiers had been to Tully before now, but those that had gave us all a wake-up call as we approached the small township of Tully. Sleeping equipment was quickly stowed into packs as we passed through the town.

Although it was only 0630hrs, it was still fairly dark outside the confines of the trucks. The cloud cover was ominous and the rain kept coming down, faster and faster. The trucks pulled over, 600 metres short of the Battle School, and drivers were quick to drop the tailgates. There the DS commenced with their torment: 'Where's you OC?' He was easy to find; he had the biggest smile on his face. 'Ah, there you are. Sir, if you wouldn't mind, I want you off of these trucks as quickly as possible. We have a lot to do and little time to do it in.' I realised that these DS knew what they were talking about because they all had big sticks, just like I'd seen in the past, and I was beginning to wonder whether or not a big stick was a part of their 'complete equipment schedule' and actually issued to them.

The trucks disappeared out of view, out of the rainstorm that was to maintain its ferocity; a sorry sight to some of the sore heads that only now had started to clear of their alcohol induced trances. This wasn't any dream; this was the twilight zone.

Section commanders were seen coming back from their orders group and information was passed on down the line to soldiers. 2IC's were then taken from the sections by platoon sergeants. Work details were now issued. Ammunition, rations, radio batteries, M30 grenades, trip flares, and an assortment of other equipment was passed around, most of which was shoved into packs: 'Hurry up you people. You have two minutes.' The DS were ever helpful.

'Hey, Nigel.'
'What?'
'You know where the camp is from here don't ya?'
'No.'
'You see that dirt road over there. Well, you follow that up and over that small rise. It's 600 metres away.'
'I don't understand.'
'You're damn right you don't. We're walking in the long way.'
'The long way.'
'Yeah.'

I continued to pack my newly issued equipment and stores, and looked Andrew in the face. 'But it's only a six kilometre walk in.'

'You didn't look at the map did you? It's as steep as you've ever seen,' and with that he started laughing.

The first thirty minutes or so was relatively easy but the ground soon took to a gradual rise, steeper and steeper it grew. It really wasn't the steepest I'd ever seen, or even that hard for that matter, but those that had had a hard night before, or who had taken care to avoid extra physical activities in their own time, found the going somewhat

The Long Road to Rwanda

difficult. There was one guy in particular to my front that just couldn't keep up with the pace. He must have been at least thirty kilograms overweight and not used to such activity. He was the company clerk. What did they do, give him a typewriter to carry in his pack? He looked like he was going to drop dead at any minute, gasping for air the way he was. Guys were ordered to push from the rear, holding him up by the pack he wore, to literally take turns in assisting him up the rise. I just prayed that he didn't fart when it was my time to push him from the rear, and when it was my turn I made sure I kept my mouth closed so I wouldn't get any fart fumes in it.

The Australian issue pack that we carried on our backs was as small as a carton of beer; big enough for a sleeping bag, two days' worth of rations, shaving kit, spare sock, a spare set of work clothes and something warm to wear at night. But now with the additional assortment of equipment issued via the DS they weighed a tonne, much of it strapped on the outside of the pack in sandbags.

The DS certainly knew how to weigh soldiers down. I could remember my first ever exercise with the BN in 1981. Back then our packs were so full of gear and busting at the seams that each man had to strap a sandbag full of equipment to the outside of his pack in order to carry the additional seven ration packs issued, simply because of 'because'. It was somewhat quite pathetic. Back then it was because of the resupply, but now it was because the DS were sadistic bastards.

Another twenty odd minutes of climbing saw an end to the steep gradient and a great relief as I could now open my mouth, and the ground levelled slightly before reaching a spur line, which led down and around to the rear of the camp, where we were to be based for the next two weeks.

And now for the commencement of training.

The accommodation for the course was five-star – compared to living in the field. Open windows, no doors, no heating or seats of any description. Like you'd imagine the waiting room for execution of a cow at an abattoir. There were two floors, several rooms to each. Some of these rooms were used for lessons, so sleeping in them was forbidden. All 30 of our platoon fit into the first room, taking up every possible centimetre of space. At least we were receiving field allowance for the two-week duration, that in itself should be enough for the purchase of another dozen beers in our favourite nightclub.

On a visit to the latrines – which consisted of four porcelain bowls, a urinal, and next door to that about half a dozen (bare essential) shower cubicles – I noticed a piece of graffiti on the back of one of the doors. It read: '22 days and no rain'. Some pogo transport driver, doing hell knows what in Tully, had gotten away without a drop of rain falling from the now covered sky. It was enough to make anyone sick. All I could do as I sat on the porcelain was listen to the rain hitting the tin roof above, no immediate relief in sight.

A voice was then suddenly heard in the background, yelling out for all to hear: 'Get your webbing and rifles, form up outside; two minutes!'

So the jungle training had definitely commenced, no less than two nights a week of which were to be spent in ambush, for anything up to five hours duration – and that bloody rain.

Ambush – the DS loved them

The Dalmatian came sniffing around again just on last light. Every time we lay in ambush the dog was there. I didn't know which of the DS owned him, but we all hated him. There we lie in the pouring rain. A rustle was heard. That damn dog was sniffing around. He would go up quite casually to a soldier lying silently in wait for the enemy, cock its leg, and urinate over him, steam rising through the jungle vines. Every ambush was the same, with at least one soldier being pissed on. Of course, if you moved or said anything then the DS was there to leap down your throat in an attempt to pull out your damn larynx. The dog knew this and so always went about his business with a smile, his tail held high in dominance; he knew what he was doing.

The nights here were the worst. You could never see a thing, ever. Even when the stars were out you couldn't see anything – so we were told – due to the thickness of the canopy above. But I didn't recall seeing any stars that trip, I couldn't even see the rain cloud. And the rain was never accompanied by wind; it just fell, hour after hour after hour.

Night harbour

Whenever a night harbour was set up, perimeter cord would be placed around the position from pit to pit. All you had to do when finding a relief for a gun picket was to follow the cord around the perimeter.

The Long Road to Rwanda

Remembering what the terrain had looked like by day and picturing this in your mind, or by tying knots in the perimeter cord, you could almost always find where you were going. The only problem being was the soldier you were going to wake up.

'Pssssst. I know you're there somewhere, Wayne. It's your picket.' The soldier would usually be awake but praying that you'd move on your way to leave him alone. 'Wayne.' A light whisper. 'Pssssst.'

'Shut up down there!'

Bloody DS.

A good trick to employ when getting back at someone was to walk past his hutchie spot just before nightfall with a tube of condensed milk or jam from the ration pack, and squirt this around his sleeping area; it would bring rats in from everywhere. But even without this tempt of ingenuity the rats would search you out eventually. Many soldiers would wake in the morning to find that a hole had been gnawed through their canvas pack, the shortbread biscuits stolen from the rations within.

We were half way through the trip when I was confronted by one of these ever-hungry rodents of the bush.

I searched for the button of my watch and from within my sleeping bag sought the time. 0130hrs. I was on picket from 0230hrs till 0550hrs (reveille).

What was it that had woken me? Why, the rain. It had stopped, just the occasional splatter of a few drops from the branches above falling onto my hutchie. I turned onto my back and closed my eyes once again.

Shit! I woke with a jolt. What was that? Something was near my pack.

I slowly removed my hand from within my sleeping bag and waited.

My pack was at my head, half of which was lying in the jungle, exposed to the elements. Better it got wet than me: I didn't like sleeping with mud in my ear. The noise came again. I could only imagine what it was, a tiny rodent trying to gnaw its way through my pack. Well, the bastard wasn't going to get my rations. I waited in ambush, and as the next sound of scratching came to my ears I lashed back with a clenched fist, hitting something hard and fury. Jesus Christ! It was huge. I decided then and there that I no longer wanted my biscuits, and that if the rodent wanted them so badly then he was

Nigel B.J. Clayton

welcome to them.

Then it started to rain as before.

And with the rain came the leeches; and as it was always raining... say no more. The next day, during the normal running of morning routine, Peter Sheer decided he needed to visit the centre of the platoon position in order to see the platoon sergeant. 'What's up, Private Sheer?'

'I got a problem Sarge. I need to see the doc.'

'Can't it wait? The trucks are picking us up at midday.'

'Not really, Sarge, no,' and with that he pulled his trousers down. A leech had crawled up his urinary tract. He received all the sympathy in the world from platoon headquarters after that, and the remainder of the platoon received a good hearty laugh at his misfortune.

NO. We truly loved Tully. No digging you see. But what time was saved through not digging holes in the ground was quickly used up trying to keep the weapons free of rust. The damn SLR was always a problem to look after in the field.

Three cleans a day whilst in a field environment, and the occasional maintenance during a five-minute break in a patrol, would still not prevent the build-up of rust. The SLR must have been the worst weapon in the world for this; a genuine rust-magnet. Thank God we didn't all have to carry the M60. But section scouts had it best, for the M16 (an automatic armalite) very rarely rusted.

It didn't happen very often, but occasionally a soldier would approach the platoon sergeant with his weapon in hand, pull-through dangling from the flash suppressor (the open end of the rifle barrel). Another barrel jammed by some fool trying to force a too large-a piece of cleaning flannelette through his weapon.

Magazines were another important issue to contend with, in particular when returning back to the five-star accommodation of Tully.

The 2IC (a captain) of Tully sprang another surprise inspection on all of the soldiers' equipment, to ensure that everything was serviceable. Without fail he would always find something wrong with just about everyone in the platoon.

We were formed up in three ranks when the 2IC approached.

The 2IC picked up one of my magazines and peered inside. 'What's this?'

I had to maintain a positive upper hand, but had none. 'I don't know

The Long Road to Rwanda

sir.'
'It's shit; what is it?'
I looked him in the eye. 'Shit sir.'
He picked up another. 'And what about this one?'
What could I say: 'Errrrr— that's shit too, sir.'
He snapped abruptly. 'No it's not. It's bloody dirt and rust.' He then proceeded with the inspection, to find someone else to chew out. Even to this day I have trouble distinguishing the difference between shit, and dirt and rust.

The obstacle course was another experience. It had to be completed in ten minutes, and if it wasn't, then you had to do it again and again until you achieved the time required. The section I was in had one downfall in the form of one rotund. For an infantry soldier he was fat, and lazy, fattest man in the company, apart from the company clerk. There simply was no excuse for someone, anyone, whether in the infantry or not, to be overweight – unless for medical reasons. More than 90 percent of cases concerning obesity can easily be put down as sheer laziness; after all, no one forces people to put food in their mouth, unless you're trying to eat your biscuits before the sun goes down at night to prevent the rats from making a visit upon your pack.

Due to his being overweight the section had the pleasure of attempting the obstacle course three times in the same afternoon before we could complete the task within the time frame laid down. We always seemed to be 30 seconds over time.

On the third attempt we dragged him, pushed him, and literally carried him over the obstacles to finish in time.

He ran up towards the ten foot wall and fell upon it, his arms stretched upwards. He was too tired to stand on his toes so he needed some friendly persuasion – I think I saw someone accidently smack in the face. Two men then bent down and lifted him by the feet. His fingers reached for the top but he again fell short of helping us out by trying to pull himself up, and he decided, then and there, that he was completely exhausted, and he needed to allow the two men atop the wall to reach down before lifting him up and over – I think I saw an elbow accidently slip and knock him in the mouth, but I might have had some of that Tully, 2IC shit-in-my-eye.

We were always helpful and tried our best to persuade him to try harder. We were always thinking of our mates.

We were given a tick in the box, but I still believe that we had failed to complete it in the time required, but because of the combined section effort we had been given a pass by the DS.

The fat guy was kicked out of the army two years later with a friend, for harbouring more than 40 stolen M26 grenades and 1,200 rounds of M60 link; he was never seen again after that.

One of the obstacles on the course at Tully was a set of horizontal monkey bars that had to be crossed by the challenging soldier in one of two ways, either going underneath, swinging from rung to rung, or crawling over the top. Now due to the fact that it was wet, and everyone was drenched to the bone, the bars were found to be quite slippery. Due to this reason, most went over the top. Mick Wakelin was one of these soldiers.

During rehearsals all were met with one of the funniest things seen all trip. As Mick came crawling over the top of the obstacle, his 'manhood' fell from its quarters within his unbuttoned fly, and as he proceeded across the bars, his 'manhood' hit every single rung. He was well gifted in that region of the anatomy.

The last night in the field before our return to Brisbane was one of my most sleepless. During stand-to that particular day, and as the sun was disappearing once again, the man who shared a pit with me whispered: 'Don't move.'

'What… what is it?'

A second later and he let out a quick sigh of relief. 'Ah; it's okay now.'

'What is?'

'Ah, nothing. Just a sort of fist-sized spider sitting on your back.'

'Where'd it go?'

He pointed: 'Just over there somewhere.'

I had a good look around at the base of the tree next to which we were lying behind, near where the spider had supposedly vanished. It was full of large holes, all of which disappeared into depths of darkness, and each was covered in cobwebs.

'I don't fancy sleeping here the night.' There was never any hint to his bending-of the-truth, so I took it all as gospel. In Shoalwater Bay blokes used to dig up bird spiders from time to time, but we were a long way from there at present.

But time flies when you're having fun, and having fist-sized spiders running freely across your back is almost as fun as wearing a spider on your face.

The Long Road to Rwanda

But it wasn't long before the two-week trip was over with and all were exuberant about seeing the coaches turn up. No time was wasted in stowing gear below the coaches and then clambering aboard for a window seat. This was by far better than travelling in trucks.

As we hit the main road and passed what had been our drop-off point some fourteen days earlier, we could see B Coy. They were packing their packs full of rations, ammunition and other equipment. Section commanders were receiving orders and DS were yelling out commands, each and every person preparing himself for the six-kilometre walk into Tully. All A Coy could do was point and laugh.

And as we drove off I think someone flashed a browneye.

Tobruk

June 1983

Although the exercises of 1982 were repeated again this year, Diamond Dollar did come about a small change. Movement to SWBTA was by way of the Tobruk, Australia's troop carrying vessel. Many hated the trip but others absolutely loved it.

Seasickness seemed to be a very small problem, with most going unscathed and free of sickness. It could also be said that the battalion was lucky that no individual suffered from claustrophobia. I couldn't recall the exact amount of equipment, or numbers to personnel that this seafaring vessel was capable of carrying, but two battalions housed in dog boxes was something of a sound estimate. There were also ten tanks below deck, and sixty odd vehicles, of all descriptions, above. If there was a human equivalent to the RSPCA then the army would have been under fire from all quarters.

It was a ship filled with sleeping quarters [berths] and little else. The chow area only seated a small portion of those on board, but had a system of rotation and displayed all timings for all to see, eg; lunch was rostered for up to five or six sessions, taken between 1100hrs and 1400hrs.

The bunks were just large enough to sleep upon, with legs pulled up slightly, every cubicle, to every room/wall, housing soldiers in areas not much bigger than coffins. When taking into consideration our packs, webbing and weapons, it meant that no room whatsoever was available to move around in. If there were ever a case where we needed to abandon ship, well... most men would have to try and tuck their heads between their legs and kiss their arse goodbye... but for lack of room wouldn't be able to bend over: It would have been easier to kiss somebody else's arse goodbye, a true haven for any homosexual, and I suspected we had a few of those in our midst, but nothing could be proven.

A small canteen did exist on board and was open for business for an hour at lunch, and for several more after dinner. Here you could buy cigarettes, chocolates and soft drinks, all tax-free; and for the homosexuals, lollipops to curl their tongues around.

The Long Road to Rwanda

Beer was 25 cents a can and the distribution of such worked out to a plan. At 1800hrs, if you wanted your ration of two beers per man, then you reported below deck to one of the storage areas. 'Come on fellahs. Keep the bloody noise down. Form a single file. That's it.'
'I didn't think you were a drinker, Scott,' said one man.
'I'm not. Andy saw me earlier on. I'm getting my share for him. What about you?'
'Bloody platoon sergeant nabbed me. He said I was too sick to drink on account that I missed out on working in the heads this morning. Had to report to sick bay with a crook gut.'
'You seasick?'
'No. I just didn't want to work in the heads. I don't swab shit for no man. I've estimated that the platoon sergeant got six non-drinkers earlier on today. That's twelve bloody beers.'
'Andy got seven of the bastards.'
The platoon sergeant gave two raffle tickets to each man as he approached. 'Sign here. Here are your two tickets, Private Smith.'
'Thanks, Sarge.' And once Smith had signed for them, handed them back to the platoon sergeant. 'Enjoy.'
And Scott was next. 'Didn't think you drank, Private Wheelan.'
'Thought I'd have a couple, Sarge. Didn't want to let the team down,' and the cans would be ceremoniously handed over to one of the other hands.
Who ever said you couldn't get pissed whilst on the Tobruk, was absurdly incorrect. Cards were a favourite pastime for some. With four packets of tax-free cigarettes in hand, a game of pontoon would commence. For six hours or more they would play, and when one player was finished, another quickly took his place. Malcolm Peters departed with a smile on his face; five packets up.
'That pays double.'
'No it don't.'
'Where I come from it does.'
'It pays triple in Melbourne.'
'Who asked you, idiot? I said at the start we weren't playing that bloody rule.'
'You're just making the rules up as you go along,' and suddenly the alarm bell went off. 'Shit!' Time for battle stations drill. What were the chances, the one and only drill for the entire trip, and it had to happen when I was trying for a five-card trick. So three days was more than

enough experience for all. Roller coasting waves wasn't everybody's forte. But with the lack of water arrived the expedient digging of shellscrapes. APC doctrine was maintained, and as each stop was only a short one – but longer than that required for a five-minute durry (Cigarette) – shellscrapes were a desired and called for principal of nature, a real necessity if life was to be maintained – due to the fact that the enemy carried 60mm mortars. The area of operations was praised however, for one thing, if not another, for digging a shellscrape took as little as 15 minutes in the sandy soil; venturing inland a few days later proved to be much harder on our hands. A count of seven shell scrapes in one day was our best. One of the niceties of working with APC support was that you certainly got around.

I had been promoted to section scout for the trip and absolutely adored the opportunity to carry out all tasks assigned to the job; early morning clearing patrols, reconnaissance duties, and other short excursions into the bush when accompanying the platoon commander on his appraisals for firm base and ambush position. Due to my present duties I also had to be paired off with the section commander whilst in a harbour position, whether it be night or day, during any type of defensive activity; except the old you-beaut contact drill, when contact with the enemy turned fruitful, and the scouts first job was to return fire into the enemy and/or the enemies likely firing position.

The section commander in my case was a big thug, and when a digger himself was reported to have started fights for the promise of a schooner. 'How come you Poms are always marrying blacks?' he asked.

'I say what?'

A burst of 'live' machine gun fire cracked over our heads.

'You Poms are always marrying blacks aren't ya? Your countries full of the bastards. The Indians and all of them Arabs, and such.'

A burst of fire again ripped through the air.

I gave him a strong look of protest and then changed my look to a sarcastic grin. The section commander had just been married to a Thai, although I certainly wouldn't classify them as black. And by all standards, I was nowhere near as racist as some of the others in the platoon.

'Don't say it, Nigel. I'll drop ya like a bag of shit.'

Machine gun fire.

'I wasn't dreaming of it,' I replied, and before I knew it a message had arrived for the section commanders to report to the platoon commander, and 2ICs to the platoon sergeant. Another opportunity for the elements of PHQ to share in a brew.

Machine gun fire.

A warning order accompanied the runner's news. The section commander gave this to me. 'Go read this out to each of the pits.' Machine gun fire. 'I shouldn't be more than twenty minutes,' or when the brews have been drunk.

He was back sooner than expected, along with the section 2IC, who started without haste to give each soldier his work details for the coming assault. Looks like the corporals didn't get to wet-their-whistle after all. By the time the 2IC had finished with his tasking all were seated on the ground, looking out periodically towards the platoons' killing ground, awaiting orders. This 'glancing out' was a force of habit more than anything else, and wasn't really necessary during this exercise, for the assault to come was of the live fire variety – no 'flesh and blood' enemy existed.

Machine gun fire continued throughout – unopposed friendly fire.

'Listen up, men, someone's stuffed up again and forgot the digger at the bottom – as usual.' The normal practice or teaching was for the hierarchy to ensure that time was allowed for all members of the assaulting force to receive proper orders. This allowed ample exposure to administration time for allocation and carrying out of tasks, for the preparation of ammunition and other essential stores. This very rarely happened. The apparent reason in this case was due to the fact that safety staff had to be fully briefed and pioneer platoon fully rehearsed – in respect to bangalore torpedoes that had to be positioned. The section now had ladders to make, to which we would climb over enemy wire obstacles, and later put them to good use as litters for the carrying of the dead and wounded. The Battalion live fire attack did go well however. Two rifle companies up and one in depth.

We all approached the enemy position with the invaluable Vickers machine guns continuing with their fire support. They'd been firing for ten solid hours now, straight over our heads, through the night and into the day. The CO at the time wanted this exercise to portray all in its most realistic quality. It was then that I saw something quite remarkable. A DS was putting his stick to good use, brushing aside a man's rifle as his live ammunition was being fired, the rifle pointing dangerously close to another man in the distance. What would they think of next? This was initiative at its best. And here I was, thinking that DS really stood for 'Dip-Shit' or 'Dopey Sergeant'.

The pioneers moved forward and laid their bangalore torpedoes, blowing gaps in the wire in the hope of gaining quicker penetration of the enemy fortification, as opposed to climbing the ladders we'd made. Once again we'd wasted time and resources to manufacture something for no good reason. Those bastards! They knew we weren't going to be using the ladders; not for climbing, nor for carrying wounded.

The bangalores would prevent us from being drawn into enemy firing lanes, or becoming bogged down, and would help us maintain a little conformity to the coming assault. And there was at least one thing that could be said about these figure-eleven targets; as enemy, they certainly knew how to stand their ground.

The assault itself went as many others, and that was that for the exercise; the following day would see an evacuation back to Brisbane; oh, but one thing remained. The battalion had to form up in an extended line and go back over the ground we had just crossed, to pick up every piece of brass from expended ammunition as was humanly possible. A minimum of 75% had to be returned to the manufacturer for recycling. It's too bad that 75% of the trees we'd chopped down for the ladders couldn't be replaced.

Malaysia

December 1983

All members of the company clambered aboard the aircraft with great anticipation for that which lay ahead, arriving at the RAAF air base in Butterworth Malaysia a little before 2000hrs on the 29th NOV with pockets filled to the brim with condoms. Tasks met during this trip seemed to be somewhat belittling to most of the members of the rifle company, from the hierarchy, right down to the administrational staff. Mind you, if anything was to go astray, be blown up, or someone was killed, then look out; somebody's arse was going to end up in a sling for a long, bloody time.

So the task ahead was that of security, a job that had been maintained by the infantry since Australia's arrival some time back when Humphrey Bogart's Great, Great Grandfather was still in diapers and had a snotty nose.

An early rise on the first morning saw the company move into its accommodation, our home for the next three months. The day was surprisingly short with all of the tasks and speeches being met by the troops, those in front nodding their heads periodically and those towards the rear shaking off yawn after yawn. The Malay way of life, customs, and 101 rules and regulations, were spilled out at a hundred miles an hour for the soldier's complete absorption of what life was like in this country. Most ignored this ritual. 'Young men' brought up in a white man's environment normally did shun anything which was alien to them, but an understanding would slowly come about – with the passing of time. But even politicians of years' experience sometimes found a bad word for immigrants (please explain); it all stems from what we are taught at a younger age, regardless of whether we were intelligent or simply sold fish and chips, or what we might have been exposed to at times of hardship: was selling fish and chips hard? Australia itself was a great nation that understands the fundamentals of a multinational society, and a rifleman coming out of his years of adolescence needs a bit of breathing space in order to grasp that same understanding.

Protection of the Australian air base was the obvious priority, but there was no way in which any of us was going to miss out on this opportunity for a free holiday and a little cuddle. But with this opportunity at hand also came abundant time to train, for without the battalion breathing down our backs, every minute of the day seemed to be stolen by the platoon and company headquarters elements in order for them to train their soldiers as they believed best suited the current situation. So training did start in earnest, but at times infantry training seemed to be nothing more than glorified. We all felt a bit like a train driver, each of us training to do a job, but never getting to fulfil; and the older soldiers were even worse off, for rust was being to show on the old-horses of the Coy. So even at this early stage of my career, I was thinking of whether or not I was ever going to get the opportunity to serve overseas; other than what was currently being experienced.

The system for duty in Malaysia was quite simple. The company consisted of three platoons and each platoon had three rifle sections. Each platoon would take on full responsibilities for the task of security for three days [again that number three] whilst the other platoons conducted training, and took time to visit other areas of this wonderful country when time was permitted. For example; a visit to Pulada, a live firing range: Whilst we were here we were going to take full advantage of the ammunition allocation to which the company was receiving, and Pulada was one of the greatest chances we had to blow-away live ammo. We were in the infantry, firing weapons was our bread-n-butter, and to a man of experience cleaning weapons no harder than cleaning a toaster.

The three tasks assigned to a platoon on roster were very straightforward. One section maintained a rove-and-picket, which was a 'foot' mobile patrol around the living quarters and rifle company armoury; another section on QRF, designed for immediate call out to any part of the air base from the QRF guard room; and finally, a section on stand-by, responsible for replacing the QRF within minutes, if the QRF was called out to respond to insurgence. The third section (replacing the QRF) would then prepare for possible reinforced call-out, or call out of their own to a secondary location. On call out the rove-and-picket would continue with their task whilst the original QRF were carrying out their task, speeding around the airfield, in an open-air truck, in order to cordon off the supposed infiltrated area.

The Long Road to Rwanda

Each section task also had numerous pages of Standing Orders that had to be read and understood by the persons conducting any of the duties above. No matter how many times we'd been read the orders before, all were to be read again next time we mounted duty, and our signatures had to be put to paper indicating that we understood those orders. Live ammunition was carried by us; we weren't on Active Service but at any time of day or night we could be called upon to load live ammunition into weapons and deal with any situation which presented itself to us.

The members of the QRF carried live ammunition in magazines; the tops of these were secured with black tape for identification purposes and as prevention against accidental feeding of ammunition into the chamber of the weapons we were assigned, at a time when such hostility wasn't required. Magazines were then placed into basic pouches, to be carried on our person during call out. Call outs 'rehearsals' were conducted twice a night, one before midnight and one after.

On call out – which was initiated by the battalion orderly sergeant – the QRF would leap like startled Gazelles onto the back of the truck with webbing and rife. (Webbing during the trip consisted of a bum pack, ammunition pouches, water bottles and other varying necessities that each individual saw fit to carry, or by which had been laid down by platoon/section SOPs. Needless to say, if you were sitting on the toilet and halfway through your business, you would have to grab whatever you were 'doing' and snap it off, finishing the task at hand at a later date. The allocated driver would then speed off to the area of concern. If you didn't have time to clamber aboard, then you held on for dear life as your mates tried to pull you over the tailgate, another bend in one of the many roads being attacked with savage screeching of tires and griping of gears. All of this was conducted to the aggressive tone of the section commander – sitting next to the driver – whose only words of comradeship were: 'Step on it, arsehole, or I'll drop ya like a bag of shit!'

Once at the destination all would de-bus the truck and race off to secure – for example – each corner to the building of concern (to cordon off the premises of all entry or exit as indicated by the section commander). The section's entry into any of the buildings was not permitted – unless ordered by a higher authority.

Once the area was secure, the section would await the arrival of the local Malaysia Military Police – MP. This was followed by a routine of nationality-meets-nationality, heads being nodded in friendly gesture, and the call out being given the all clear for immediate stand-down of the section on the ground. The section would then return at a leisurely pace back to the QRF room where the toilet was once again employed and your business continued.

Only one other duty was maintained 24hrs a day, seven days a week. There was a small holding pen – concrete shed/bunker – that had been transformed into an armoury, in which all of the company's weapons were stored, some 50 metres from the QRF room. It was fitted with a bed, shower and toilet. A member of the company would be locked up inside this small dwelling to watch over the weapons during the course of his duty. All meals were brought to him by the QRF and this was also the only time in which the cell doors were opened – apart from when relieved of duty each morning. Other occasions for which the doors were opened were in the case of a medical emergency, fire, or when weapons were required by any member/s of the company for training purposes. When this occurred, the weapons register was filled out and the said article/s signed for.

The cell wasn't much more than a cement block with vertical bars set at the front – which also formed the door to the armoury. It wasn't uncommon to have drunken mates return home in the early hours of the morning, waking this guy up, and then dropping stink bombs into the cell. There was no escape from this as opening the cell door was against orders, and such a breach of orders wasn't to be contemplated. You might imagine a tired and weary man with his head pushed up against the inside of the bars, his hands clutching hard his encumbrance, snarling at his mates as they laughed in their drunken stupor. But that was okay, because there was always a way to get back at the bastards; like waiting for them to get drunk when you were free of the cell and then shaving off one of their eyebrows, as shaving one was twice as wicked as shaving two. Some mornings you'd wake to see a man wearing a single bandaid above one of his eyes, on other occasions you'd see a man leant over a sink in the ablutions as he attempted to shave the other eyebrow so that the pathetic look was more evenly spread across his face. Vengeance was so sweet.

For a meal on the base it was best to catch the trucks shuttle-run which the company provided, as the distance to the mess was not a favourable one for walking, in particular when you were suffering from a hangover with a bandaid hanging over your eyebrow.

If you missed the trucks shuttle-run then a visit to the Chow Wallah was essential. Situated in the same building as the boozer, but with a wall separating the two, a short walk of 40 metres would be carried out for the purpose of purchasing cigarettes, soft drink, and a variety of other essentials – which included vegemite sandwiches.

An Indian fellow who'd worked on the air base for a good many years, ran the 'Chow Wallah's' store. Prices in his tiny shop were considerably cheap but money easily spent. His shop – for the use of a better word – was also christened by stink bombs whilst his family was inside. As the stink bombs were crushed under-foot, the door was pulled closed and held from the outside to prevent any escape. The stunt didn't go down too well with the CSM and others, and such activities ceased under the weighty threats of 30 days in the armoury given by the key figureheads from within the company; 'you are here as 'Ambassadors' of Australia'.

The Public

January 1984

One of our favourite drinking establishments was the BC bar, the Butterworth Cafe, usually referred to as the Bat Cave – very cool in mid-December due to the ceiling fans and coolness of sweet beverage. It was situated not much more than a few hundred metres down the road from the front gate to the air base, but then again we were usually inebriated when attending this abode, so we lost two steps in three through staggering.

One of the young ladies here had some problem of sorts, whether it be that she didn't have a tongue or simply suffered a traumatic incident at some time in her life, she just couldn't use speech as a means of communication. The platoon's favourite of all section commanders soon arrived at a firm decision. 'I'll make her talk. Watch this,' and of course, meant no harm.

The ceiling fans were now to be employed as a crucial element to the man's plan of attack. The section commander came in from behind her and placed his hands around her thin waist, allowing support enough to lift her to the wrath of the spinning blades. Without haste her friendly neighbourhood pourer-of-beer came in from behind and started to punch the man in the back. He then let down the silent mute with nothing more than a chuckle escaping his lips. All the young lady could do was convey her thanks for his use of psychology against her infliction, expressing her thoughts by means of rapid hand movements, known in simple terms as obscene sign language, to which even the dumbest of grunts could understand.

Other fun activities could be found further afield.

It was just after 0200hrs when Stallone and I were making our way back towards the ferry, for the thirty-odd minute return trip across the bay, not a soul in sight. Now Stallone was branded the ex-heavy weight champion of an island not so far away, big and placid looking, and full of kindness.

Suddenly two females approached from a side street with smiles across their faces and offerings of sexual pleasure for only ten Ringgit. Stallone took control and commenced negotiations.

The Long Road to Rwanda

He soon had the sexual pleasures down to two Ringgit each. With this he was more than pleased.

On accomplishing this my dark comrade pulled me aside and said: 'Hey, Nigel, watch this,' and thrust his hand under the skirt of one of the wenches before retracting it, himself stepping back a good two metres. For a fleeting moment I thought that he'd discovered a string hanging from the woman, but what he'd discovered hanging there instead was a penis. 'Bloody shims, Nigel!' A man with tits usually recognised by the Adam's apple, and at other times harder to spot: But I guess a penis in the hand isn't as easily mistaken as an Adam's apple to the eye. For a moment there I also saw the shim's eyes light up and a smile fall upon its face; 'it' must have thought that all its birthdays had come at once.

We were on our way in no time at all, being showered in threats of violence as we took off down the road, several trishaw drivers looked up and over towards us briefly before continuing on their way – what did they care for the antics of two Australians. Stallone could do nothing but laugh.

Not all soldiers in the platoon learnt from their lessons early on in the trip, and several of the much-much-older members of the company found themselves in quite a bit of embarrassment when in Singapore. But even now, the truth behind these stories will forever remain top secret.

Close Encounter

January 1984

It was always suggested that no man proceed outside of the barracks area by himself for reasons of safety. But that was like telling a little boy that he couldn't have any candy until after dinner and then placing the candy jar in front of his face with the lid removed. Anyway, the Malaysians on the front gate certainly didn't regulate these rules and were more often than not seen to give us a hearty wave with a smile as we came and went as we desired.

So I weighed up the odds, Yep. Stuff it, I'd go.

So within no time at all I was on the ferry and approaching the docks of Penang, one hand in my pocket having a good scratch and the other on my wallet. The ramps were secured and off I stepped, straight into the throngs of trishaw drivers who all insisted that they were the cheapest for only two Ringgit.

I was suddenly grabbed on the arm and as I swung around a short guy wearing a scar across his face said: 'You come, me cheap. Two Ringgit anywhere you like go.' He wasn't intimidating at all, but I wouldn't want to have met the fellow who'd given him the scar.

'Why not,' I said. 'Just take me to the Hong Kong bar thanks.'

So I followed, and as we approached his trishaw, another man, but slightly older in appearance, tugged at my sleeve. 'Hong Kong bar, one Ringgit, very cheap; you come.'

'Bloody oath I will.'

As I clambered aboard his trishaw, a smile cascaded over my face in recognition of the windfall of luck I was having. Today was going to be a lucky day. I turned to look out towards my left as I sat upon the wooden seat, for no apparent reason, and as the driver of my urban convertible peddled off a silver blade could be seen to glint by way of the sun's rays. It was the other trishaw driver, obviously displeased with the loss of a potential customer, trying to stab me. I was fortunate to escape from serious injury, just in the nick of time. Yep. Today was my lucky day.

The trip was slow, the peddler of this contraption breathing in heavy gasps as though preparing to take his last. I could have walked faster.

I don't know who was more inconvenienced; myself for the slow ride, or the trishaw driver for having to pull me along for a single Ringgit.

A doorway then caught my eye. People inside were sitting around seemingly waiting for something or someone. A mouse was then seen scurrying around the walls of the small room in which the people waited, and then another.

'Hey, what's that over there?'

'Is Doctor Lim's clinic. Not far now. Hong Kong bar come soon.' I had to presume the worst from the scene, that the doctor wasn't a veterinarian and that those seated in the waiting room weren't there for an animal show.

Later that same night I met up with some friends on the ferry back to the mainland. I soon departed company with them however and found myself someone more interesting to converse with. I don't know which was more interesting; the smile on her lovely face or the breasts popping out of her blouse.

Time travelled quickly and my Malay company departed. Once again I found myself alone and ready to disembark. The ferry was docking. Now, I was so drunk that I had somehow found myself below the main deck where vehicles normally made their way onto the ferry, but that didn't pose a problem, for I knew my way around.

'You. Hey!' I turned to see a stranger approach. 'You have cigarettes?' I was as drunk as a skunk, so I should have some somewhere. I padded my pockets and looked the stranger in the eye, rocking slightly upon my feet. He seemed armless enough and wore ragged clothes. Why not. 'Take the pack mate. Here. And the matches too.'

'You Aussie?'

'Yeah.'

'You go air base?'

'That's right.'

'My Brother is taxi driver. I tell him to take you for cheap.'

So I followed in earnest.

On reaching the taxi I found five men dressed in below standard dress. Normal enough. 'I need a taxi to the RAAF base,' I explained to all.

My newfound friend looked at me. 'No, you wait. I fix.'

He went to the side of one of the waiting men, and commenced his explanation, not quite audible enough for me to hear, and not spoken in English.

The man came back with the response, standing between our two parties, the now official interpreter. 'My Brother, he say ten Ringgit.'

'Bloody what? That's more than normal.'

'No. is cheap.'

'Piss off. I want me cigarettes back,' and with my hand held open I stepped closer, 'and my bloody matches.'

I was handed two cigarettes nervously and the taxi drivers shuffled in their places. 'I want more. I gave you a whole pack.'

'No. You go now. You walk.'

I stepped closer still, and as I looked out to the side a further twenty odd taxi drivers were seen to come out from nowhere.

'Nigel!' I stopped and turned about. 'Get your arse over here now. And don't bloody run.' My mates from the top deck. 'Time to go home.'

'But that bastards got my durries.'

'You can have some of mine.'

Two close calls in one day. It 'was' my lucky day.

On reflection I think that if the shoe was on the other foot, and places and countries were traded, in this given situation, that the group of Australians would have kicked the hell out of the Malay. So I never really did have a bad thought against the man and his taxi-driver friends. They were far less racist than most of us.

The Bunny Bar

January 1984

One of the more highly classed bars of town in which we sometimes frequented, and found ourselves admiring, was an upstairs palace known exclusively as the Bunny Bar. Ladies of the night – and day – could be found here, more pricey than normal, but rather gorgeous – or so we were led to believe. Only two entrances existed to the Bunny Bar, one was a small elevator, the other was a narrow staircase.

The whole platoon had managed to find its way here; all except the boss, platoon sergeant, five non-drinkers, and the boxer Stallone.

I turned to one of the older guys, Smithy. 'Where are all the whores, mate? Doesn't seem to be any around.'

He turned on his stool. 'See that door over there with those two big bloody gorilla type bouncers?'

'Biggest guys I've seen in this country.'

'Well, behind that snot-blowing door are the whores. All ready and waiting. All you have to do is buy them a drink and the negotiating starts. You have to be pretty nifty with your mouth to get a good price in there, I tell you that for nothing.'

'You want to go in then, Smithy, Just you and me? I'd go myself only I'm a bit pissed.'

'Why not.' And with that we entered the insalubrious hindquarters.

We soon found ourselves a seat and had no sooner ordered our drinks when two females came along and sat down beside us – by-far more beautiful, characteristically cheerful, and open minded, then any Australian-born counterpart, but then again, I guess they had to be, for this country was so full of whores that you couldn't walk into a bar without knocking one over.

My smile soon dissipated however when I received my change from the first round of drinks, looking up at the waitress with a gleam of murderous intent. Jesus Christ. No wonder all of the boys only came to the Bunny Bar to drink in the other lounge. This backroom business was a rip off – though still cheap by Australian standards.

'I think you might have been right, Smithy. If this place was anything to go by the price of these two piss-ant drinks of ours, then we're in trouble.' I turned my head to the young female that sat beside me and tried a smile. 'How much, sweetie?'

Her lips parted sexually with a starting price, when a commotion was heard to rise from the main area of the bar.

Smithy was already at the door. 'Hey, Nigel. The boys are leaving for the next bar. Let's get the hell out of here.'

'Right with you mate,' I said and turned to the others at our table. 'See you ladies later.'

We joined our comrades in arms at the elevator that was designed for 14 persons, the 22nd man pushing from the rear as he too, stepped into the box. 'Get in boys.' A bouncer grabbed the last man by his arm. Big mistake. The section commander turned on his heels and bang, punched him hard; smack in the centre of the head. 'Piss off.'

The door closed, the platoon descended in the elevator, and the doors opened. We had missed the ground level by three feet – too much weight. One by one we now climbed out as the manager of the hotel pulled at his hair, screaming obscenities in a language none understood, and then more in broken English, looking much like the Malay answer to Basil Fawlty.

The following morning, and for some strange reason, we found that we'd been banned from going to the Bunny Bar again during our stay in the country. From that day on, all visits were cut to just a few, and on entry we would inform the management that we were RAAF, and that we hated the AJs to death – ID was rarely asked for. They too had to enforce their rules and regulations by standing behind their ban, but on the same token they needed customers for the lovely ladies in the adjoining room. It would seem that our wallets were able to negotiate practically anything.

New Years - Palada

1983 – 1984

Just a few days after our return from Thailand, we were packing our field gear in preparation for Pulada. It wasn't what you'd call a bush trip; just 'a part thereof'.

Most of the nights were to be spent in the comforts of a featureless building that was large enough to take all 30 members of the platoon. The only comforts of home were what each individual carried in his pack. Not even cots were issued, an item used extensively during non-tactical deployments into the field, usually seen in most BHQ and rear echelon areas during large scale exercises, where the distance between those elements, and the minor infantry call signs, was anything from ten kilometres to one hundred. Kangaroo exercises in the late eighties were a prime example of this. Never let it be said that a pogo had it hard.

And as promised, there was a shower block with sinks, and discoloured walls where the mirrors had been smashed years before and removed, no doubt, by the few residents who lived in these parts. It was a fine thing to have if you didn't mind putting up with cold water and scorpions. You could almost guarantee that death would be around the corner if bit by one of those little bastards, not like the Australian cousin which just made you a little queasy.

Early mornings and nights were repetitious, brought on by the fact that there was no lighting available for late night card games or the reading of novels and stick books. New Year's Eve here was one for the memory, something never to be forgotten. On this occasion the coming of the New Year would be seen from the comfort of an all-night ambush.

We'd returned from the ranges early for preparation of the ambush to come; cleaning weapons, last nap, last feed, camouflage those faces, check magazines and get ready your warm weather gear. Mossy repellent on, stretcher tops packed in case of casavac, orders groups and rehearsal sessions. Carry out preparation of claymores, trip flares, early warning devices; test fire machine guns, M16s, SLRs and pack signal flares. Prepare gun stakes, night sight devices, and comms-cord;

have your last cigarette, last piss and shit and prepare to move. That was the icing on the cake, for a reconnaissance was needed as well as a safety DS brief, a necessity for all live fire activities, and that's exactly what this was. Nothing we'd never carried out before.

After the ambush was initiated all went through the procedures – tactically mind you – of reinitiating, searching for the enemy, taking of POWs and medical treatment to wounds sustained. Then came the withdrawal to the firm base and the move from the firm base back to the barracks with the cold water and scorpions. Time for a quick shave and onto the trucks; we were going to the anti tank range for the firing of the 84mm Carl Gustaf. It was here that one of the biggest flukes ever was performed. A guy named Pugsy achieved a headshot with the weapon from over 550 metres. Definitely more arse than class.

The best thing of all however, was what lay ahead of the platoon; for at the fortnights end was a three-day trip to Singapore. Good byyyye ambush.

Singapore

January 1984

The three days in Singapore was hectic to say the least. Every man seemed to do nothing more than race around in an effort to see as much as humanly possible. This certainly didn't interfere with our heavy consumption of the amber nectar. You may imagine a taxi being driven down the main road of the city, a few heads sticking out of the windows, and with can in hand all you can hear is, 'come on, driver; hurry up, hurry up; next bar, next bar. I've seen this bloody road before – ah look. Looks like a museum or something – step on the bloody thing, driver; I'm nearly empty'.

Shopping in Singapore took care of most wages, with many of the soldiers being caught surprised that none had come across a Mickey Mouse Rolex. Bugis Street saw to what cash remained. All the good looking females were her, and all were shims as well – what a waste and a shame – most with distinguishing voices which were deeper than any of those in the platoon, Adams' apples bobbing up and down as they spoke. You should have seen the look on the CSM's face as a shim sat down either side of him – he didn't know which way to look; left, right, or down at the two hands that were making a move towards his fly.

During the first two nights in Singapore the precedent was set. All would congregate in Bugis Street as though to the call of nature and led by the star that brought the three wise men to Bethlehem. A hangout was formed at the crossroad, smack in the centre of the two streets that formed a huge café-type area with seating and tables, where all would eat and drink like it was going out of fashion. Even late at night the kitchens could be seen smoking away, cooking rice dishes to fulfil our needs, and those of any tourists, each of the chefs seemingly cowering under the onslaught of flies.

Beer and spirits were downed one after the other, everyone was laughing and having a great time. It made for a late night and even later rise.

I thankfully never made the third night to this congregation. The mate I was shacked up with had made a reverse charge call back to

Nigel B.J. Clayton

Australia from his hotel room against all advice. I'd informed him to check with reception as to cost, but no. The extent of damage ended up costing me all I had. Someone had to bail the guy out.

Anyway; that night down on the legend hangout came screams of blistering pain and mayhem. For whatever reason unbeknown to the Australians, but caused by mischievous goings on, the stall holders and residents from around commenced a reign of terror with iron bars, wooden bats, and buckets of boiling water. A few of the platoon were taken to hospital, but nothing too serious. Bugis Street was closed down and we holidaymakers were moved by C130 back to Butterworth with hangovers as big as our ego's.

It stands to mention that American and British sailors were also present on Bugis Street during the clash of the titans. During this battle it was the yanks that turned tail and fled, leaving the Poms and Aussies to conduct a fighting withdrawal with honour. Damn Yanks; always late to enter a fight and always eager to leave one, and anyone claiming them to be the best soldiers in the world should be ashamed for the lie: if anything they are one of the worst.

Rogue

February 1984

Of the three months in Malaysia, all the platoon could muster in respect to days in the field – in a tactical environment – was three (although the trip was initially planned for seven). The OC at the time explained why. Simply put, the first exercise area to which they were looking at was under the constant harassment of guerrilla activities, and the second was flooded by way of natural disaster. The third choice was accepted, although deferred for several days. You can imagine the images going through my mind when he said 'guerrilla'. I thought that there were silverbacks thrashing through the scrub and beating their chests; it took me a while to realise he was referring to rebels.

Finally however we headed off.

The platoon was tactical from the moment we set foot on the soil, pushing out into a defendable position, whilst a work-party of five grabbed packs from the trucks, the trucks in turn took off down the road and vanished from sight at the same instant that the rain commenced to fall. The enemy (a small group of three soldiers from the company) had been given map coordinates. The platoon was now to search them out and attack their position. To move without being seen – to aid in our approach – a nearby creek-line was used to our advantage. The foliage was thick for a good fifty metres either side of the approach. The map also showed the entire area of operations as a low depression, which was why the weather had almost claimed this area as a victim of flood. So here we were, up to our waists in stagnant water, and being showered upon from the thickening clouds above. The move forward came to a stop. Had the scout seen the enemy? No; just a deadly snake taking a swim across the front of the scout's path. 'Okay, keep moving. It's okay, if it bites you'll be taken to hospital; don't worry,' said one of the officers. That bastard; who did he think he was, my mother?

The third day in semi-jungle had drawn to a close and the platoon was preparing for night routine when the platoon sig came down to my pit. 'Your 2IC wants me to tell you that you're on picket first. You and me.'

'How come you're with us?'

'I'm not really tired and your section's got the least number of blokes.' An extremely light whistle was heard. The signaller turned to receive the stand-down signal from the scout. We both picked ourselves up and headed over to the machine gun, to find mud upon mud around our ankles. We sat down, the rain continuing to fall. I could feel the mud in the crack of my arse so quickly moved over a foot and found a sharp rock to sit on instead.

'Anyway, Nigel,' he continued as the look of discomfort faded from my face, 'there's a rogue elephant loose.'

We watched our arcs continuously, although very little could be seen in the dark of the jungle. Ears and other senses played an important role here. I quite honestly thought that after many years of experience that there was truth behind the sixth sense, although I would only experience it a dozen times or so during my 16 year career. Decisions had been made on such instincts, and usually for the better. But here is the reality: ie; six billion people in the world, each one experiences four dreams per night, that's 24 billion dreams each day, and even if only 0.01 percent of those dreams were to come true then that would be… ah…. Come on grunt… quite a lot. Coincidences are no different. Is there truth behind the sixth sense, behind the saying 'I knew that was going to happen, I had a dream last night'. Sorry, no; just a dream; just chance, simple luck.

'A bloody what?' I whispered. Did he say road or vogue? I'd heard of Vogue Magazine, but never a vogue elephant, but I could see how it would be on the 'road'.

'A rogue elephant. It broke loose from its chains earlier on today. It was being used in a chain gang just up the road a bit.'

'Bullshit,' I said. Why would it be in a chain gang, come on! Did it commit a crime or something?

'No; fair dinkum.'

'I don't believe you.'

'It's the bloody truth, Nigel; I'm telling ya straight. The enemy group were brought in through another section's gun fifteen minutes ago because of the danger.'

'How come no one's said anything to me about it?'

'I'm telling you now. I was told to pass it on as I was coming down to see you.' So I turned my head to face the front once again, the beauty of the night taking control, although the rain still fell, insects giving eternal resonance to the surroundings as they always did, no matter what jungle we happen to be in – even in the openness of the training area of Shoalwater Bay. Then in the distance a groaning was heard. Was it distant thunder, or a pissed off elephant?

    The following morning, after all tactical routine had been completed, the exercise was pulled to a halt. The platoon headed off for the nearest road in single file. The trucks would be there to meet us. It wasn't until we were heading out of the area that I really believed the story of the rogue elephant, and the piles of shit we saw along the road on the way out of the jungle simply added testimony to the fact.

Disease

February 1984

We returned back to Australia on the 22nd, and for those that were married it wasn't too soon. About two thirds of these had been unfaithful to their wives, and those that had been faithful had well-trained hands.

One particular guy, a day before returning, had reported to the medic that he'd been pissing razor blades. He was given a few shots for it and told to abstain from sex for a few days. 'But I'm married. My wife was going to expect it. I can't tell her, no, I'm sorry, I have a headache.' So he devised a plan that could easily have backfired.

On the first night with his wife, they made passionate love. The following afternoon he confronted her. 'You bitch. You've been with someone else; haven't you?'

'No. No, it's not true!' she said.

'Then why am I pissing razor-blades?'

'Okay. I only did it the once. I promise. Just a one night stand.'

It would seem that the women back home were having just as much fun as the men.

Duke of Gloucester Cup Squad

May 1984

The Duke of Gloucester Cup competition team was known as the DOG squad by members of the 8/9th Battalion, a competition that was brought back into existence in 1983 after many years of absence. Apparently the yearly venue used to compare shooting results between Infantry units and the team with the highest average took the line honours that came in the form of a large cup/trophy. The cup would then be proudly displayed in a cabinet case of the winning battalion, in BHQ, where only a small percentage of the BN members would actually get to see it; namely the hierarchy. Soldiers do the work, rank gets the trophy. There was a little conjecture that the cup should have been displayed in the OR's boozer; after all, it was a section competition and had nothing to do with officers. It was in prime position near the entrance to BHQ where an officer could stand beside his wife and proudly state, 'look, darling; we won this last year,' to be met by her puppy-dog eyes, and she thinking how hard he must have worked, and how deserving he was to get some extra special sex that night.

The competition had now been given a face-lift and each battalion's representation had to compete over a five-day period. Each team consisted of a section of ten men – along with several reserves in the case of injury.

Infantry style events were the key to the new précis that saw a specific activity being completed for each day of the five-day period. The competition was conducted in Singleton NSW, the home of the infantry soldier, a home where mummies and daddies weren't allowed and boys had to learn to become men.

Monday

A Test of Elementary Training (TOET) was to be conducted on the M16, M60, SLR and M203, along with a short rifle shoot with the SLR down at the 25m range. During this type of shoot/test, the DS would place drill rounds amongst the live ammunition. Two ten-round magazines with two and three drill rounds respectively in each would force the shooter to carry out his 'Immediate Action' (IA) and 'Stoppage' drills to see how proficient he was with the weapon. Time and time again was spent rehearsing the IA and stoppages until they became second nature: Weapon fires, weapon stops, tilt right, cock the weapon, lock the working parts to the rear, tilt left and look in. Rounds in the magazine, no round in the chamber, release the working parts forward and continue firing. Weapon stops again, tilt right, cock and lock, tilt left and look in. Rounds in the magazine, no round in the chamber, gas stoppage. Release working parts forward, apply safety catch, pull weapon back, re-adjust the gas setting, weapon into the shoulder, safety to fire, and continue firing.

That mind you was just one example of many. All weapons have specific rules which govern its operation and these have to be applied in specific order, to force habit upon the soldier, to hopefully enable each individual to remedy IA and stoppages without the need to think about what he's doing – like I said, second nature. Like approaching a busy road, you don't say to yourself that you have to check left and right before crossing, you just do it; or you see a beautiful girl across the road and your tongue suddenly flops out upon the footpath and you have to spend the next few minutes trying to tuck it back in. Nobody likes to look like a fool or to spend free-time scraping gravel from their tongue, but it's natural that these things take place when seeing a good-looking chick. I always say that it is better to be pestered by your tongue on the footpath when seeing a pretty girl, than it is to choke on it from seeing an ugly one.

Tuesday

A half-yearly 'Battle Fitness Test' (BFT) was conducted, 15km's of running in boots with ten kilograms of webbing plus an individual weapon – be it M203, SLR, M16 or M60, an additional 3-10 kilo's.

The new health and safety act doesn't allow for a soldier to run more than two kilometres of the 15, but back then there was no such explicit directive, and as for everything else this had to be trained for. Most of our fitness training involved several hours of physical training per day.

1 hour 17 minutes was the best the others and I could muster in training for the 15km run, and on the day of competition this proved

to be inadequate.

At the completion of the run, the second phase of assessment came into effect. This came in the form of a shoot, after all, the idea of conducting a battle fitness test was to be able to run 15km and conduct a battle of some description at its conclusion. If this was the case, why was it that during my entire 16-year career, I never once got to conduct a platoon or company attack at the end of a 15km run, organised as a battalion test of fitness? Wasn't I always being told to 'train hard, fight easy'? The army was sometimes so contradicting in its ways. I personally had never heard of so much bull. No matter how hard you train, during battle conditions you were going to be pushing yourself to the max. If your personal fitness was going to have a direct effect on your mates' lives, then you would take care to maintain your fitness, if not, then you were unreliable and inadequate as a soldier. But how can you take care of your fitness if you were stuck in the depths of the jungles of Vietnam for 12 months. Most rely on guts. Fitness – to a certain degree – was a statement of mind.

Anyway, today's shooting test was a modified falling plate. Balloons had replaced metal plates. The scoring system had something to be desired.

By the end of the day's activities our section didn't feel the best. We wouldn't know the results until Friday, but it wasn't looking great at present.

Wednesday

A marksmanship shoot was usually offered to soldiers who had passed the previous elementary practice; if you don't pass the elementary, you don't do the marksman. A minimum of 200 was required from a total score of 275. Doesn't really sound like much, until you do the shoot.

The lead up training for the boys of 8/9RAR went well and all were expecting to achieve the 200 required, with myself anticipating a score of 210. The 210 soon ended up being 178 as a funny thing happened whilst at the manufacturer. The scoring targets were normally cut from a single piece of ply, three targets being obtainable from the wood in question. Today we found – after the shoot – that by way of 'someone's' ultimate wisdom, 'someone' wanted to get four targets per piece to save on funds. I guess this must have been the first of the defence cuts, and all the while I thought there was something horribly wrong with my eyes. So out of the six battalions – a possible 60 marksmanship passes – only three passed due simply to the width of all targets being drastically reduced.

According to statistics of the representation down here there should have been a good 35 to 45 passes. Stuff the cut backs, and that's all I have to say about that, because I knew as Gump does; that life was meant to be a carton of squirrels, or something like that.

Thursday

Drill day. The test today was the pro-forma still being performed throughout the battalions in 1996, except the battalions in '96 performed this with the steyr, and slight modification on its march-past and march-off. It was a guard mount format of 30 minutes duration dressed in polyester uniform, embellishments, grade one slouch hat, black belt and spit polished boots – back in the good old days 'high shine' boots were never used, just spit, water, parade gloss and elbow grease attacking an everyday normal boot. It usually took many days to get a good shine, if not weeks.

Black belts also had to be lacquered and polished – not just a piece of car seat belt cut to suit the wearer as was the case today. It was no wonder that discipline fell through the roof in later years. Too many easy options were coming into play.

A dress inspection was followed by a weapons inspection. One DS looked us over whilst the other deducted points for faults, all one million and one of them; then came the drill, more than 50 verbal orders, some requiring three to six separate movements.

Discipline seemed to be the key factor here, simple concentration on the job without infringement. Keep the eyes looking directly to your front, if you didn't, and the eyes wondered, then you lost points for it. Quite simple really. And as for the women watching the parade from the front row, as a friend of mine from the rear rank would say, keep your damn legs together.

Friday

The big finale. Obstacle course day.

The weapons which we took so much care in refining for the perfect shot to be fired, and hours to clean with toothbrush and toothpick in readiness for the inspection during the drill on Thursday, was now going through the mud, water, knocks and basic abuse; all of which was part and parcel of any obstacle course. This would be the biggest buster and lung burner of them all, because today we had to push ourselves beyond that which we'd trained. Every second counted here. Can you imagine coming second place to a battalion who had beaten you by a matter of one second? This was all-possible and could never be lived down; better to lose by several minutes or not at all, so there was no choice, we had to go for broke.

A little under 20 minutes was the estimate for a section to complete the 17 to 20 obstacles ranging from vertical ropes, horizontal ropes, and swinging ropes; four, six and ten foot walls; 20 foot ladder wall, monkey bars, height reducing jumps, tunnel, bear pit, wire obstacles and others. Teamwork was the only road to success.

An equipment check was to be carried out prior to the obstacle course being conducted and on completion was to be conducted again to ensure that nothing was missing. All was to go with us; webbing and individual weapons, spare gun barrel, all remaining CES to all weapons, med kit, full water bottles, two grenades (M30) per person and other field equipment such as toggle ropes, and stretcher tops/ground sheets.

On conclusion of the second equipment check, after the course had been run, came the throwing of the M30 practice grenades. An infantry soldier was supposed to be able to throw one 35 metres, a big ask in itself.

So two grenades per man were thrown at a small fighting bay some 25 metres away. What do you do; a straight throw for accuracy but a smaller opening due to trajectory, or do you lob the grenade up for higher trajectory giving less accuracy but larger target opening. It all averaged out to be the same, each to his own, but throw both the same way in order that the second throw can be adjusted to suit. Most BNs only received an average 25 percent achievement in hits.

This brought the comp to its conclusion, all apart from the announcement of the overall cup winners and grinners. It wasn't the 8/9th battalion. Maybe next year.

Reconnaissance Course

November 1984

The course this year was not much more different than the previous; it was still out in the field. During the course there was one incident to which I could recall as though it occurred yesterday; it was the only thing that differentiated it from the previous, apart from the new faces.

It was during the final week of the course and all had been given orders for the close reconnaissance and surveillance of a suspected enemy camp sight. The squad's orders were the same as always, to obtain as much information in its broadest of terms on SALUTE HIM; strength, arms, logistics, unit, tactics, equipment, habits, intentions and morale. A field sketch was also required, which included details such as the distance between enemy pits, gathered by way of counting the amount of paces the enemy took from one to the other and then converting this into metres (depending on the enemies average height). We were also required to record things such as weapons arcs of fire, attained by way of compass bearings.

At present we had one pack, this contained the radio, one sleeping bag, a hutchie and a one-man ration pack between the five members of the squad, as two days earlier the DS had purposely informed the enemy of our recon patrol's position. On encountering the enemy – under specific circumstances – our recon force of five was to tactically withdraw in the opposite direction. Due to this the enemy now had nearly all of our equipment.

A message was received over the radio; it was 1400hrs. We were to move to a pick up point designated by the DS via a 'safe route' as indicated by him. He would accompany us for ease of navigation. Any blind man, without a seeing-eye dog, could see from ten miles that it was a set up; unless of course you were a dumb-smuck or a drop-out-uni-student.

So here we were, strung out in single file and moving alongside an animal track, when all of a sudden a vehicle could be heard just out of eyesight some 50 metres to our front. The lead scout turned to signal this information back down the line when the brush to the right woke up all the dead by way of several hundred blank rounds and several

The Long Road to Rwanda

grenade simulators being consumed in a matter of seconds. We hit the deck, laid down covering fire, and withdrew as taught.

Realistically we'd all be dead, but so long as we carried out our procedures as taught, and to the letter, then the DS was quite content to let us live on under his ever watchful eye – how kind of him.

Within a minute we had broken contact with the enemy. The DS appeared at the acting patrol commander's side. 'You've got a wounded soldier, Pete. Your scout's been hit in the arm and is suffering from shell shock.'

The wounded soldier was shuffled onto a shoulder.

Pete deployed a man to either flank, and we all raced off up the hill towards the road and the waiting rover; our method of exfiltration. Twenty metres remained until safe evacuation... ten. The men on the flanks dropped to counter any likely enemy movement from the rear as the vehicle was approached with the fireman's carried scout.

Another surprise was confronted. The driver, another DS, eyeballed our group as we approached from just three metres. 'It's too hot! It's too hot!' he hollered, and sped off into the distance leaving behind nothing more than a cloud of dust with a few words like 'you bastard' escaping our lips.

No time to reflect on what could have been. A quick whistle and heads turned. We headed off into the creek-line on the reverse side of the spur for protection. 'What you going to do, Pete?' asked the DS.

'Give first aid and get the hell out of here.'

'Where?' probed the DS.

'Out the creek and up this re-entrant. It's a covered route. A hundred metres and we'll take off on a bearing towards the AO boundary.'

'Go to it then.'

'Nigel; fix the scout up,' allocated Pete, 'we're leaving in one minute,' and with that Pete briefly assessed the situation whilst I went about the business of applying a field dressing to the scouts proposed wound.

The DS was at my side. 'What you going to do?'

'Just apply this to stop the bleeding.'

'Is that it?'

'He's conscious so I don't need to worry about nothing else.'

'Well he won't be for long unless you treat him for shell shock as well. I want to see you reassure him.'

That's the last thing I would have thought of in this tactical situation. What the hell. I'll reassure him; couldn't hurt.

The DS said: 'What the hell you doing?'

'Reassuring the patient and fixing his wound.'

'You're talking too loud, the enemy will hear you.' Five seconds later. 'You're still talking too loud.' I lowered my voice to a fine whisper. 'It's still too loud.'

'If I whisper any more the bastard won't hear me.'

'Right, that's it.' The DS stood. 'You're lucky I don't put you on a bloody charge for insubordination.' He looked around at the others, as though he'd been a naughty boy. 'End of exercise, fellahs. Move yourselves up this spur till you hit the road and head back in. Clayton, you make sure you stay a good one hundred metres behind us all. You hear me?'

'Yeah, sure.'

He took off up the slope that led towards a road and then the course administration tent.

When I reached the road the other four were waiting, the DS not in sight. 'What's going on?' I asked of the other members of the squad.

'He said that you stuffed things up and that we should beat your head in before taking you with us back to the admin tent,' replied Pete.

'So what's going to happen?' I was inquisitive for obvious reasons.

'Nothing.' And with that we ventured into the admin area to prepare the patrol report; we were also given our packs back.

Four days later I was informed that I'd failed the course for the second time. It seemed to me that the chief instructor didn't like having anyone that was smarter than him on the course, which I guess is why he didn't have many friends.

3/4 CAV

March 1985

Due to commitments with the DOG squad some members had inadvertently missed their opportunity to partake of the Subject One for Corporal Course with the 8/9th battalion. The CO, however, managed to arrange something for us; or was it the RSM with his god-like influence.

Four of the team – including myself – now found ourselves on the doorsteps of 3/4CAV, ready to tackle the subject course for corporal along with 30 or so members of that unit – it was interesting to note that the unit ended up moving north some years later, the 2/14 Queensland Mounted Rifles taking its place in Brisbane, only a few hands of regular remaining stationed in situ.

We were divided up into the three different sections and during the three day field phase at the back of Enoggera Barracks were given positions as section commanders within the sections due to the cav private soldiers lack with experience in employing minor infantry tactics (not dissimilar to the infantry jumping into an APC as crew commander; we'd be more than lost). The fourth Infantryman acted as platoon sergeant, and we each rotated through the task over the days spent in the field.

At the completion of the six week course we all found that we had all come within the top five places of the course, a very reasonable effort considering our understanding of infantry minor tactics. As we departed their hospitality many things came back to mind, one of these was a cav soldier's method of arousal during the introduction phase of his weapon lesson. He was being tested on his instructional technique, primarily; giving a structured lesson to a section group on the pistol 9mm L9A1.

A friend of his had met with an unfortunate accidental, whereby suicide was endeavoured, and did prove fatal. So what was wrong with his lesson? Well; it doesn't go down too well when you point a pistol to your head, indicating that a good use for it was in committing suicide; it wasn't as though he had a feather duster in his hand. It was at times like this that people needed the utmost support possible, and

Nigel B.J. Clayton

the gentleman in question was removed from the course, less the smile on his face which might have been present if he had in fact held a feather duster. A lot of stories commenced to float around at about this time, in regards to the incident, but we can't very well adhere to hearsay, for it was sometimes incorrect, and in this circumstance, rumours quite troubling. No one person was safe from ridicule, but at least with the army you had a family in which to brace your fall; or so we all thought and were led to believe.

Exercise Close Country

June 1985

Glenn Innes was about 300 kilometres South of Brisbane, and down there, somewhere, was a wonderful little place which could be classified as nothing less than rain forest – the rain never ceased during the course of our stay. Thank God that was only two weeks. It never really surprised me that the army could find the worst training areas with the highest rain fall; it's as though they organised the rain, the CQ having placed an order for 'dark skies and thunder'.

It wasn't uncommon to have guys come down with heat illness, even in weather conditions as those experienced here. The Coy CSM was more concerned about this than anyone else. His only comment however, used to be something along the lines of, 'come on, fellahs; get him squared away and fixed up. I don't want him dying on me, there's too much paperwork involved'.

Many a man came down with something. Never on Civilian Street would you see guys like this, doing what they were doing, and in the condition that they were in. I for one hadn't eaten in three days, had a heavy cold, was coughing up phlegm, had a runny nose, diarrhoea, and just literally felt like dying. The section commander had me share a pit with another to watch over me, to report on my eating habits. I'd been told to eat but found it extremely difficult. I missed out on three nights of gun picket due to the illness but found that I couldn't sleep anyway. It was suggested that I be removed back to barracks due to ill health but I stubbornly refused and desperately tried forcing the food down my throat. The section and platoon attacks had to be conducted though, and as the section was down to six men I still availed myself to the assaults, in order that the work could be spread more evenly around.

Time and time again the same hill was taken in grotesque similarity to the movie Hamburger Hill. Fire and moving up the slope was accompanied with a quick dry reach and then coughing up of all sorts of shit, then move again, another bound towards the dug in enemy defensive position.

And then one day we pushed the enemy off. Look out for counter attack; rehearse the procedures tactfully over and over again. Then we withdraw from the position, and I have no idea why; so let's take that bloody hill again tomorrow morning, and without a sigh, for we were to start all over again, all from scratch; and that's no lie.

A section patrol was required; an aggressive search for the small groups of enemy that still existed was required. The section's departure from the platoon position followed brief orders.

Only 500 metres of the patrol route had been covered when I made my first pit stop. Three more soon followed, each stop accompanied by the pulling down of my trousers, dropping a load of diarrhoea, and then taking a few seconds for the luxury of a wipe with wet paper in the never relenting rain. Up with the trousers and continue with the patrol. The section was now down to five men so I had little choice but to continue with the tasks handed down from above. I felt sorry for those behind; you could see them screwing up their face as they closed the gap, seeing me dump a load of diarrhoea and continue on with the patrol. It was the only time the section commander didn't insist the men behind me patrol their arcs professionally as he was aware of the problems associated with stepping in runny shit. You can imagine a man returning home after work, his girlfriend or wife traipsing behind him and looking for shit stains on the carpet as though he was a naughty puppy.

The following day I was feeling much better and approached the section commander about being put back on the gun picket, and he was happy that I was back to normal. He was hesitant at first but needed the manpower for the 12-hour shift – no one enjoyed four and more hours of picket. (No dead man on the gun was heard of these days, not in this platoon in any case).

Hutchies were permitted at night due to the downpour from the heavens above, until contact by the enemy had been made.

Then the enemy arrived with an aggressive initiation of fire from several weapons. Stand-to was passed around, each man scrambling from his sleeping bag, feeling around for his webbing in the dark still nine tenths asleep, eyes only a quarter open. Hutchies were quickly pulled down to prevent any possible silhouette, for the enemy may use this as a reference for our likely pit position. Then with webbing on and the rifle in hand each individual would get down in the mud, usually next to a large tree, behind a log, in a depression in the ground, anything to give protection from enemy small arms fire and shrapnel from grenades and other foreign matter. No digging was permitted in the forest so we didn't have pits to get into – which would have been filled with rain in any case, a situation I had faced in the past: we were not stranger's to the brutal nature of working tactically in the bush.

Suddenly all went quiet. Ten seconds later and the creatures of the night commenced again with their serenades, a rustle in the foliage from all around being heard; bush roaches, rats and all other manner of night-life poking their heads up once more. I thought it was marvellous. Here we were, young men lying in the dirt and the rain, and the only things with an ounce of brains seemed to be the tiny creatures of the night.

Then an exclamation of horror was heard as our platoon arachnophobic stepped into another palm sized spider similar to the St.Andrews Cross, then more silence – you should have seen him a year later when he dug up a bird spider in Shoalwater bay; it was quite a time before he returned to his fighting bay. I didn't know what was better; the rats and spiders of Tully, stealing your rations and clambering over your back, or the spiders in-your face at Shoalwater Bay [and other places like Glenn Innes]. I loved the bush, but sometimes it simply didn't love you back, no matter how many days you accumulated in the field. It was like having a girlfriend who always complained of having a headache, and no matter how many painkillers they took, they simply wouldn't submit to letting you enjoy the full reward of sexual pleasure unless you went out and brought her something special, like a dildo with a smiley-face painted upon it. You always had to take the good with the bad, which is why many guys were happy to take to the bush and leave the girls back at home: it was easier to live like shit in the bush than it was to put up with the shit dribbling from a woman's mouth, or so I'd been told, because I had nothing but the utmost respect for woman – never before have I seen a female with her mouth shut for more than five minutes, even when asleep... that's what my mate says.

The rain hadn't changed, it still fell at a constant drizzle, more a worry in regards to weapon maintenance than anything else. A five-minute break in a patrol constituted time for cleaning of your weapon. Never in my four years within this battalion had I seen so much rust; clean the weapon last thing at night and the following morning your rifle looked like it'd been covered in red dust; those with the M16 usually slept with them in their sleeping bags. But you could always draw from the 'signs' indicated by the platoon sergeant; if he went bush with steel wool in his weapon cleaning kit then you knew you were in for a very uncomfortable trip - this place was worse than Tully but would have been heaps better if the bloody rain would simply STOP!

The enemy soon bumped our position again to ensure all were alert, section members returning SLR and M16 small arms fire, maintaining a silence with the machine guns in perfect defiance to the enemies search for their whereabouts. They were circling the position, trying to single out the platoon's gun positions in the hope of neutralising these for a dawn assault, either before everyone was awake and at stand-to or during the platoon's morning routine when 30 percent of all weapons would be field stripped for cleaning.

Twenty minutes had elapsed and stand-down would be passed around soon. Then out of nowhere a combination of shots was fired from deep within the scrub. The enemy was still in situ. Maybe the guys in the platoon would be better off at home with girlfriends, at least they'd get some sleep.

The platoon returned fire as indicated by the fire control orders issued by platoon commander and section commander alike.

A further twenty-five minutes had passed and a guy approached unseen from the rear. 'Stand-down.' And the bush was lit up with another bout of exchanged fire. 'Shit,' and the messenger disappeared back to the Boss.

Another thirty minutes of silence brought the platoon sig back to my pit. 'The Boss wants 50 percent stand-to all night; 100 percent on contact.' Well, there goes all hope for sleep. There was still six hours of night remaining, so if the enemy didn't fire another shot all night then each of us would receive about three hours' worth of... shit. Another shot fired in our direction. Would this harassment never end?

Junior NCO Training

July 1985

A seemingly new concept had been brought into the battalion known as JNCO training. The 'course' duration was two weeks, and was conducted in similarity – so all students had been led to believe – to that of a SASR patrol course, though in comparison, extremely easy. Whether or not that stood to be the truth was beyond most of us and farthest from concern, as very few would ever get to find out, and a majority simply were not interested in attempting that arena of infantry skill.

All we really knew was that the officer in control of the training had just returned from the West after doing the course previously mentioned, whether he passed or not was another question; going by his attitude I would say 'not'. He certainly mused to put Adolf Hitler to shame with his antics and mannerisms, seemingly big-noting himself at every opportunity, but then again, it was more than likely that he was simply making the most of his training, and endeavouring to pass onto us what he had so far learnt, which must have included putting his foot in his mouth. Maybe that particular SAS course never did 50 push-ups as punishment/amusement, but foot-in-mouth exercises instead.

There were 40 of us on the course and all were bedded down on cots in a hut within the administrative area of Shoalwater Bay Training Area. We were soon to learn that the cots would be lucky to see use as we were to average only five hours sleep a night during the two week period, and then not usually on the canvas stretchers.

Many push-ups with pack on backs were forced upon us all. It seemed pure luck that no back injuries were caused through such needless feats of physical abuse, but I'm sure that wear-n-tear upon our bodies would have taken place to some degree.

The following is just a minor example of a day's routine.

We'd just returned from a patrol at 1600hrs. The members of the section were then rotated through all jobs within the section formation of 12 men. The new section commander now reported for an orders group and the section 2IC for administrative details, the remainder of the group took to the cleaning of weapons, preparation of mud models for orders, and conducted a general equipment check on all that the section carried.

Orders were then received.

We were on the truck by 1900hrs and taken to an insertion point. Quite ironically, after de-bus from the vehicles, the rain commenced to fall very heavily. Drenched in seconds we pushed off on patrol through the scrub, to a destination where a standing patrol task had to be met.

2000hrs; we were in position on a small knoll that was found at the end of a spur, itself belonging to an even larger knoll. After a short five minute stand-to period in the downpour we prepared for the digging of our fighting bays – the dimensions of which allowed two standing men room to fight from, using the ground to the front edge of his pit as an elbow rest, being chest height in depth.

A picket on the machine gun was maintained as well as a 50 percent stand-to in the other pits around; therefore, if you didn't dig, you watched your arcs for enemy movement and changed over tasks with the man in the pit with you, every twenty minutes or so.

0100hrs; the pits were down to fighting bay depth. The rain had not stopped and a command to stand-down was given to the section as indicated by the accompanying DS. 0220hrs; stand-to, enemy movement to the front of the position was evident. 0400hrs; still standing-to. A message was then received over the radio informing the section to marry up with the other minor call signs of the platoon. Fill in those pits first, packs on backs, and let's go.

0530hrs; we were in position watching a road. One of the other minor call signs had already joined us and we were now waiting for the other. Ten minutes later and the last of the students arrived. 100 percent stand-to was maintained.

The truck was then called for over the radio. 0615hrs and no truck. It was bogged two kilometres up the road. It was still raining.

The platoon made an administrational move up the dirt road, as we were all required back in the administrational area no later than 0715hrs. The truck took 20 minutes to reach, and after a further 20 minutes of failure to budge the vehicle, the truck finally gave way to our persistent pushing and digging.

All students quickly clambered aboard and headed back to camp in readiness for another re-shuffle, more orders and another patrol to God

knows where, and duration unknown.
   The rain stopped as we entered the barracks area.
   There just had to be a job better than this – not.

Rappelling

November 1985

The DOG squad came and went once more, every minute of which was enjoyed by all, myself being awarded with an engraved knife as reward for being 'best soldier'; and it would seem that fortune was to follow this competition, for I had missed out this year from being bored to death by sitting on an unknown course full of theory instruction and no action. Instead I received a spot on an airborne rappelling course that was to be run over a period of just three days – short and sweet.

The 18 students were to be taught all they needed to know about the rope, knots, carabiner and aircraft. Safety was the prerequisite to their first descent from UH1H (chopper). 15 jumps had to be made for qualification; two practice jumps were made clean skin (no webbing, rifles or packs) followed by several in patrol order (webbing and rifle) and finally marching order (the pack and everything in it as though going to the bush on exercise).

Five guys approached the aircraft, two from the starboard and three from the port. The loop of the figure-eight was offered to the aircrew. This was the secure end of the rappelling rope. A floor mounted metal pin was to be placed through the loop, hence rendering it secure to the centre of the chopper, so that when it finally came time for jumping out, you wouldn't fall to your death.

They now faced each other, and on indication that all was secure, placed the rope filled sandbags from their left hand, into the right, prior to turning on their butts and facing outwards. The chopper now lifted from the ground to make for a quick trip around the airfield prior to the jump.

The two-minute safety check signal was given by the loadmaster. Ensure the rope was secure in position, and by logical sequence follow the rope down from the figure-eight knot to the figure-eight descender (carabiner), check that the gate to the carabiner was closed securely. From here the rope should flow unobstructed into the sandbag that was held securely in the right hand.

As you approached the jump zone, the signal to move out onto the skids was given. Now you stood on the skids facing in, holding onto the rappel rope as each waited for the chopper to make its final manoeuvre into position some 25 metres above the insertion point. Another signal and all threw the bags containing the rope down to earth, the Bluewater revealing itself from the sandbag so that each had a secure line from the helicopter all the way down to the ground in which to travel.

All would now lean backwards with toes on skids so as to achieve an 'L' shape position with their bodies – unlike that of the Blackhawk. The final chopping signal from the arm of a member of the chopper crew arrived and all twisted their ankles, relinquishing their foothold on the skids, making for a controlled descent to the ground below.

Once on the ground, take several steps back so that the load-master can see you, if everything was okay, give the thumbs up and the rappel rope falls to earth on being released by the air crew withdrawing the metal pin. Feed this rope back into the sandbag as taught and then await your next jump.

Quite a thrill.

Mortar Platoon

1986

It was a decision of the hierarchy that as I had been in the battalion for several years and hadn't yet been posted to support company, that it was prime time I extended my experiences and received a posting to mortars. 'But,' I had pointed out, 'I haven't even done a mortar course.' 'No need to worry,' was the reply, 'you can do one next year.'
Fine.
Being sent to a platoon to do a job that you didn't want to do was quite terrible, my entire year was spent in miserable temperament.
How could I get out of this? I soon decided on a rather simple solution. I would use this year to do whatever I could to stay away from the platoon. Volunteering for bush trips was one way, another was to stay busy with the SASR Cadre Course, and if that failed I had the DOG squad and Reconnaissance course. That would do for starters. But anything to prevent from receiving a mortar course.
As I hadn't done a mortar course I wasn't permitted by law to act as a number one on the mortar tube during live fire practices. I wasn't even supposed to be on the mortar line, but they couldn't exactly employ me in the command post; that was an even bigger no-no. I was absolutely forbidden from having any involvement with that. The CP was where charge settings for bombs, and calculations of bearing and altitudes were derived, as well as basic receipt of fire missions, and registration of targets from soldiers in the field.
So working on the line it was, as number three, although there were several occasions to which arose where I was involved in throwing bombs down the 81mm tubes and getting experience with assisting in misfire drills.
Each tube – to which the battalion had six, but during war entitled to eight – consisted of three men. A number 1, number 2, and you guessed it, a number 3. The No 1 was primarily responsible for setting the direction and altitude onto the C2 sight system as indicated by the section commander via the CP – two tubes per section. In most cases a red and white post, similar to the look of a barbershop pole, was positioned around ten metres from the tube, but not always to the

front. This was the aiming post and used specifically to get the tube in alignment with grid North so that all bearings set on the sights were in correspondence with those on the ground. A good No1 could have sights set and a mortar tube laid on target ready for the first round within 90 seconds of deployment.

The No1 would receive commands from the section commanders to fire; he would then relay this to the No2. After each round was fired (dependent on orders) the No1 would confirm by looking through the sights that the tube was in-fact aligned with the aiming post, being both vertically and horizontally correct in reference to the plotted target.

The No2's prime task was the placing of bombs down the tube after being handed it from the No3. He also swabbed out the tube after every five rounds to prevent obstruction on the interior wall of the mortar as the charge bags on the bombs were disintegrated on detonation, but did leave some debris on occasion. He would also assist the No1 in the carrying out of any misfire drill – in most cases this was where a bomb was prevented from striking the firing pin due to debris becoming lodged between the tube and the bomb.

The No3 prepared ammunition as indicated by the CP by removing the appropriate number of charge bags and arming the round by pulling the safety pin from the bomb. He would prepare the number of rounds as indicated by the CP or section commander.

It was quite a remarkable little unit when firing a mission. It was a great support weapon capable of giving indirect fire up to a distance of five kilometres, but I was still happy to see the end of the platoon however. At the end of the year I was posted to C Coy on promotion to LCPL. I think the platoon was also sad to see me go because I was quite often employed as a pack-horse, and on one occasion carried two radios with spare batteries, with my own equipment on top of that.

DOG Three

Mid 1986

It was time for the DOG squad again and volunteers dribbled in from the different companies.

This year it had been given quite a face-lift. An offer for an Australian rifle section to compete in the Cambrian March in the UK was given. Their yearly competition involved more than 40 teams from across Europe. It took the shape of a section being put through its paces, as a real section should; in the field doing it hard. AMerican soldiers didn't attend this, I guess it was deemed as being too hard for them to do.

The Australian-epic area of operations was chosen wisely. As the Barrington Tops (near Singleton) was climatically similar to the area in which the English competition was to be held, it was decided to have the Australian teams compete it out here. This year the team was literally competing for a trip overseas, for a ticket on a plane to take them to the Mother Country, to compete against a rival of mind, for a prize which could only ever be seen by the heart and never with the eyes. The 8/9RAR team members were just sorry to say that one of their main figureheads, from within the section that year, didn't have the same aspirations and drive as others for the winning of the competition. This became ever evident over the three days and nights of competition. The Corporal did an extremely poor job that year and received a lot of criticism from the section. The A-hole was from pioneers, if I recall, and we mostly held little respect for him.

The army took advantage of this activity and made a 29 minute documentary on the competition. Since then I've never heard of or seen the army display the piece as a publicity stunt. Here was a prime tool for the recruitment of soldiers into the forces and yet it wasn't being employed. Was there going to be another cut back of funds and numbers within the Defence Force, or didn't public relations and good clean advertisement come to mind? Maybe I watched too little TV and drank too much beer.

Before the competition kicked off we all spent the afternoon relaxing and carrying out battle procedure. Several hours later we were 100 metres down from the School of Infantry HQ, waiting for the first of the choppers, to take the first of the teams to the freezing heights of Barrington.

The 30min chopper ride concluded with the section being purposely dropped off at a position some distance from the insertion point as decree by the competition program, quite a shock surprise to us all. The only information we received from the chopper pilot was that we were within two kilometres of our supposed drop-off point. A position was finally determined after 15 to 20 minutes of trying to decipher what we couldn't see, which included farm houses several kilometres away, and the car headlights off in the distance.

Even from this early stage in the competition most realised that no matter how hard we tried, that a win would not be within our grasp. This was evident when the section commander wanted to stop at 0200hrs for the purpose of giving all a short break. A few others, along with myself, commented on how we could rest at the stands we were to encounter enroot, and that even if we didn't get much sleep over the next three days, that it didn't really amount to anything because it was only a few nights. What was the loss of a few hours gonk? 'No. We'll stop for a few hours.' Sometime in the morning, just before sunrise, our 'team' – the word being used lightly – continued on our 'not so' merry way. The morale had now been given the kick in the guts it didn't need. We were out here to do a job, not to sleep; damn it!

The next decision shattered all even more. That afternoon at 1400hrs it was noted by the section commander that one of the navigation legs on the 40km trek was off by itself. A plan was soon arrived at to send himself and one other – less their packs – to retrieve this check point whilst the remainder under command of the 2IC – very competent in his ways – would continue to other checkpoints and then wait for the section commanders return at a specific location. In other words, going against the rules of the competition, but using initiative to try and make up for the time he'd already lost the group: what a dumb arse!

By 1600hrs the 2IC's group had arrived at the marry-up point, but no section commander. 1800hrs and still no contact with the section commander. 0800hrs the following morning and he finally made an appearance. How the hell did they keep warm – they built themselves a fire of course. So instead of making up two hours in time, the section commander had lost a further 15 odd hours. We were now a good 18 hours behind our best possible time. We could only hope that the other sections were having the same problem with their commander.

Two days later scores were read out and 8/9RAR were informed that they had lost with flying colours, but hadn't come last, that honour was given to a team with obviously less ambition than can be found in a pile of shit – well done 5/7RAR.

1RAR took the line-honours that year and went over to compete in the competition overseas. The Australian team came first, winning the competition with ease. Just goes to prove which army was the best in real terms, just as the Australian competition proved which sections had pride in their jobs as Infantry soldiers, and which NCOs cared not for their rank and position within the battalion. My mate reckoned that our section commander would have done better as an officer.

Some NCOs certainly didn't deserve their rank, but the thing is, bad NCOs were so far and few between. The competence and professionalism of the Australian Army was simply beyond reproach.

It would also be fair to say, however, in defence of my accusations against the individual above, that the platoon in which he was posted (in SPT Coy) had different aspirations than those of a rifle section. It was therefore possible that his attitude towards the task at hand, wasn't entirely his fault; he may well have been against the temporary posting from the start, but as an NCO should have continued without complaint to do the best that he could.

SASR Cadre Course

March 1986

I knew during BRL in Melbourne that my application to try for the SAS had been given the thumbs up, and that the initial course of 24 days was to begin on the 6th March. I thought it might be fun being a special soldier, and I loved the idea of having extra pockets in which to hide things.

I had decided not to commence with my preparation for the course until my return to work in late January, allowing for a good six weeks of physical build up. As it turned out, this was more than ample, as I'd already had a good foothold on my fitness. I even surprised myself one day by completing a 15km run in patrol order, with M60 machine gun, in 91 minutes. It was no wonder my heart rate was down to less than 40 beats a minute.

The day of concern however was soon upon me and the course of 100 odd students, and as I sat in the belly of the C130 in Townsville, awaiting the final leg of our journey to Perth, I couldn't help but to look around at the others who had decided to try out for the course. This was their preference for career progression, and as I looked around I tried to evaluate them by expression; some showing nervousness and uncertainty; what were their motives for putting themselves on such a course as this?

There was a guy of 25, spoke very posh and snobbish, a bloody good hand; another who read women's magazines, fantastic guy; both passed the course. And there were several – just a few – who boasted how tough they were, what they had done, how good they were as a soldier, how they picked up women by the dozens – they were some of the biggest losers it was my displeasure to meet; extremely self-centred. These 'tough guys' were some of the first to go back to their units after just five days on the course, a course that had been designed so specifically. Here they ran, running with tails between their legs, and with excuses as big as their now deflated egos and looks of embarrassment. It seemed to me that a majority of those that passed the course were 'mind' wise, with the attitude, mentality, and temperament, to go along with it – no need for a personal trainer here.

Of course, not all of those removed from the course were big-headed; most were genuine and friendly.

Food was plentiful on the course, which was a good thing. I'd lost five kilograms in six weeks of training and was about to lose a further seven kilograms over the next 14 days – no bull.

During the course we were to be assessed during two physical training periods a day, an hour in the morning and another in the afternoon, not to mention punishment activities and other sprints around the area surrounding Northam Camp. All of this was carried out in order to get from one activity to the next. That was certainly one thing that could be said about the 'selection' course, it was a hell of a lot more physically demanding than anyone had said. I'd tried to imagine what the PT during the course would be like when I was conducting my own training periods, but never visualised it as being so hard. Only the extremely exceptional of the hundred that were here found it easy, most found it difficult, though refused to say so – a good mental attitude, so long as it worked for the individual.

A 3.2km run was the first of the major tests. It had to be completed within 16 minutes – one kilometre every 5 minutes; 200 metres in 60 seconds; shouldn't be a problem. All students waited for the starting whistle to be blown, dressed in uniform, boots, 10kg webbing and carrying 4.3kgs of weapon. The run was conducted around an airfield so you could see the start/finish line. Several laps of the airfield were required, quite a psychological hit to the head; but then again, any track would have been. And another thing, the DS weren't afraid to point out, just before the whistle being blown, that 70% of all those in the past had failed this activity the first time around. At least this meant you got to try again if you failed.

The course this year managed a good 40% pass, myself only scraping in with 13-odd seconds to spare. The second major test on the course, however, was the 20km route march. The students on the course reported, forming up into three ranks with their marching order placed at their feet, all ready for inspection by DS. Ten guys were to be hand-picked by the DS so as to have their equipment weighed. If any of these were caught underweight then two things would occur. Firstly everyone would undergo a weight check and secondly, the culprit would end up with an additional five kilograms overweight in the form of rocks being placed into the top of his pack; oh, and if he managed to finish the 24 day course, his chances of being denied a pass were huge – for he would have been found guilty of an attempt to cheat. For these reasons most on the course ensured that they carried a few kilos more than that required; just in case.

The forced march was soon under way and men slowly spread out as the distance covered, grew. A funny thing happened here. A DS passed me by and put mention to the fact that I was leaving some members of my group behind as others had done before me. The DS said that the test should be completed as a team. Now if I was to fail to finish the march in the 3hrs 15min allotted, would my remaining 'as a team' become a defence against my being removed from the course; was it worth the risk in finding out? I decided not and continued, for my chances of survival were better if I went it alone (and this was the way in which I'd trained, by himself, pushing myself along by use of personal pressure and self-motivation, not having to rely on others for support.

After only eight kilometres I felt that I wasn't going to pass the march. I just wasn't stepping out enough, each stride seemed to fall short of that achieved by the previous, and what about those guys behind me, were they mentally calculating the distance travelled? I had done this enough times in my career to know how far I'd gone – not to mention the checkpoint at the five kilometre mark. My feet were also starting to tenderise in the heat of the day. I'd have to do as some others were doing, I would now have no choice but to run a light shuffle, and as I commenced to double time down the road a thought came to mind. I'd read a book years before, some guy on the British selection course had failed to pass a navigation test because he was several minutes late to finish, and he had a fractured ankle. I decided to go a little faster.

The 15 kilometre mark came into visual and I slowed the pace slightly, I had enough time remaining, surely – watches had been banned from all other activities on the course, except this one; but I couldn't recall being informed of that. A guy passed me by and told me how much time remained. Good, ample enough.

Two minutes later and the DS informed him differently, and as I was determined not to take a chance on the DS having been wrong I continued with the pace – or was he trying to psych me out? Five more clicks and fifty minutes to do it in.

I finally approached the finish line and crossed with 15 minutes to spare, 20km in 3hrs – not too bad. I was soon informed that the first to cross the line had done so in 2hr 40min. That soldier was apparently pulled aside by the DS who were unimpressed with his effort. He'd completed the march with ease but had refrained from giving any boost of morale to his mates and only strove to please himself – just like most of the others had done, whether they finished under time or over. It seemed that in some cases mateship was the key to success, but then again that could have been a hidden front to aid in the study of each individual's reaction to suggestions of a varying sort as given by the DS.

On our return to the rooms the following morning – after an hour of PT – we found that a member of our group had been removed from the course. This was obvious as his chair, bedside table, and bed, were gone. Nothing remained except an empty space. No messing around here, when they take you off of the course, they take everything except the bloody floorboards. It was said that they did this so as not to affect the morale of other students, but the thought of this scared some guys shit-less – the DS, were again, messing with our minds.

The 24hr navigation test was upon us. We stepped off individually mid-morning and had a specific amount of checkpoints to achieve by day, and three checkpoints (minimum) by night. The day phase wasn't the problem.

It had just turned 2200hrs and I had left my first compulsory night checkpoint and was beginning my manoeuvres for the second. To go across country and numerous creeks was asking for trouble, so I decided on the alternative. I would head on a bearing for 1200 metres, turn right and take off on a different bearing for a further 1600 metres; both were along spurs with only one re-entrant to be crossed on the first leg, and several others on the second. Shouldn't be a problem.

I came upon a small bush, and as I pushed through, tripped on a loose stone, my leg falling out from under me, forcing me to overstep my mark, to meet with a six foot drop to a dry re-entrant floor full of boulders. I sat still for several seconds, thinking. Does any part of me hurt? Have I damaged anything? No, all was fine. I climbed the six-foot escarpment on the other side and continued on my way until I reached my pivot point. I pulled out the map. With the torch held close to the ground I searched for confirmation of my next bearing. The next portion of my trip involved two more re-entrants similar to the one I'd just fallen into. It just wasn't worth the risk of injury.

I bedded down for the night. Maybe if I completed the navigation test within the 24hrs without all three-night checkpoints up my sleeve, and did well in other aspects of the course, they would forego getting rid of me.

I continued with my journey the following morning after breakfast, a can of corn beef and a quick coffee.

Reaching the last of my checkpoints was no relief as I now had to get myself back to the start point, the final leg of my journey. The distance was just over seven kilometres and I had 1hr 45min remaining. I would have no choice but to take the distance in one hit, there was no time to break the distance up into more easily to manage navigational bounds. I placed my bearing to the compass and just as I was about to step off the DS called me over.

The picture was painted. A guy from the Navy [yeah, sure] whose job didn't involve navigation as such – but the individual had skills required by the SAS – had but one leg remaining as I – or was he a spy planted within the course? [of course]. It was requested that I take the man with me. No problem.

I'm sure I was being tested: It was soon evident to me that the guy liked conversation as during the fast pace through the scrub he continued to chatter on about numerous subjects, and here I was trying emphatically to navigate and count paces for accurate measure of the metres covered. Something had to be done, even at the expense of seeming unnecessarily rude. 'Listen mate. We've got more than another six clicks to travel, less than an hour and half to do it in, and I'm trying to count my paces. The last thing I need right now is conversation. Would you mind not talking?' Quite a simple solution.

Time passed us by quickly and when next I looked at my watch I discovered that we had three minutes remaining, and according to my calculations about 200 metres to travel. I stopped and looked around.

'What do you think?' I asked of my 'Navy' acquaintance.

'I'm not sure,' was his reply.

The ground around was flat but a creek junction was marked on the map. 'This foliage around us here; does it look strange to you?'

We assessed the ground alike. 'It's certainly different.'

'Look at the way it lays on the ground,' I pointed out, 'like a 'Y'. What do you think? Could this be the junction?'

It was a near impossible decision, and I was receiving no aid. If it were a junction then our angle of approach would have to be altered slightly, if not, we should go straight ahead. The time ticked by. We now had two minutes remaining.

'It certainly looks like the foliage here was lower in comparison to the stuff around. Could be....' And there in the distance. A generator had just been turned over. An army generator by no mistake, just through the scrub a bit. This was a creek junction. 'That's it. Quick, let's go!'

We walked into the camp two minutes late. Would they fail me for this, only completing one night checkpoint and being two minutes late? To tell of my fall in the creek line would be futile. I should have continued regardless.

It was day 12 on the course and I was standing outside the office of decision, myself and three others (two of whom passed the course, and several months later finally marched into the regiment). I was called into the office – being told basically the same as the others before me.

The officer looked up. 'It's been brought to my attention that you've been taking it easy and haven't been putting the effort in. I require a one hundred percent effort, one hundred percent of the time. I find your report disturbing to say the least. If you don't pull your socks up sunshine, you'll find yourself being marched off of this course. Do you have any questions?'

'No sir.'

'Get out.'

Oh well. What could one say?

That night I phoned home and was informed that an Aunt was coming out from England for a short stay, that she would be dead from cancer before the year was out, her trip coinciding with the SAS patrol course – as far as I could determine. I put the phone down and crawled off to bed.

The following day the students who still remained on the course loaded themselves onto the coaches for the trip to the Stirling Ranges. We were to find ourselves here for the next five days, climbing mountains, by ourselves, navigating over five peaks in the process. This was supposedly the test of all tests. The mountains were just that, mountains of shale and rock that were near on impossible to walk upon. It wasn't uncommon to find yourself falling time and time again, many times in an hour, and with an extremely heavy pack on your back, injury was very possible.

The first of my checkpoints was Mt.Hassel. A close look at the map showed two possible routes to the top. The first would take me around

The Long Road to Rwanda

to the far side and an extra two or three kilometres in march. The short leg was up the wind shattered portion facing me, very steep, but very short in distance. For some strange reason I chose the steepness. The steepness soon became a cliff face and as I climbed I realised my mistake. It was too late now to turn back, as to do so would make it near impossible to complete all checkpoints in the five-day period, or so I thought.

I occasionally looked back behind me, ensuring my backpack didn't throw me off balance. The drop behind was a good 150 metres. This was definitely no slope. The wrong placement of a foot would see me fall to my death upon the rocky outcrop below, and that wasn't even the bottom, there was another hundred metre drop beyond that [or so it seemed] - I was hoping that my 'perspective' had created an illusion. Never again would I be so quick to try and take the shortest leg. I should have known better, experience should have told me that I had made the wrong decision in my approach.

Two and half-hours later and I finally made the checkpoint. It was worth the climb just for the view, but I wasn't here on a sightseeing venture.

I met with the DS and reported my location to the centre administration area via the 77 set radio: Each of the students carried one. The DS then made a comment. 'I wouldn't spend too much time here if I was you.'

'How come?' I asked.

'You were one of the first of your group to leave, but the last to achieve his checkpoint.' The individuals of the group he was referring to were sent on their merry way at 30-minute intervals.

I took this new information on board and was soon on my way to the next destination.

At 1100hrs the following morning I could clearly see the monstrous feature to my front. That was my next checkpoint, Mt.Magog. I calculated that I'd be lucky to get to the checkpoint by 1700hrs; then I weighed up my options and all that had occurred over the past week.

I'd been warned that my effort wasn't good enough, probably due to the navex. Then there was the fiasco with Mt.Hassel and the coming death of a relation. Should I quit now, because it certainly looked as though I was heading for failure? Should I take the opportunity to visit my Aunt when she arrived in Australia, to see her before she died? Was family more important than a career with the SASR? Was I going to receive a tick in the box – doubtful?

I chose the hard option and pulled myself off from the course, and to this day still don't really understand why I chose to quit, whether for my Aunt or for my inability to complete the navex under the time restraints. But I do believe, after contemplating it all, deep down, beneath the surface, that if I'd not made that phone call home that I would have completed the course. I don't say this to make myself look bigger and better than I am, but because being in the SAS had been a dream of mine. I had what it took but I also had a conscience which allowed for my aunt to see me one final time.

I would leave the course till another day.

Five years earlier, in 1981, during my posting in Singleton, I did request a chance to conduct the SASR course. I was provided an interview, possibly out of sheer courtesy – which I appreciated immensely, for it showed that they understood how genuine I was. I was however turned down – I was only 17 at the time.

In 1988 I again withdrew from the course even before getting on the plane, this time due to a back injury incurred two weeks before the commencement of the course, and though it was only minor, chances were I'd really have a problem if I attempted the course – this I knew from experience.

In 1992 I was denied the opportunity to make another attempt. It was probably for the better, as my injuries were playing up extensively. My body was becoming broken. The more I did, the more broken I became, and the more serious matters appeared.

Was this maturity or did I just need a swift kick in the arse to put a smile back upon my face, because I wasn't smiling much these days?

Cooktown

1987

Exercise Diamond Dollar was an exercise with a difference for the battalion this year as an emphasis was to be placed on aid to the civil power. One of C Coy's first tasks in the exercise was to give protection to the local police station as well as some other buildings of particular importance. Concealment from the enemy wasn't of great concern for the company over the first week of exercise, for as all well knew, security arrives in its best form with the actual presence of an authoritative figure. In this case authority had been given to the 7.62 ammunition that most carried, although the M60 machine guns were absolutely forbidden to be fired, unless specifically given the order to do so by higher elements. Showing just cause for firing an automatic weapon, or weapon on automatic, in the case of the M16, couldn't be justified if a civilian was killed, unless the enemy had launched a large scale assault against any of the key establishment to which the company was protecting.

The enemy had blended into their atmosphere rather easily, made up by individuals, and small bands of soldiers from a variety of battalions and the SASR. They grew beards, had boats, maintained jobs, and had become one with the population – in some cases but not all – and had reportedly established themselves a routine. The locals became a great source of information here. The police as well could easily point the finger at those who were new to the town.

Routine on the ground was quite slow and tedious. It involved basic security work; maintaining pickets around the key installations, conducting ID checks with suspicious persons; and eating the mangoes that were given freely by the trees that grew around us.

It was during the first phase of the exercise that a DS approached me and two others.

He informed us that a bomb had been placed into the letterbox, that stood on a post at the gate to the police station, just five metres from where we sat – no one actually carried this action out mind you, but the DS had been informed that casualties were required. We three had supposedly received cuts to the faces and were suffering haemorrhage from the ears.

The rules governing this exercise, in respect of exercise casualties, were very simple.

The medivac system had to be tested and exercised, the same as everything and everyone else. We were further advised by this DS that we were to be taken by rover to the battalion RAP and from there wait to be picked up by military ambulance, to be taken to the field hospital where we were to be treated for the wounds sustained. We would then stay out of exercise for a period of 24hrs before being returned to C Coy as a replacement to the lost numbers.

Very interesting; I wonder if it were officers that had thought that one up? 1. To RAP; 2. To Field hospital; 3. Return. Huh; three, the magic number. Yes, it was an officer initiative.

The rover evacuation to the RAP took no more than 30 minutes to organise and execute, then three hours was endured before a decision was made that the ambulance wasn't coming. We would therefore have to be taken by rover the short trip to one of the rear echelons, namely the 8/9th Battalion's location of field kitchen. Other elements were also to be found here, those required by the battalion for the administrational purposes of running the exercise.

We were off loaded with our packs and approached by an officer. 'Look men. I haven't got time to talk to you now. We've got our arses hanging out doing security patrols and manning sentry points around the echelon at the moment. You boys shouldn't be here too long, maybe 24 hours. As soon as the first available vehicle heads back to the front, I'll give you a ticket. We're a bit understaffed though in the field kitchen. Hope you don't mind helping out?'

'No sir,' and with that we commenced peeling the potatoes required to feed six hundred men. Mmmmm... You've got to love the army.

Two days later I approached the officer in reference to being taken back to the company in Cooktown. 'Sorry son. Haven't got any vehicles. I told you that the other day.' Thanks, arsehole. 'Now, I'll get back to you soon,' (Meaning next week some time).

With that being said we commenced to peel more potatoes and some carrots, just like we'd been doing for the past two days. I did suggest that we help out with the security patrols [as they were supposedly short in manpower], but no; spuds were more important than security, which directly contradicted what the officer had said a few days before in regards to security patrols. Officers were

The Long Road to Rwanda

sometimes so full of themselves.

On the afternoon of the second day a CPL cook came up to me. 'Listen mate. We're a bit stretched at the moment. Would you mind doing some sentry work?'

'So long as it doesn't involve peeling spuds.'

'No, but the shift is about three and a half hours.'

Whoopee bloody do. 'That's okay.' Bloody oath it was. 'What about the other two guys with me?'

'You'll all get a turn.' I was shown the sentry position.

Now, to the rear of the field kitchen was a stretch of thick bush, and forty metres beyond that was a small creek-line. That's where the sentry position had been placed. I couldn't believe my eyes when I saw it.

There was a canvas stool that you sat on and under this was a pile of stick books ready for the reading. It was in the shade and perfectly cool. On relieving the cook that was there – and had been for the past five hours – I asked for the orders on the sentry position.

'What orders?' replied the cook.

'The 18-odd points which need to be covered when relieving a sentry; arcs of fire and actions on contact; everything.'

'I haven't got any orders,' he said. 'Just watch the road.'

'What road?'

'It's beyond the bushes over there, somewhere. It's just two metres past those.'

'I can't see anything.'

'No. But you can hear vehicles going up and down. If you hear one, just go and look. But I wouldn't bother if I were you.'

So this was what they needed the man power for, to peel spuds whilst the cooks sat back reading stick books, doing sentry work on a road that was never going to be seen. A plan of attack was decided upon. I wrote a quick note and took this to the cooks. This was to be delivered to C Coy's CSM along with the fresh ration dinner that night; no room on the vehicle for anything (or anyone) else mind you.

The following morning I was pleasantly surprised to find that all three of us were to be sent back to the section, reinforcing it back to its original strength of seven men. It was then that the CSM made a firm decision not to send any further casualties back to the RAP unless told to do so directly by a DS – but under protest of course. All worked out fine for the next few days and by then it was time for the company to change roles with another company, and we headed for the wilderness. We were going bush housed snugly in the back of APCs.

It's stories like these that really make you feel sorry for the poor officers back in the echelons. It's no wonder the padre was always there; they needed him to help relieve their stress.

As for the officer, whose mouth did the work of his arsehole, the less said about him the better.

DOG Squad Four

June 1987

Exercise OTBO was once again being held in the wastelands of SWBTA. All of the fieldwork during this exercise was of a live fire nature. The DOG squad however was exempt from this due to meeting the training criteria and basic bulk of training requirements that included the dreaded 20km march with packs every single day.

The logistical support of the battalion during the exercise was bountiful. Here the team could conduct ambush drills, section attacks and basic field techniques, until they were coming out of our ears. This was certainly the most training we'd received as compared with any other DOG squad of previous years. Once again the team consisted of a ten-man section, with two reserves and an allotted driver.

The Ambush (training)

We lay in ambush with blank ammunition exchanged for the live that we'd been used to carrying. Simply put, several members of the battalion were being employed as enemy for the night.

The scope of the DOG competition was completely known but not solid. It was a logical and realistic assumption that a live fire ambush conducted for assessment by the DS in Singleton would be sprung within 30 minutes of being set up due to restrictions in timings. Besides that, the RSM had been informed of some competition stands for ease of
section preparation, and he was standing in silence just behind our team alongside the training SGT, both of whom were watching with a keen eye and obviously full of interest.

It was a comfort to know that the night was fairly well lit. Not a cloud existed and the moon was a quarter full. This would certainly aid in all aspects of the sections standard operational procedures and conduct of the withdrawal from the ambush site.

Movement was detected within the half-hour. Three bodies were walking along the track to our front. The section commander would now wait for them to move into the centre of the killing ground prior to initiating the ambush with his M16, and on this failing to fire, for any particular reason, the alternate method of initiation would be used; the scout would fire his M16. All weary heads were turned to face the front with fingers on triggers as the enemy moved past. Suddenly, a tenth of a second after the section commander's initial application of pressure upon the trigger and firing of the first round of ammunition, then the bush commenced to echo with five seconds of automatic and rapid firing from all section weapons, into the killing ground.

Then silence. Time for a quick assessment; was there more enemy approaching; should those caught in the ambush be fired upon with a second initiation? All seemed fine and only seconds after silence befell the surrounding dark the command for searchers out was given.

As the order was being carried out the DOG squad training SGT came in behind the section commander. 'Scott; you're wounded.' So as section 2IC, the show now belonged to me.

Quick orders were all that were required. All were experienced men with common sense to suit.

Two riflemen grabbed Scott by the harness and dragged him away from the ambush sight to the rear some 25 metres where they had prepared several stretchers as per ambush SOP requirements. One was dismantled as Scott was placed onto the other.

The section was quickly deployed on the ground as medical aid was carried out on the supposed sucking chest wound that the section commander had received. I then called in a fire mission by using the direct fire support we had in the form of a section of mortars.

This was used to cut off any likely approaching enemy at a road junction some five hundred metres away, and having spent eleven months in mortars, the target registration numbers were somewhat easier for me to remember.

By the time the fire mission had been called in and a quick but short adjustment had been made to counteract another likely enemy approach, the section commander was wrapped and ready for the 500-metre move to the administration area where packs had been left.

All the while this was being conducted the training sergeant and RSM were watching in silence, assessing any faults, to be used as debrief points after the short exercise had met with its conclusion.

I quickly deployed a scout either side of myself and followed the compass bearing in the direction of the admin area, with the stretcher party close in tail, and the gun group split either side of these as rear and flank protection.

Visibility was good for about fifty metres but none of the ground we were covering looked familiar as yet, but I was also to remember that the light was different at 1800hrs, for it was still dusk back then.

We'd soon covered the distance required. I signalled for the scouts and asked for a confirmation on the distance so far travelled. The group average was slightly over the distance required, so the two scouts were sent off to the flank for a quick reconnaissance.

This was the likely solution to our problem, the only solution. They reported back within two minutes that they had indeed found the packs.

On arrival at the administrational area all threw their packs onto backs, rotated two of the guys on the stretcher, and were informed by the training SGT that the ambush scenario was now complete. We now had to stretcher the wounded section commander down the road a short five kilometres.

As for the ambush – the RSM was quite content with the test results and seeing first hand that all SOPs were being employed to the satisfaction of the section commander and training SGT. A month later we were down at Singleton awaiting our chopper insertion to the Barrington Tops.

The team this year was the best I'd worked with. We all felt that a 'win' was on the cards. Our section commander was more than competent and looked up to by all in the section.

The First Night (competition)

The competition was off to a blazing start and it was all good news to see that the section commander this year was more than interested in giving his best to the competition and the soldiers.

The first day's competition came to an end and as it turned dark a DS approached Scott with the requirements for the night's activities. We were to move to the top of a large feature and set ourselves up a night harbour position in a location indicated by another DS, who was to meet us there. A distance of no less than thirty metres would segregate each of the six battalions. Once in position, sections were to conduct night routine, and this would be assessed by several DS during the night; they would venture around to visit each of the sections at undisclosed times.

Nigel B.J. Clayton

This was the most disappointing of the stands for one reason, and one very good reason. It was disappointing to note that some of the other battalions had decided not to run a proper gun picket that night because of the rain and cold. The weather was that bad that they probably figured that the DS wouldn't be around. As it turned out, they did. They saw firsthand that the section representing the 8/9th battalion, and several others, were filling all requirements as laid down, but 1RAR were not – just to mention one. It was then the DS's prime decision to declare that this portion of the competition not be assessed. They would instead assess the night harbour another night when – hopefully – the rain had ceased; it never eventuated.

So here we were, doing all the right things, spending a miserable night in the scrub, conducting night routine from within a section harbour position. We sat and watched the rain drop off of our hats, periodically looking out drearily over the sloping ground to our front, to some house a good twenty kilometres away that had its porch lights turned on. All of this whilst other battalions – one in particular – slept without concern or worry.

According to the competition criteria, each assessed stand was marked out of a score of 100 points. It was therefore logical that if 8/9RAR had conducted the test to the best of their ability and someone else did not, then they would surely out score them by as much as one hundred points. It stood to test patience when at the conclusion of the competition we had lost by 65 points to 1RAR who didn't do their night routine as laid down in orders. 1RAR... scumbags. 8/9RAR, having completed it correctly, received no points whatsoever as it was decided the morning after the test that it wouldn't be fair to these 'other' battalions. Well let's all have a nice little cry. I was led to believe that 1RAR enjoyed their trip to England again that year – thanks to the DS and their unscrupulous ways. Did the DS take a bribe? And to think that I had always thought that honesty was the best policy. It was quite obvious to me that 1RAR had more NCO's and soldiers, that cringed and made a fuss, at every opportunity, than what could be found elsewhere. 8/9RAR was more disciplined than the battalions to our north, and we had just proved it.

The DS obviously held a different point of view when it came to moral equity, they being tainted with the love of their former battalion.

As for the overall results, the 8/9th battalion came second in the Duke of Gloucester and first in the McDonalds cup (a new aspect which looked specifically at ambushing, navigation, and shooting).

This was prejudice beyond belief, but it wasn't until I met with someone of 4RAR that I knew something was mighty wrong with the people whom made the decisions as to those that received promotion to the next highest rank; but my posting to 4RAR was still a long way off yet, and a story which should remain shrouded in darkness… in other words, the less said about the men of the 4RAR BHQ element, the better.

Fighting Bay to Hospital Bed

1988

I soon found myself in Reconnaissance Platoon after being awarded a plaque as student of merit (best soldier) for my efforts in late 1986, and digging a fighting bay whilst posted to the platoon was one of the last things on my mind.

The BN's major exercise for the year was EX Silk Purse and Recon's first task was the conduct of a reconnaissance of a beachfront vehicle track due to the heavy rain the area had received that month. We were checking it for its ability in taking the weight of rovers, APCs and trucks.

Information needed to be recorded on all aspects so that a decision could be made as to whether particular types of vehicles could use the road. What detours – if any – were needed, establish whether any changes to the map were required, and mark these changes as appropriate to our map, recording the widths of the track, inclines/ depth of creek lines, etc, etc; and the list goes on. During the three-day task we only once encountered hostile activity and that was a small enemy group boarded up in an old shearing shed. We took them out via unrealistic fashion – vehicle assault. It had all been prearranged with compliments of the PL SGT to help keep everyone on their toes and to aid with the writing of SOPs for vehicle mounted patrols, to which this was the platoon's first. I still recall spending many, many hours writing the SOPs which never seemed to be employed by the platoon due to changes in policy a little later on. Again, I had wasted many, many hours of work.

At the task's conclusion the patrol married up with the remainder of the battalion not long after dark. The position was under construction on our entry to the position and we could hear the digging going on around us. We were now shown our area of responsibility.

The platoon was to remain here in the Battalion Firm Base for the night and commence tasking the following morning, meanwhile fighting bays had to be dug as quickly as possible as the enemy had the capability of directing mortar fire upon our current position.

It didn't take long to pair off, and with entrenching tool in hand, each man commenced pounding at the ground. Shovels and picks would be brought up from the stores area as soon as possible but meanwhile we had to use our entrenching tools.

The job took a good five hours as the ground was fairly hard, and on completion I reached down to pick up my 45kg pack.

Quite suddenly I found myself in excruciating agony and in a position on my elbows and knees, the most comfortable posture possible - back pain. After I was lifted to a stretcher I was taken down to the RAP in the centre of the BN position. The RMO soon had drugs injected into the cheek of my arse. I now had 15 minutes to roll over onto my back before I fell asleep; it took a minimum of ten just to roll onto my side.

The following morning I was evacuated by road to another medical centre and after five hours here transferred to a hospital bed in Rockhampton.

Whilst I was there I saw two nurses. The first on my being admitted – who also took time to ask if I wanted any pain killers – and the second was three hours after I'd been lying there in more pain than I care to remember.

'Are you still here, Mr.Clayton?'

'Yeah, that's right.'

'Well you can't stay here I'm afraid. We need the bed.'

'What exactly would you like me to do? I can hardly move.'

'If you give me a phone number I'll get someone to come and pick you up.'

Unbelievable. Here I was, unable to do anything, still dressed in the stinking fatigues I'd been wearing and sweating in over the past four days, and they wanted me to 'phone home'. Who did they think I was, E.T. or some local. 'I don't come from here,' she must have thought I was from the Army Reserve, they had a unit stationed close by.

'What about the barracks phone number?'

'I don't know that. I don't come from here.'

A look of scorn fell upon her face, 'that stupid fat cow'. 'I suppose I'll have to do it myself,' she said in the most sarcastic of manners and departed, with a waddle.

An army ambulance picked me up several hours later. It was around 1800hrs and I hadn't had anything to eat all day. I was taken directly to the barracks where I was helped very slowly to a bed in a spare room and told that I should get someone to get me a meal, as he, the driver of the ambulance, had other things to do. With that my help departed. I was once again by myself.

Two hours later I finally saw someone. It was a transport driver from my battalion.

'What are you doing here, Nigel?'

'Not much, Brett. Done my back in. Apparently I have to stay here until the next available aircraft South.'

'That's not for almost a week. You'd be better coming back with us in the truck.'

'I can't travel in no truck. My backs stuffed.'

My friend thought it over for a few seconds. 'I think I can help you there. We've got a load of parachutes in the back, picked up from an airfield after 3RAR's drop. They're all loosely thrown in. I reckon if you take enough pain killers, and we avoid the potholes,' which was doubtful, 'between here and Brisbane, you'll not have a problem.'

'I guess you're right. No one knows I'm here. If I don't go with you guys I'll be dead in a week.' So I took the option open to me and returned to Brisbane – which turned out to be ten times more comfortable than the ambulance drive – and on arrival was informed that

no one had heard, or seen, a report of my injury, nor knew of my returning. They found it all very strange that I should have been dumped the way I was and forgotten about. I was asked if I needed to be put in hospital, or whether I had a home to go to.

'No thanks. I have a home to go to,' and spent the next few days in my room on the barracks, whilst another guy brought back from the exercise due to a sprained ankle, fetched meals for me from the mess hall.

After all, one hospital experience was enough.

As for the fat rotund at Rockhampton Hospital, I have a message for you… but do I really need to spell it out?

Interrogation

April 1989

During the running of the reconnaissance course this year, platoon headquarters extended an invitation to 1 DIV INT to come along and carry out their forte of interrogation techniques upon all of our students. All of the instructors from the platoon had been through it before at some stage or another during their military career, and it was an experience never to be forgotten.

The students were gathered together one afternoon and told that they were being taken down the road two kilometres so that they could all watch a movie called 'The Iron Cross', to be watched on a bed sheet that had been set up against the wall of a toilet block on Greenbank Range. This camp was used exclusively to house soldiers during live firing exercises/practices through the course of a normal training year. The movie was to give them a deserved break in training.

They were soon on the back of the truck and some started to become suspicious when the rear flap to the vehicle was pulled down and secured to the tailgate: 'Don't worry fellahs, it's just to keep the dust out.' The welcome they received on arrival at the toilet block was well orchestrated.

1800hrs. All 20 students on the course now had their hands tied, were blindfolded, and wore not a stitch of clothing on their bodies. The interrogation was about to commence.

For 12 hours they remained in a mosquito filled shower block listening to a Thai music tape that was played none stop for the duration of their supposed capture. An interrogator sat in one corner, and every now and again, CLANG! He would hit a bucket once with a wooden spoon. The soldiers sat in a squatting position. CLANG-CLANG! They stood. CLANG-CLANG-CLANG! They spun around 360 degrees.

One by one they were taken by a different interrogator who set upon to use his skills of interrogation upon his victim, first a soft and mellow approach, and then later the harsh and threatening approach; and again the physical wear-him-down approach.

This was all an introduction to interrogation for the benefit of the soldiers' learning.

Years before on previous reconnaissance courses however, where I had been the student, a particular SGT (who in the early 90s was posted to Range Control and 'is not' permitted to be in command of troops any longer) ran things his way. He had been seen tying a guy to a tree and punching him, and forcing another underwater in a creek bed, almost drowning the poor guy (who was saved from death by the hand of another instructor). He had forced another to put his hand into a box and made him keep it there, though the snake was dead (and if you didn't know, a dead snake is still quite capable of killing even 24hrs after death) but the student didn't know this; and last but most certainly not least, he was seen to have thrown something out of a fast moving army rover he was driving – and the less said on this, the better. He was known to have done numerous other things that could only be expected by someone the likes of… 'Censored'; and if the RSPCA were to hear the stories of him, would have him put away for the rest of his natural life.

In regards to the interrogation being conducted, a few things had to be remembered.

All students had received a lecture on the Geneva Convention 48hrs prior to the interrogation as required, asked if they had any medical ailments such as a bad back ten minutes prior to the interrogation being undertaken, and were entitled to a night free of interrogation if they'd gone through the process before. All students went through the process without complaint however, as all wanted to march into Reconnaissance Platoon at the conclusion of the course with the knowledge that they had persevered all that we threw at them.

The 12 hours of interrogation passed without incident. Activities such as this had specific and strict guidelines; quite far-fetched compared to what would really happen. All had to remember also that a private soldier – when speaking of the infantry in general – only has limited knowledge on up and coming events with concern to friendly forces. All he needed to do was refrain from talking to the enemy for six to twelve hours; after that the soldier may as well spill his guts, especially if it meant getting a decent meal. Chances are he didn't know anything important.

The SAS – for example – were another kettle of fish. Here it's said that they undergo a minimum of three days interrogation and forego most of the niceties that had been given to the students on the 8/9RAR reconnaissance course. One more thing of importance should be remembered; civilised countries such as Australia are 'supposed' to be bound by guidelines as laid down in the big book of rules governing interrogation, where as other countries not abiding by such rules give themselves an open slather – so what was taught in practise isn't what you'd normally experience in real life.

At the conclusion of the course five new guys were welcomed into the platoon, along with a further half of the course having received a pass on the course as a whole.

Unfortunately, a platoon of our size couldn't take them all.

Suspended Extraction

Mid 1989

It was with luck that a proposed, combined course to qualify students in the art of repelling and suspended extraction, as well as others already with the qualification of repelling, to become qualified instructors of the same, was to fall the platoon's – Recon's – way.

The first two days of the course was conducted in Brisbane, with the student instructors learning all they needed to know about the ropes, accessories and teaching of techniques. This was followed by the student instructors teaching the students the art of repelling, all under the watchful eye and scrutiny of their instructor, a SGT from commandos who had apparently spent some time with the SASR. His technique of teaching, the general structure, and his mellow temperament, allowed for an enjoyable and easy flowing course.

After two days of basics and dry repelling from the mock tower positioned to the rear of the Enoggera Barracks fire station, the student instructors were ready to teach the same again, but from Blackhawks. The only two real differences between Blackhawk and UH1H was that when you jumped there was no need to move out onto the skids, as Blackhawks

didn't have them; and secondly, the ropes were secured to the ceiling of the Blackhawk aircraft, not the floor as was the case with the UH1H. Students were not, however, going to teach the forward exit style of exiting an aircraft, which involved the taking up of a metre of rope in slack and simply stepping from the chopper – as we'd done on numerous occasions on the mock tower.

For the final stages of the course, a trip to Townsville was voyaged, as this was the area to which the Blackhawks had been primarily stationed. It was like thrusting a tool into a babies hand, where 1RAR and 2/4RAR would have enjoyed themselves immensely; after all, we were quite aware as to how they cried their eyes out when on the Barrington Tops, and none of us wanted to see them upset further, in particular the politicians who were bent upon military cutbacks.

The course was soon underway with one of the soldiers continuing even with a badly sprained ankle, making sure he kept his mouth shut as he well knew that loose lips sink ships and in this case, no more jumps if the injury was known about by the hierarchy present.

After the initial phase of the hands-on it was time for the suspended extraction phase of the course. Here the chopper would land to allow groups of four to hook up, before the chopper lifted to a height of 25 metres above the students. The throttle was then gently engaged, and the students would be lifted from the ground, arms linked, and taken for a quick joy ride around a five-kilometre circuit. It stands to reason that in the real situation that the chopper wouldn't take to landing for hook up, but would simply throw the ropes down to the ground for the troops there to secure themselves to the rope in seconds flat. Flying around beneath the chopper was quite exhilarating to say the least.

The course was a definite must and all felt as though they could quite honestly say that they could see why so many people loved hang-gliding.

It must be the most fantastic sport.

Exercise Kangaroo 89 - Movements

Day 1
Sunday 6th August
1600hrs

Parade timings for roll call had been set on the Friday dismissal parade and became a disappointing reality, which fell into step with other exercises, to the point where they always seemed to commence and conclude on weekends. It was supposed by many that the Generals wanted to get their money's worth, considering that we were paid on a theoretical basis of 24 hours a day. Very convenient indeed was this rule, calling upon us to work 24/7 whenever they felt like it. Most married members found themselves struggling to keep their heads above water as it was, and it was said on numerous occasions that most infantry soldiers were below the average wage – according to statistics. As for me, I didn't really care; so long as I could afford to put a stubby in my hand it really didn't bother me.

Every soldier had all of his equipment placed into three ranks to the rear of A Coy, the pre-pre-embarkation assembly area which catered for recon platoons specific flight number, a flight which was to take us via the comfort of a QANTAS flight to the airport in Darwin. Once there we were to wait for transport to take us to another airfield before a final flight by C130, across the border into WA, was carried out.

The CQ was one of the first HQ element persons to arrive. He soon had the Q-store opened and armoury unlocked. Soldiers of A Coy lined up and one by one signed for their particular weapon – Reconnaissance platoon had been directed to move their platoon's worth of weapons to A Coy on the Friday for ease of final administration. All of the controlled stores that the patrol required for operation in the field were also issued on the Friday and marching order secured in Support Coy, to be picked up prior to weapons issue; this alleviated the problem of mass panic that was the usual outcome to pre-bush admin – we were ready for bush within minutes.

The gear that reconnaissance platoon carried looked quite cumbersome and could well have been given to them to savagely add weight to that which they already carried.

The Long Road to Rwanda

Within my patrol of five we carried an F1 radio and accessories, four claymores, claymore multi-firing device, patrol ambush light, night scope, binoculars, scout regiment telescope, helicopter landing panels, strobe light, all equipment as required for living in the field and a minimum equivalent of eight water bottles per man – more if you knew your appetite for drinking brews was significantly more than the average. This didn't include simple necessities such as smoke grenade or to the basics normally carried on patrol. In some cases we carried two radios, an F1 and a 77. This all came to quite a weight, and we were still yet to receive rations and ammunition. A good book was also a must and was usually rotated through the platoon, and sometimes these had dirty words in them, like vagina and arsehole, but we didn't really mind that much because we were real men – not like those plastic ones from the reserve.

1800hrs

The patrol had been moved to the Enoggera area theatre for the 'dangerous cargo' brief. The entire battalion was here, apart from a few odds and ends that included the road party that had departed a week earlier. They were charged with taking a whole heap of stores into the training area, along with several eskies for the road trip... but I don't know what they needed the eskies for. One guy said it was to help keep him cool because he hated to get hot and fidgety, and he couldn't sleep properly at night without a XXXX – I guess he said it like that because he didn't like swear words much so I wasn't going to offer him a read of our platoon book. If it was up to me I would have put a few good-old Queensland beers in the esky and had a few on the way, but I guess not everyone was as smart as me.

The brief went for at least five minutes and could have been significantly cut shorter with the following: 'No lighters, matches, ammo, hexamine tablets, pressure cans or batteries in cameras are permitted on this flight. If you have any on you, declare it now'. It was no wonder guys were getting out of the army in droves, fools taking five minutes to deliver a five second spiel. With talks of this nature, and petty rules to accompany them, who of a sane and stable mind could prevent themselves from yelling out obscenities at the top of their lungs? I thought that we must all be mad in one way or another.

Then came the inspection. One by one our gear was inspected for the prohibited articles mentioned above, and just for safe measure, so that it was all above board and legal, the MPs were there to watch over the procedure.

Tags were placed onto webbing and packs after inspection, and once equipment had been repacked, another transport corps wallah came forth: I could tell he wasn't from the infantry because he had a really big gut which hung over his belt and his teeth were shitbrown from drinking too much coffee from behind a desk. He cleared his throat, just like my

friend did once when flying over Townsville beneath a chopper, having swallowed a fly, whilst performing an extraction, and said something really stupid. He now wanted all breechblocks taken out from weapons and placed into packs. I wondered how high an IQ you had to have to think up these ideas, that individual would then know the theory behind the metaphysical structure of black holes and warp time factors of equimolecular proportion.

Soon after the movements brief and assignment to buses, the patrol was on its way to the airport. At 2210hrs we were finally in the air and heading for Darwin.

Exercise Kangaroo 89 - Drugs

Day 2
Monday 7th August
0100hrs

We arrived in Darwin to find the temperature sitting on a sticky 26 degrees. If this was the temperature here, and now, what was it going to be in Kununurra by day?

All of our equipment was soon moved onto awaiting trucks and on this task being met we moved ourselves into the foyer where a short wait for buses was to be endured. The short wait turned into a two-hour thumb wrestle fight with boredom. What the hell was going on? One of the guys had reported seeing the coaches; they were just out of reach behind one of the airport complex buildings. The drivers were also present and sitting behind steering wheels. At first I thought that maybe the drivers were too stupid to know where to drive too, even though they could clearly see us, but that wasn't the case at all.

The battalion soon learnt of the reasons behind the delay when a vehicle carrying members of the SIB rolled in and the battalion was formed up into six ranks. An announcement was then made by the CO who indicated his displeasure on a specific article that had been found on the aircraft after the unit's departure from it. A syringe with illegal substance had been found in one of the toilets: For a moment I thought it might have been our book. Then I thought; 'maybe one of the soldiers from the 'hygiene section' had been scrubbing the toilets out'; I mean to say, you'd have to be high to have your head stuck in a toilet all day, scrubbing everyone else's shit from a porcelain bowl.

The entire battalion now found itself being sniffed by dogs (who had already been through our packs) and we were asked to roll up our sleeves. I was glad that the dogs didn't sniff too hard because I think I forgot to put clean underwear on. The battalion medical officer then went around to inspect arms for puncture marks – assisted by some officers of the battalion – and gazed deep into each and everyone's eyes for signs of drug use. I could see him as he walked past each of the men. He would look into their eyes and smile. Now I don't know why he did this, but two things crossed my mind. Either he was happy that the soldier was 'clean' or he was a homosexual trying to get-it-on; and then I suddenly remembered, he was an officer, and smiling was a part of his duty.

They found nothing wrong with anyone and finally arrived at the conclusion that the syringe must have been discarded in the toilet before we had even boarded the aircraft.

The last guy kicked out of the battalion for drug use was an officer. I dare say that the CO would have had the officers checked behind closed doors, because they weren't checked then and there with the remainder of the battalion. How would it have been for morale to see an officer break down into tears in front of the entire battalion, confessing to a sinful life of drug use and prostitution? It reminded many of an incident some six years before when a thief was actually drummed out of the unit, being stripped of his embellishments by the CO in front of the entire battalion. Great stuff for morale to see that justice was being done. That was one thing that never used to go without a bruised face or harsh word, thieves and bludgers – thank God they were a dying breed; or were they?

At 0530hrs all were on board the coaches and on their way to Larrakeyah Barracks where we received one more brief and placed into further groups for the flight by C130 into Kununurra some 350km's South West South, 27kms West of the WA/NT border.

Once in Kununurra our Recon patrol was placed into an administrational area where we received our ammunition and hexamine tablets, those brought up by road convoy.

Tomorrow the main body of the battalion would be placed into their tactical environment at the FSB Stan, a flat dust bowl of searing heat.

Exercise K89 - Late Infiltration

Day 4
Wednesday 9th August
2000hrs

Our patrol (63B) made for its insertion point; we were loaded onto UH1H. 63A (another 5-man call-sign) was also along for the ride in another chopper just behind ours.

We were in the lead chopper and as we approached the insertion point dropped abruptly into the safe hands of a small clearing, where we commenced to debus.

Within seconds my patrol had dispersed and was secure on the ground, packs on backs. Seconds later the chopper carrying 63A could be clearly heard to fly overhead. Once the chopper with 63A aboard passed us by our chopper commenced to build on its accumulation of revolutions, lifting from the ground to follow behind. The charade, a method of leap-frog movement, was conducted to aid in the concealing of the chopper's change in pitch, to deny the enemy information by sound as to our being inserted.

We soon picked ourselves up from the ground to be met by a small band of pioneers of the battalion. They had arrived here earlier in the morning, along with a boat and small outboard motor, a motor that according to orders wasn't supposed to be employed.

Visibility across the river to our front was very poor, but the landing point was known. It lay almost three kilometres downstream.

We clambered aboard and found the small paddles anything but helpful. The river was more like a lake, rather motionless. A snail doing breaststroke could have moved down stream with more speed.

The first task was to cross the 200 metre gap and then move stealthily down the river to the point over a kilometre away where boats would be left behind to be taken away by pioneers.

Time passed slowly, and with the passing of the first 60 minutes came the chalking up of only 500 metres. At this rate we'd be worn out before mission parameters could be met. A decision to make land was made then and there, take a short breather for assimilation by sound of what may lay in the immediate vicinity, confirm navigation details, and move off on our merry way with packs on backs.

The move wasn't too difficult, although many homes were encountered. Luck seemed to have changed slightly in favour of our patrol. Each house we passed seemed to have some kind of interior light on, or even a small porch or other outside light. Now I wasn't Einstein, but it wasn't hard to figure that it would be near on impossible for anyone to see us from within their homes, even though the distance between the homesteads and ourselves was as little as 40 metres, as we were in the open but shrouded by the dark of the night.

By 0100hrs we had arrived at a water pump and a ten metre wide canal that stretched out some 600 metres to the West. A white ute also had itself parked near the water pump, seemingly facing the river in such a position that the occupant would be able to see the entire waterway pass him by. If it was the enemy then we were lucky to have left the boats where we had, to then continue by foot, or we would have been seen sure enough.

I pulled the patrol back into the natural depression that had the best tree and bush cover around.

This act brought about a warning we had received the day before, about crocodiles.

Any time we found ourselves closer than 20 metres to a river, we had permission – as laid down in the safety guidelines for the exercise – for the commander of that group to load up with live ammunition. The commander was also the only man in each group not to have been issued with a BFA, for to be issued with such could have been rather dangerous if called upon to fire live ammo.

We were now ten metres from the riverbank and in such a depression of mangroves that my 20 round magazine of live ammo was secured immediately.

The sun commenced its climb at 0500hrs and the single picket during the night to maintain a watch on the ute overlooking the river turned up nothing of consequence.

Information was more easily available now however; the vehicle occupant's age, description, vehicles make, registration, etc. All was collected, encoded, and sent via the radio we carried. It seemed quite suspicious that someone should be watching the river like this, but due to the slope of the ground and shading of the interior, it was hard to say whether he was asleep or awake.

By 0530hrs the guy in the Ute was off on his way, and so were we, across the small canal and into a LUP, a location just as attractive to crocodiles than earlier on.

Day patrols were sent out; two two-man groups, with the fifth member given the live ammo, and informed to remain behind and hidden with the packs, codes and radio.

The groups remained out all day, five buildings coming under the watch of several hours' worth of surveillance each, all in the aid to determine whether or not they were safe houses used for the harbouring of enemy forces or individuals. One such building was a banana shed, where several workers were found packing the yellow fruit into crates. This area must have been literally swarming with snakes, and here I was, me and my mate, crawling around in the long grass, but none were encountered.

Shortly after midday all had returned to the LUP. Several hours sleep would now be taken advantage of prior to a more formidable reconnaissance and surveillance being conducted on buildings (at night) that seemed to be more suspicious during the passing of the daylight hours.

It was 2300hrs. I approached a suspect house with another man, a building that was hidden well amongst the palms of a banana plantation. It would have been virtually impossible to get in here during the day – an effort was made, but penetration was limited to just fifty metres due to the throngs of workers. Our skilled two-man patrol had been fortunate not to have been compromised earlier on in the day, and lucky we were to have withdrawn from our task when we did, for more workers were brought into the area soon after lunch.

Twenty metres now separated us from the building thought to be suspect. We stood and listened. Fifteen minutes later and all remained quiet. The lights were off and not a move made from within the wooden walls of the old Queenslander style homestead.

We turned to retreat, and as we did so a dog commenced barking.

We stepped off slowly, hoping the dog was barking at something else, but no. The distance between it and us was quickly halved – it was coming towards us.

The outside lights of the house were turned on and the owner stepped out. We were thirty metres off from the porch; the distance between the dog and us commenced to decrease. The dog was now backed up by his master, courage instilled. It was now ten metres to our flank, and joined by another four-legged friend. 'Get 'em boys!'

was the master's command. And the dogs were upon us. A torch beam followed the dogs who were now at our side. We stood our ground with steadfast will – in any realistic situation, I would have offered my left forearm to the menacing jaws, before thrusting a knife into the throat of the attacking dog, drowning him in his own blood; but this was an exercise, and such methods of defence discarded quickly.

'You guys,' he immediately recognised us as the army, 'you enemy or friendly?' He soon calmed the dogs down.

'Friendly, mate. Definitely friendly.' We introduced ourselves.

'I'd ask ya in for a beer but I don't suppose you'd be allowed.' He smiled, several teeth missing from his upper jaw. 'This here be my oldest dog. He's a bit deaf though. A damn snake bit him yesterday as well.'

'Poor dog,' I said.

'Yeah, but he's a good dog.'

'I don't suppose you've seen anyone acting suspicious around these parts?'

'Only you two. There's been no new people around here for years. Just the owners and plantation workers. All the locals have dogs too, ya know; all around these parts.'

'Is that right?'

'Yeah,' and the discussion continued for a short time.

'Well thank you for your time.' What else could be said? 'Hope you have a nice night, and see you around.'

'No worries, mate.'

And with that we parted company.

We decided to give several other houses a going over, but as each of these was approached, dogs would start to bark: 'Locals.' So an early retirement of the mission was encountered.

63B were extracted at 0430hrs and returned to Fire Support Base Stan some three hours later. It was here that we found out from a reliable resource that the enemy, those that we were searching for, had been extracted from the area some 18 hours before our insertion.

So much for military intelligence.

Ex K89 - 15km Close Surveillance

Day 7
Saturday 12th August
1330hrs

Once again, we of 63B, found ourselves bound for the wilderness by courtesy of the newbeaut army chopper pilots; destination; some rise in the ground known as Bluff Mountain.

To be flown directly to its peak would have compromised our position, so a landing zone 1.6km away was considered to be the appropriate measure of security required in hiding our true destination to any nearby enemy – we would have to climb.

During orders – given by the reconnaissance platoon commander – an order to carry out water resupply was given. The patrol was to descend the mountain every time water replenishment was required. After several minutes of discussion it was decided to carry a jerry can to the top of the mountain instead. This turned out to be hectic to our health, by way of its weight, and by the time we'd reached the top of the feature one third of the water had been consumed.

Once at the top of the mountain, the major objective could be seen. It was a road that ran parallel to the line of sight with objective two; the road's extent couldn't be seen. The second objective was a farmhouse near a three-way road junction; it was fifteen kilometres away. The patrol's task in regards to this was to watch and record all vehicle movement, in and out of the farm, and to which direction they approached or departed. The occupant number, registration, colour and make of the vehicle were also required. With the SRT set up, the best we could manage was the obtaining of the type of vehicle and its colour.

One of the more unusual orders was also met with this trip and directed that there was no need to encode any information prior to broadcasting it over the radio. This was apparently so that the CO back in FSB Stan had the option of acting immediately to any incident as quickly as possible – which didn't mean much to us any more due to past experiences.

That afternoon, and the following morning, our patrol reported seeing an SAS patrol using the road; once to the farm, and once from it. This information was apparently acted upon some 24 hours later by way of B Coy on trucks, paralleling the road from just short of the farm, and up to and past Bluff Mountain. On initially sighting this platoon, a confirmation was made with the remainder of the patrol. Was it not stated in orders that 'no' friendlies were operating in our area of operations? Correct.

If I found it difficult to distinguish a vehicle's make which sat in the open at 15 kilometres, how on earth was I to establish whether this was friendly or enemy, as the trucks in question were hidden well by the surrounding countryside as they traversed the road towards us.

The call was made and I describing the movement as enemy. Some minutes later we were informed to disregard the sighting – meaning it was friendly.

It sort of contradicted what had happened to me during my first ever-bush trip; back then I'd gotten myself in the shit for not considering those on the motorbikes as enemy; now I was in the shit for considering two trucks as enemy when in fact they weren't. No matter which way you looked at it, no matter what the rank, all persons tried with great effort to hide their inadequacies by blaming others for things that went wrong; and then again, no one was safe from making a simple mistake, and all should be forgiven. Consider for example a reverse to the decisions that had been made by me, that was to say, not reporting the trucks, but shooting at those on the motorbikes. Everything would have worked out fine and nothing further said, for luck would have taken a ride on the back of a 'stab-in-the-dark' guess.

It seemed to me that all things needed to be taken on merit, and decisions had to be made by the man behind the trigger at the time of the confrontation; if that decision should be wrong, then so be it. Contradictions like the above occurred all of the time in the army, but regardless of its outcome, or regardless of who was in the wrong, it always seemed to be that 'you' were the one with 'your' name in the dreaded black book. As before, it was as simple as forgive and forget.

That afternoon the call we were waiting for finally arrived. We were to be airlifted back to FSB Stan. A question was asked as to the pick-up point, it was to be 1km to the West. Why not to the top of Bluff Mountain? The answer; the enemy may see us being picked up and the position compromised. But we weren't coming back here. But then again, what did it matter? The soldier at the bottom of the ladder couldn't do much for any particular circumstance or situation, when someone above him was unwilling to stick his own neck out for that particular individual, and officers rarely stuck their necks out. This was apparent to me, and probably why I was always upsetting someone, for I always liked the ability to voice my opinion, whether it be right or wrong, and many of the officers above me didn't readily accept that type of behaviour; in a strange way I could tell, because there seemed to be fewer smiling officers when I was around – or was the army changing.

The move to the exfiltration point took two hours, numerous cliff faces of no more than ten metres in drop, revealing themselves as every step was taken, and not a single one of them seemingly marked on the map; they were like giant thumbs sticking out of the ground, joined by buttresses of solid rock.

Once at our destination we were required to cut back the foliage for the chopper.

But weren't we trained for suspended extraction?

No, best not interfere this time around; let the officers have their wicked way with us.

One thing was for sure; the army in general was growing more pathetic with each year that passed. Here we were, trained with the ability for suspended extraction, but unable to perform it; and as for not being picked up from atop the mountain, that in itself could just not be explained. I personally felt that even in these fairly early years that it would be hard to recommend the army to anyone. It was a shame that good times were forgotten in times of bad.

Exercise K89 - Wasted Effort

Day 13
Friday 18th August
0430hrs

Orders revealed that a reconnaissance of some low ground, namely a basin, needed to be cleared visually of all enemy presence. The area of concern was the buffer between two areas of operation, that is to say, it was the responsibility of no single unit in particular and required specific permission from Brigade for any such move into it to be undertaken.

Permission was granted and all of 63B's equipment was readied for the three-day task.

The insertion point was to be on some of the higher ground near the basin as it was strongly suggested that this would once again deceive the enemy as to the true objective, and also permit the insertion to be conducted out of view of the basin in question.

The tactic of using two choppers in the aid of concealing the change in chopper pitch was once again employed. A small force of three men was also being inserted for the three day long reconnaissance, to aid in communication. The men from signals platoon were to set up a re-trans station and remain with this on some of the higher ground in the vicinity. Many problems were being encountered with comms, due primarily to the ionosphere.

1200hrs

The UH1H came into a hover some eight feet from the rocky terrain below and over the headphones to which I wore came the voice of the army pilot suggesting that we get out 'now'. He handed over a piece of paper with the grid reference location and I looked at this as he spoke into his headset.

'Aren't you going to land?' I asked.

'No. It's too risky. Now get out. I haven't got all day, mate.'

I removed the headset and signalled the others to climb out onto the skids. I was then met by several horror stricken stares. 'Get out. Hang

The Long Road to Rwanda

from the skids and drop,' I yelled.

One member being only five feet tall shook his head.

'We aren't landing so you better jump,' was all I could say.

I climbed out, followed by the others. Hanging from the skid with 40 to 45 kilograms in pack on your back proved arduous (not to mention the weight of weapon and webbing) and we were still half a metre short of the rocky surface below – if you happen to be six foot tall. It wasn't like dropping onto a football field with nothing on your back; this was a landscape of hardened steel, and of the five men in 63B, three of us had a history of bad ankles and back problems due to conditions of employment.

Each dropped with packs on backs and weapons in hand. The chopper took off. A quick survey proved that all ankles had survived the fall. Now for the first of the navigation and radio checks, both of which proved unconvincing and inoperable; so much for re-trans.

We commenced to move towards the known basin area and by 1300hrs had confirmed our exact location on the map.

The lay of the ground compared with the 1:100,000 map proved mind provoking at times, many of the cliffs being unmarked as per the previous mission; boulders sized between that of a golf ball to a basketball also made the move slow and dangerous.

We continued down what at first appearance, and according to the map, was a good line of approach towards the basin. We were in a creek line where the banks rose a good fifty metres on either side. The journey was short lived however as we soon came to another cliff face; this one being of an eighty metre drop and once again, not marked on the map.

It was late afternoon and coming up to scheds. It was decided to stay there the night, 20 metres from the cliff face, protected by that and the 50 metre high – 70 degree – sides.

There was to be no moon tonight and movement in this country in the dark was asking for trouble. Tonight would also be a bad time to find out that you were a sleepwalker for the cliff was ever on my mind.

The following morning at 0600hrs we commenced to climb from our predicament, down the 50 metres in 30 minutes. The trek to the basin was remarkably easy from here, travelling the 800 metres down the spur in two hours; less than half-a-click per hour – not bad for this country.

By midday we (63B) had established ourselves a LUP and tried emphatically to reestablish comms. Even with the re-trans station this proved to be an impossible task. It was about then that a boat was heard travelling the river some two kilometres to our front.

It didn't take much common sense to realise that it was meant for us. Who else knew that we were here? Why was it apparently moving up the river, making ten-minute stops along route, and firing the odd shot from a rifle? We headed off towards the source of the noise.

We finally emerged from the brush to find a small group of 8/9RAR pioneers. BHQ were apparently worried over the lack of communications that they had received from us.

The re-trans had been airlifted out, we were required back at Stan, and the BN was closing a cordon on a large group of enemy somewhere to the north. The recon PL COMD was also becoming disgruntled with our efforts; but then again, who really cared. It was obvious to me that the only reason he was spitting venom was due to the kicks in the arse he was receiving from higher, which was by no way 63B's fault. More encouragement was needed from higher, not kicks in the pants for something that was not directly our fault. There were always two sides to a story.

63B received two missions after this, but both proved to be of little interest. The enemy never came to view during the exercise, although we were fired upon once from a distance of two hundred metres during a reconnaissance of an area which was already being patrolled by a friendly force; a waste of time and effort on our part.

All were returned to Brisbane on Monday 28th after 23 days bush; less than anyone would have liked, but more than ample for an exercise which gave little interest; most of the large exercises were like this. But then again, what was our job in the infantry? More than 95 percent of an Infantryman's time was supposedly spent searching and waiting for the enemy, less than a few percent being spent in engagement or under fire.

This exercise was not common. Although displeasure has to be voiced, it was not uniform throughout the army. All-in-all the army was an adventure that will last in my memory for eternity. We also need to keep in mind the military argument of 'the big picture', which, as it suggests, means that there was more to 'it' than met the eye.

In short; although I am peeved, I did understand.

Papua New Guinea

July 1990

The Australian Army has more than a few instructors/advisers in PNG at any given time. Most of these are of the rank of Warrant Officer and are quite obstinate in their ways. There were however, Sergeants doing the same job back in the 80s, but not any longer (to my knowledge). These sergeants were of no less merit to themselves or their country.

On the 7th February 1990 the 8/9th Battalion was given the news that a 65-man contingent was to head for the sunny shores of PNG on 12th July and establish themselves at the training establishment known as Goldie River.

They were to be known exclusively as the Australian Army Training Project Team, the first training team since Vietnam. Compared with the backdrop of Vietnam, our task was substantially less fragile in terms of its diplomatic importance, but not by terms of merit. We weren't going to be shot at or killed by the hand of a well-organized unit, but in comparison with the growth of social standards within Australia, faced a formidable task that was just as exciting to mind, and as impressively important to the growth of individual pride.

Why were they sent here? Simply to increase the strength of the PNGDF to a sizable force for the protection of its borders – this was the political statement shared by most. PNG only had the strength of three regular infantry battalions and the Indonesian/PNG border was a large undefined area where clashes between forces of Indonesia nationality occurred quite often. But of course, others would say that the instructors were there to train soldiers purposely for Bougainville.

On the 12th day of July the contingent boarded a QANTAS aircraft with great anticipation for what lay in wait for them during their six-month deployment. The contingent arrived in Port Moresby at 1320hrs that same day.

Goldie River

12th July

The road to Goldie River Barracks was for the most part unsealed, as were many of the roads out from Port Moresby's industrial, commercial, and residential centres. It certainly appeared to most, that the 'welcome dollars' that the Australian government was sending over in aid, was going to waste. It was originally felt and confirmed that the money was being spent on roads and schools etc. Many of the 65-man contingent believed, however, that the corruption of the government was brought out into the open that year, but unsure as to the measures that the Australian government took against actions such as high officials accepting bribes for votes of confidence. But I guess this was a better option than allowing PNG to have tried to pursue aid from the communists [Russians] back in 1973.

The surrounding countryside was in tune to that of Townsville, the major difference being the basic living standards; the way in which they led their lives, the poverty and way of society, and its wave of crime that put Australia's to shame; thank God.

It took about 30 minutes to reach the gates of Goldie. It was a pleasant change from what had been seen so far. But the scene around was a masquerade that hid Goldie's problems so easily on that first day in country.

The barracks themselves were very similar to Lavarack Barracks; a blueprint had apparently been brought up from the North of Queensland and used to build some of the camp. Even the OR's kitchen was a mirror image to those in Australia.

The camp boozer must have been a local initiative. No walls, two pool tables, several picnic tables, and a wooden box that normally housed a TV, were all the commodities of the dwelling. The TV itself had been confiscated by the PNG CO of the area, due to horseplay amongst his soldiers one night, and was probably still stashed at his home for his own personal convenience.

Here the soldiers of Goldie would come, every payday, cash in hand, and blow nearly the lot in one hit. Fight after fight was normally the outcome, but we of the contingent would just have to wait and find

The Long Road to Rwanda

out for ourselves.

I had seen very little of this place which was to be my home for the next six months, but a tour of the area would be conducted on the morrow. Were we to be impressed by anything here? I strongly doubted it.

The ration store was in a shambles. Snakes and rats had to be beaten back with sticks and clubs. On showing the medic the standards of the store, he confessed that all had a big job ahead of them. Even before the clean-up had commenced he realised how lucky all were that none had come down with any serious illness.

The transport yard needed attention. The PNGDF TPT PL had quite an ill effect upon all of the vehicles in the vicinity. If a vehicle didn't start for whatever reason, then it was towed to the yard and left to rust, and fall apart.

Maintenance on vehicles was pretty much non-existent. Tools were minimal; usually borrowed by the soldiers working there, who in turn failed to bring them back to the workplace. Light fingers were a major problem in Goldie.

Most of the vehicles were found to have small deficiencies of some description, such as having no oil in the engine, no petrol in the tanks, or air in tyres; all of which could easily have been fixed.

A $40,000 cooling system had been purchased for the RAP some years ago and just two months before the contingent's arrival it had broken down. Instead of getting it fixed for a price of $5,000 it was decided by someone in authority that it required replacing. So they brought another one of inferior quality for the low price of $25,000.

They had already proved that they had little common sense and a poor attitude towards their equipment. The logistic and administrative system certainly failed to operate effectively, or was it the men who worked (couldn't work) the system?

125, brand new, military compasses, were supposed to be in a safe, in the Q-store, that the instructors were to be operating out of. On approaching the PNG SGT, our SSGT was advised: 'No. We don't have any compasses here.'

Our SSGT decided to push the issue further and inspected the safe himself, shazam, 125 compasses.

The PNG SGT would still deny their existence however, as he had no paperwork on them, although he did admit seeing someone writing something, somewhere, some years before.

The RAP had a hell of a job ahead of them too. Not only did it take them all week to scrub back the filth from the walls in this 'operational' RAP, but also mass bribery was to meet them at every corner they turned.

To the rear of some of the rifle ranges – which were required for the training of the 300 PNG soldiers – were large chicken coops. The local tribe of the area owned these. They would be willing to move the chickens to a different location so long as they received free medical treatment. So once a week the RAP had to pick up sticks and visit the local tribe.

Most of the locals that worked in the area, or who were related to someone of the military in some way – living on the barracks – visited the RAP frequently. Most came due to children that had been affected by mosquito bite, and many were infected with malaria/polio.

The RAP witnessed many deaths and was always confronted by long lines of patients each morning. Two children in particular couldn't be helped. They were so sick from infection that they were half brain-dead due to lack of preventative measures being taken against the dreaded mosquito.

The RAP organised a dousing of the area, fumigating the entire camp, and killing off the uninvited mozzie. Once a week seemed to do the trick.

It took a considerable amount of trouble to sort out all of these problems, and we hadn't even started to climb the ladder as yet.

Atrocities

16th July

The contingent soon found themselves with the opportunity to converse with the regular soldiers of the PNG Army. I was more than surprised to find that some were very keen and knowledgeable, others deserve nothing less than a firing squad.

UH1H aircraft, of which were given to PNG as a token gesture of goodwill by the Australians, to be used for medical evacuation of ground troops in Bougainville, and for the ferrying of medical supplies, weren't.

I had found myself a veteran who had a mouth most humble. He couldn't help but to spill his guts, to tell of his stories, to tell of his heroics.

A member of the BRA was taken aboard one of these choppers and was questioned, or more specifically, interrogated. Whether or not he gave into the wishes of the PNG soldier was never told, but I was informed how they threw him out of the chopper to his death, into the Solomon Sea. This certainly coincided with a story I'd heard of a body being washed onto the silky shores of the Solomon Islands earlier that year.

And another: A Company of 32 soldiers, carrying out operations in Bougainville, soon became fatigued; they had been there for three months – quite a stint (without rest) by anyone's terms. They were informed that they were to be relieved in place by another company of regulars.

A lot of the men were unhappy with this arrangement, as they had not yet killed anyone, unlike some their wantoks before them. How could they possibly return home without first doing the job for which they had come, to inflict death? They were on the verge of a mutiny.

The company commander finally gave his orders. They would attack at dawn, an unsuspecting village which could quite easily have hostiles in their midst. The village was taken out and the soldier's egos satisfied – many innocents died.

And yet again: A sniper fired upon a PNGDF section on patrol, the very section that was under command of the guy I was speaking with.

Nigel B.J. Clayton

The sniper had killed his lead scout.

One of the sniper pair escaped unharmed, but the other had been wounded in the shoulder – the man responsible for the kill.

The section commander approached the scout and looked into his eyes. The sniper had done his job, nothing more and nothing less. The commander of the section lifted his SLR and placed the butt firmly into his shoulder; and holding the barrel against the sniper's head, pulled the trigger. No prisoners would be taken.

Miscellaneous Affairs

25th July

Diarrhoea had spread throughout the camp overnight. Our bodies just weren't used to the bacteria and other constituents found within the water.

A test on the water source proved it to be unhealthy for human consumption, so it had to be purified by the individual prior to drinking. Two purification tablets, to every water bottle of water, was the order of the day, and some of the guys who weren't affected applied a smaller dose of purification, administering less and less as each day passed.

Was so much purification in the water bad for our bodies, our inner organs; it certainly couldn't be doing us any good.

Sometime later a report proved that the problem did lie in the water tank situated upon the hill overlooking Goldie. It was the direct responsibility of the local caretaker to purify the water on a daily basis, the water itself being pumped directly from the river, the same river that flowed down from that which was used by local tribes. It was enough to make your stomach turn over backwards and do cartwheels: faeces in the water.

The caretaker had decided not to purify the water, as the climb up the hill was too much for him to be bothered with, which was the same way in which he looked at the hot water system for the barracks. The reason no one had any hot water, wasn't because the system didn't work, but because the caretaker had failed to keep the gas-pilot lights, lit. The medic soon had words with him about matters of health and safety. This must have had some effect upon him, for the problem with the purification of water soon ceased to exist.

One bed and a single locker, per man for the six months in the country. During the six months we were permitted in town on less than eight separate occasions [give or take].

26th July

Tuarama Barracks, just on the fringes to Port Moresby, had been placed on alert. There was expected to be a riot in direct response to the K4,000,000 (kina) given as bribes to officials for their votes of confidence. The riot never eventuated.

27th July

One of the contingent found himself in a situation which could have been rather messy, not because he was faced with possible injury or death, but because he was the only married member of the contingent who was seen or heard to try and play around, with the opposite sex. PNG was much different than Malaysia; in particular from when I was there last, for this place was dangerously overflowing with disease.

He had found himself a young lady and took her for a walk down to the pier. Here they sat and talked – amongst other things.

Sometime after their arrival at the secluded spot – around 2200hrs – a group of no less than six rascals arrived.

They held him at knife-point, told him to hand his clothes over, and went through the pockets. They then took the young lady with them, threatening the soldier; that he'd be killed if they returned in five minutes and found him still there. Screams and murmurs could then be heard coming from where the woman had disappeared, and as the soldier ran for help, the gang of rascals proceeding to bash and rape their victim. Maybe if he'd done what he was told and remained in place at the club, which had security guards present, none of that would have happened. I thought he was stupid and very self-centred.

The young lass spent five days in hospital before returning to the Aussie for more affection. Some people just didn't learn.

4th August

Twenty tonnes of ammunition for the course arrived aboard three Hercules aircraft. Not all was used for the Recruit/IET course: I'll let you use your imagination…

The Kokoda Trail

11th August

The course in Goldie was to commence soon. To date, all that the contingent had done was to carry out administration for the course to come. So much lay ahead of us, from erecting gallery ranges to sneaker ranges (varying types of rifle range), to moving in 300 beds, preparing lesson plans for the sixteen week course, and bringing in stores which were to be issued and used by the soldiers in question. Now it was time to take a short few days break, to either rest back in barracks and do nothing, or to see a bit of the country.

19 decided upon the Kokoda trail as a means of amusement, taking along with them two members of the PNGDF, who themselves were sergeants and instructing on the course alongside the Australians.

After being flown into Popendetto, a two-hour wait for transport was suffered. The transport had been arranged by one of the PNG soldiers, his sole reason for taking the journey was due to his wanting to see his family, to which he hadn't seen for quite some time. A cousin of his had arranged for the neighbourhood police to pick our group up by truck.

By the time we reached Kokoda village, we were ready for the big trek – the museum there was nothing more than a small open shed, but very much worth the visit.

We walked for several hours that first day, coming to a stop on reaching the first of the many hills to be encountered. As we weren't to commence until the following day anyway, we saw nothing wrong with taking an early break, to take in the surrounding atmosphere, the solitude of the jungle.

The final hours of light were put to good use, spent rearranging the packs we carried, our house for the next few days. Here we carried our food which was to last us the short trip.

It just wasn't good enough that we should rely on food from the villages – even though we would pay for it. It may have saved some the locals a trip however, as it wasn't uncommon to see men and women travelling for two to three days from the highlands down to the areas near Moresby, to sell their crop at the markets.

A minimum of one-day worth of water was also carried by each trekker, along with a group radio and other equipment for communication with Goldie. Essential warm weather gear, sleeping bag, and hutchies were other necessities.

The first day of walking was quite breathtaking, but certainly not the best; much more was to come. The jungle was a most peaceful place, by day and night.

We spent our first scheduled night in a place called Alolo Village. Here we found a Kokoda Trail sign that had been ripped from the post and thrown to the ground to rot. It was in fairly good condition, so was picked up and carried the remainder of the walk, to eventually find its way into the Rams Retreat – the 8/9RAR boozer.

We passed all of the places seen by any adventurer willing enough to make this most worthwhile of walks; Mt.Bellamy, Lora Creek, Templeton's Crossing, and of course Owen's Corner.

All the sights were seen; the foot bridges, mountain streams, foxholes and shellscrapes. Ammunition was easy to come across as well, old 303 ammo and mortar bombs.

At one stage during the adventure, it took almost four hours to travel a distance of 400 metres – due to the lay of the ground. It was quite harsh in some places. Another thing that was a wonder to see was the aircraft landing strips. These rolled with the contours of the ground and suddenly stopped, the edge of the strip dropping away to a valley hundreds of metres below. Not much different to an aircraft carrier really, which rolled with the waves, creating its own rolling curves and cliff, so I wouldn't classify it as unique.

The 15th was our final day, a short four hours of walking bringing us out to Owen's Corner, another extremely steep climb; but at least this had fewer false crests, something which was encountered too often during the climbing of some peaks, and quite demoralising.

This was one experience that would live forever in the hearts of those that trekked the trek; it was made all the easier too; for a battle wasn't being waged as we walked it.

I noted with great inspiration that an Australian man, who didn't have the use of his own legs (wheelchair bound), literally walked the entire trail on his hands in ten days: it made our effort of just a few days seem rather insignificant.

New Recruits

23rd August

The first of the recruits arrived from outside Moresby today. They were met as one would like to have been met, speaking to them firmly but not belittling them – quite dissimilar to the Australian Army recruit/IET system which only forced an opinion upon the soldier that, yes, the instructors were immature fools with no real hold on reality. So much for the system of fools. But the opinions of men and women not open to ridicule or military training, would naturally find it hard to cope with harsh words and a cold stare. Kapooka and Singleton were not holiday camps, but training establishments of the hardest kind.

43 heads were counted, as they were loaded onto the trucks, 45 had been expected.

One of the older guys from Mt.Hagen pointed out that four of the recruits had run off down the road when the buses had turned up to bring them into Goldie. All they were after was a free air flight to their capital in the hope of finding other employment. But if four had made a run for it, there should be 41 heads, not 43.

A check was conducted by name. Two of the men here weren't recorded on the list we'd prepared earlier. Unfortunately they couldn't be taken. They were informed to go through the correct channels of enlistment and advised on how to go about it, being told that they had exactly one week before the course actually commenced. They would miss out on most of the preliminaries but could catch up on these later – dependent on how long they took to join us in Goldie. They immediately made their way to the recruitment office as advised.

29th August

They arrived in large numbers, most by foot, few by bus. Once through the gates of Goldie, their names were taken down, and after cross-reference, they were placed into a platoon in order for administration to commence.

Most of the platoons had been arranged in such a way that those members marching into a platoon would find themselves amongst others from their place of birth, or near as possible to it. But after the preliminaries week and introduction to the course, they would be split up once more into a more logical pattern for training, along with a large diversity of age groups combined within a single section. Here a mixture of experiences and knowledge would be sought, separating certain recruits from any high authority that was found to be present from their highland's tribe or birthplace. There was a situation encountered on Goldie where a regular private soldier was of a higher order of rank within his province than that of a warrant officer he now worked under. Whilst in camp everything was fine, but once outside of the front gate, and no longer on military soil, the private was in charge and in complete authority over that of the Warrant Officer.

There was also a situation in Moresby where a truck driver had run over a little girl. Being from a different province, the little girl's wantoks claimed compensation; k1,000,000 and several thousand pigs was the going rate. All you could hear over the radio for the next three days were announcements trying to persuade the two groups not to clash in bloodshed.

An arrangement was met and compensation paid, but not for the amounts requested – several hundred pigs was the outcome; that's what her life was worth in the end.

Age was also a factor in recruitment. One of the recruits looked extremely young, and on further investigation was found to be only 14 years of age. No real proof could be gained and the PNGDF seemed not to care about his age. The contingent had no alternative but to allow him on the course. He passed all objectives on the sixteen-week course and with better results than some of the older soldiers; so on completion of the course he was 14 years of age and ready to kill.

One of the recruits enlisting did so under a false name. The only reason he was caught out was due to the fact that the real owner of the name was already in Goldie – most didn't have birth certificates as they were born in the highlands, in places like that found along the Kokoda Trail and sometimes even more remote than that.

31st August

All of the recruits were brought together today and arranged into ten platoons of thirty men.

This was the big adjustment to separate the provinces as best as possible and equally between the platoons. There were now two companies, each comprising 150 men.

Of the 30 men in the platoon I was operating from, we received only two of our original soldiers back. The other twenty-eight were new faces. Now came the first of the crunches to time and space for the first week of training, for we had no idea if these soldiers had been inducted correctly, or even if they had all of their administration details taken care of. This could bring about a lot of late nights – but it was only for one week.

Problems

1st September

The course was under way, but not without its headaches, all of which were brought on by the recruits.

'Corporal, I don't have a knife and fork.'

'Corporal, I lost my towel.'

'My shorts don't fit.' It wouldn't help to explain to these soldiers that they had a variety of nine different sizes to choose from, where-as the last course which had just marched out, under the guidance of the PNG instructors, had a choice of just two – a choice of only four when it came to boots. Boots were something else, for most of these guys had never worn them before. 'Corporal, my shoes don't fit and they hurt my feet, do I have to wear them?'

'I think I'm twenty one years old, Corporal; but I'm not sure.'

'No, Corporal. My Father's first name is my last name, and my first name belongs to someone else; I liked the sound of it so took it for myself.'

'No, Corporal. He's name is Namor.P, mine is P.Namor.'

One of the questions asked was why they had decided to join the army.

'To protect the borders of PNG.'

'To serve the people.'

'To get away from my province. I hate the people there.'

'I have nothing better to do.'

'My crocodile farm will need three more years to mature. I'll join the army and get out later.'

What could you say: 'Well done men; you all passed the questions with flying colours.'

A quick explanation on 'flying colours' was then conducted.

Another recruit was found emptying the contents of the bag he was carrying into his locker. Instead of containing clothes, it contained 200 buai nuts, a drug similar to that of the coca leaf of Peru (as far as I understand it).

A search was conducted, each of the instructors searching his own section. No buai was found in our platoon, but the 25 odd knives were confiscated until march-out.

2nd September

The instructors were informed to conduct their own medical parades in the mornings due to the influx of soldiers reporting for sick parade each day.

'Oh, Corporal. I have pains under my chest and around my armpit area. I need to see the doctor.'

'How do you think you got them Recruit Siaoa?' (see-'ow-'a)

'I think it was doing push-ups.'

'Then I suggest you get back into the ranks and cover off, before you get another 20 push-ups for wasting my time.'

Three recruits approached me, asking to see the doctor. They were complaining of constipation. When asked how long they had it for they said since they'd arrived at Goldie some six days before. After one owned up to the problem, more and more started to come out of the woodwork. Half of the platoon was infected.

I gave each a pill and told them to see me in the morning.

The following morning saw the same guys complaining that they now had diarrhoea.

4th September

Four recruits were taken to the medic. They were each diagnosed as having Malaria. The CO of the Australian contingent was soon informed as all platoons had started to show signs of having the same problem.

A course of malaria pills was strongly suggested.

PNG officials immediately denounced the idea and forbade the contingent to treat the problem.

Each instructor was also teaching as per the Australian method of instruction. This was soon discarded. The recruits seemed to look at the instructors as a mirror image, and no matter what was done, the same mistakes arose time and time again. Lessons were then changed to suit the drill being taught, some as I stood beside them, and others as I stood with my back turned on them. The change in the methods of instruction worked and an overall faster progression made thereafter.

Platoon Commander

11th September

I found that the platoon was rather lucky, when taking into account its structure of instructors. We had the good fortune of having an Australian SGT, our only demise was the platoon commander who happened to be a PNG regular, the most hated man in the company.

He couldn't help but to show off and boast on how he was trained in Australia, always remarking on how good he was.

A few of the Australian officers were questioned reference this, and it was announced as a fact that this particular officer was indeed trained overseas, but PNG students on an officer course in Australia were subjected to a shorter course as compared to others – and, from what I understood, usually involved receiving a pass, regardless of how good or bad the student fared. Of course, there was the exception to the rule, and some PNG students made rather good officers. Our platoon commander was not one of these.

On occasion he would find a seat to the rear of the lecture room, in most cases that being a large tent with the sides rolled up due to the heat and lesson structure.

Up would shoot his hand, every time a question was posed to the soldiers. He was never asked to give an answer, and he certainly had nothing to gain, or prove, by doing such.

He couldn't help himself during some of the lessons, putting his nose in where it wasn't welcome. 'No, Corporal Clayton. Not like that. We always used to do it like this in Duntroon,' and would then go on to explain things to the recruits. One day he was pulled aside quite politely, so as not to damage his reputation with the soldiers, not that any more damage could have been done. 'Listen sir. If you want to give the lesson then go ahead and give it. If not, go away and pester someone else.'

20th September

According to PNGDF law, a soldier wasn't permitted to smoke cigarettes during working hours. The Australian instructors turned a blind eye to this fact, allowing the students their indulgence during breaks between lessons.

At one stage I could see a few of the soldiers talking amongst themselves. They didn't appear to be in the best of spirits. On questioning them I found out that their beloved PL COMD had caught one of the recruits smoking during work hours and had ordered him to put it out in his mouth, which of course the soldier did.

The soldiers were then pooled together and tactics drawn. If any wished to smoke he could, but to do so he would have to walk the short distance of thirty metres from the tent and down into a large drain that ran the length of the sports oval adjacent to them. In this way they would be less likely to be seen by their PL COMD. He seldom showed his face nowadays, having become a little bashful. He was probably tired of the NCOs' sarcastic remarks. 'And always maintain a sentry to watch for the Boss,' was our warning to them all.

10th October

The PL COMD tried pushing his luck one day. He had pulled aside two Australian NCOs from a neighbouring platoon and was chewing them out over something that at this stage was unclear to me. They were also in earshot of the recruits, which just wasn't on. If an NCO was to be disciplined, then it should be conducted out-of-sight: unlike what I did behind his back, so I guess I was no better.

I approached.

He was apparently trying to find evidence of a recruit's effort, in blaming a NCO, for something that remained the fault of the recruit. The officer took the side of the recruit, apparently a relation.

It was decided to interject with a change of subject as the officer had now threatened to charge the NCOs. 'Excuse me sir.'

'Yes?'

'I hear that you made a few of the soldiers put out their cigarettes in their mouths the other day; is that correct?'

'Why is that, Corporal?'

'Well, I'll tell you, sir. If I see or hear of your doing that type of thing again, I'll be taking the information to the OC and have you placed on a charge.'

'You are going to charge me?'

'Yes, sir. That's right. What do you have to say to that?'

'Well.' The subject, once again, changed rather rapidly. 'I just wanted to say that there will be a conference later on today; reference tomorrow's activities. That's all.'

'Fine, sir. See you later.'

That seemed to be the last time that he pursued anything reference NCOs and their right to train soldiers as they saw fit.

10th November

Today was the day of the gas tent.

A tent had been erected near the river where the breeze was strongest, so that on a soldier's exit from the tent in question, the gas crystals could be more effectively washed away with the helping hand of a splash of water on face.

Numerous lessons were the normal lead-up to this activity before gas masks were issued. Each soldier was talked through the checking of his mask, checking it for size and the refitting of gas filters when required.

The PL COMD took this opportunity to show up, announcing to everyone that he'd done this ten times before and that there was nothing to it. He looked down at one of the soldiers who was sitting crossed-legged and checking his mask, when the officer snatched it from his person. His plan was to show off as usual, and he wanted nothing more than to be one of the first to go through the gas chamber.

Now, once inside the tent, a few tests were to be conducted by the soldier. Firstly you ran in with the gas mask strapped to your leg. You have to very quickly place the mask on, clear the trapped gas from the fitted mask, and check the seal; all part of the drill taught.

Secondly you were required to break the seal, and then reseal and clear the mask before coming under the effect of the gas. If affected however, you then had to proceed with the actions of clearing the mask over and over again until such a time that you could breathe normally. Last of all, you were required to remove the mask completely and give answers to questions posed by the instructor in the tent at the time.

'What's your name?'

'It's... it's... I... Joseph... no Bob.'

'What's your girlfriends name?'

'It's ah... No it's... I don't have one,' and out he would come to receive the splash of water on his face in the loving cool breeze, wiping away the snot pouring from his nose as he stood there half bent over and gasping for breath.

It was quite a sight to see the PL COMD go into the tent and then come running out because the mask didn't have a correct seal due to it being a size too large.

The tent of concentrated tear gas had done its job.

Individuals

11th September

Early one afternoon a soldier from within the platoon approached with what he believed was a major problem.
   His act was genuine and had him removed from the course and sent home.
   He was complaining of severe pains that were shooting through his body, 'like a fever,' he said. And he knew how he came about getting the pains.
   Back in his village he had lost his parents and some close friends; they had died because a sorcerer from another province had placed a spell on them; the same spell that now affected him. He had to get back to his village so that he could render the situation harmless.
   He received his discharge papers within two weeks.

M79 weapon range.

From day one on the course, all had to be on their toes for even the slightest problem that might crop up within the section, platoon, company, and course as a whole; such things as personal hygiene, for some of the soldiers, had never:
   Used a toilet before; didn't know how to use a shower (and one man tried to defecate in one); didn't know how to brush their teeth with toothpaste and brush, or; had never seen, used, or heard of a razor blade before.
   Regardless of whether the individual needed to shave or not, he was required, as laid down in standing orders, to shave every single morning before 0615hrs.
   I walked into the latrines at 0800hrs to find one of the soldiers shaving. 'What are you doing, Recruit Pew? Didn't you shave earlier on?'
   'Yes, Corporal. But I was a bit prickly, so I thought I'd shave again.'
   He was given several days 'extra regimental training', as it was a hell of a lot easier than charging the soldiers, but only after a confession on his part had been received, that he had in fact lied, and

did not shave earlier on.

Time in training was a major factor here. The section commanders could hand out punishments of up to five days 'extra regimental training', and none ever went over-board.

Discipline had to be taught as soon as possible during this sixteen-week course; the only discipline they'd probably ever encounter during their time in the PNGDF.

That night Pew informed the NCO in charge of the ERT parade that he couldn't do the punishment drill as he had a bad headache and his arms were sore. The drill was given regardless, and 30 minutes later he collapsed. His pack was removed from his person and he was sat down to rest – for the others, the drill continued. Even NCOs made bad calls of judgement from time to time.

Recruit Siaoa used the privilege of approaching the NCOs 'after hours' quite frequently. He was keen to learn. He knocked on the door.

'Who is it?'

'Recruit Siaoa, Corporal.'

'What do you want?'

'I would like....'

'Get in here.'

'Yes, Corporal, thank you, Corporal.'

'Listen, Recruit Siaoa, you don't have to say 'thank you, Corporal' after every sentence. I want it to stop. Use a bit more aggression, especially when you knock on the door. The army will look after you if you break your knuckles.'

'Yes, Corporal; thank you.'

'Where's your hat? You know you're supposed to have it on when you come to see us. You know that, don't you, Recruit Siaoa?'

'Yes, Corporal.'

'You can give me twenty push-ups later on.'

'Yes, Corporal, thank you.'

'Now what is it you want?'

'You wanted to see me about my written medical test.'

'That's right. Tell me, Recruit Siaoa; how do you treat a snakebite wound? Let's say... to the leg.'

'First I would cut open the infected area and suck out all of the bad blood. I would then elevate his feet so that the blood could rush to his heart.'

'No, Recruit Siaoa. That's what you're 'not' supposed to do. You

Nigel B.J. Clayton

just killed a man; and probably yourself too.'
   'I think I might have got it wrong.'
   'Yeah. So do I.'

Unfortunate Events

14th September

Another of the Australian soldiers received a Dear John letter today. We'd been in the country not much more than a few months and the women were dropping their boyfriends, and fiancés, like flies.

What exactly did they think they were getting themselves into when they started going out with a member of the infantry was beyond any sane person. Here they were, sitting back in the lap of luxury known as Australia, and all they could seem to do was worry about where their next cuddle was going to come from. It was all very sad. It was no wonder that many of the guys remained happily single, playing at nothing more than to use the women they came into contact with instead of being used themselves – at least there was a little honesty in not leading a female on to think she was something... more permanent.

2nd October

One of the contingents few luxuries disappeared today. Someone had stolen the video player from our makeshift boozer, so now the boys couldn't even watch their loved ones on the videos sent from home.

Evidence in reference to the theft was easy to come by. There were large bare footprints of the culprit on the floor of the single room building, a building that had been transformed into the only means of group socialisation for us. Not only that, but his fingerprints were also everywhere we cared to look.

The PNGDF MP's were called, but all efforts to conduct a search were dropped.

Another example of the wantok system.

11th October

A crocodile was reported to have been spotted just a few hundred metres from the barracks.

This put slight worry in everyone's minds as quite frequently there was the requirement, for training purposes, to cross Goldie River by foot.

Although this water was only knee deep at its shallowest point, it still forced a decision of safety to be made.

When crossing the river, as a section was required, I always made sure that there were others around me. There just had to be safety in numbers, so the open file method of movement was employed; a standard box shape formation with scouts to the front. I figured that the croc-farmer of the platoon had a better chance of survival than me, so why not employ him?

Final Week in Papua New Guinea

End of Days

The combined Recruit/Initial Employment Training course had commenced on the 3rd September; all of the soldiers marched out on the 21st December in front of family and friends. From here they would march into their battalions.

It was only hearsay, but very prominent in its outspoken voice, that from here a reported 100 were to venture over the Solomon Sea, to Bougainville on 3rd march, 1991.

Three of the recruits – who were now classed as Private – from my section, were more than happy to hear that they would be a part of that 100.

Short speeches were given by individual instructors behind closed doors on behaviour; what not to do, to be wary of their officers and NCOs, not to fall victim to the whims of others by doing for the sake of doing, but to maintain the code of conduct as taught by the Geneva Convention.

As for the equipment that was issued to them on behalf of the Australian government, well, that would more than likely be taken from them by the other soldiers of their battalion in Tuarama Barracks; that was the way in PNG. They, too, would commence to brainwash the new soldiers' minds, to fill their heads full of unnecessary garbage, to reteach what they had been taught. Only the strong willed would overcome this bombardment of untruths.

It was a shame to say that a good 20% of the soldiers should never have been given a tick in the box, but this was a numbers game – as it was with the PNGDF officers in Duntroon – and selection of all descriptions outside of the instructor's control.

Their overall standards were less than that of an Australian soldier, but then again some of these recruits had no education, didn't know how to use a toilet, and had never seen a pair of shoes before, and yes; one guy in my section couldn't even speak English. The course was also a combined course and several months shorter than what the Australians would have received. These few did have one thing over the Australian recruit and IET; a few had more personal guts and drive, in particular when compared to those of the Ready Reserve – the university student (and I'm sorry that the truth is now out-there).

They were now to find out how luxurious they had their training and food, and see first-hand how well the Australian administration and logistic system worked in comparison to the PNGDF. From here their overall efforts would decline with the new teaching of laziness creeping into their newly found ranks at Tuarama. They were going to be shat upon from a great height on their march into their battalion.

I was personally more than happy with my section's results; the 2nd and 3rd best at physical training; the overall 2nd best soldier of 300 recruits; and a team which proved time and time again that they had the best section drills, and fire and movement techniques, than all of the others pooled together – as mentioned by the CSM and other high rankers of the contingent.

All of this would hopefully do them some good when in conflict with their Brothers from across the Solomon.

We returned to Australia on Christmas Eve, having made a little ground in respect to understanding the ways and mannerisms of the PNGDF, but we did feel as though we had accomplished, quite well, the task for which we had really been sent: to train them for conflict in Bougainville.

The first six months of 1991 would see another 300 trained, all in aid to strengthening the PNGDF.

Service in PNG with the AATPT is worth more to me than the service in Rwanda.

Initial Employment Training

February 1991 to December 1993

IET training for the Infantry was conducted at the School of Infantry, Singleton, NSW. Each course consisted of eleven training weeks, with all but two of the weekends being given to the soldiers for the purpose of recuperation and personal administration. Although it was sometimes boasted to be a physically demanding course, it was nothing that couldn't be achieved by anyone marching out of Kapooka.

I couldn't recall seeing any more than nine platoons of IET being trained at any one time, each in a different week of training; this also depended on the time of year. The school could only train what came from Kapooka, and they in turn could only train the numbers enlisted in accordance with the yearly quota.

The town of Singleton depended quite heavily on the School of Infantry for its survival, no less than they depended on the miners from down the road. At one point, when rumours were spread about the infantry centre being relocated, the locals were said to have screamed blue murder and began to protest via petition. I never saw this petition, nor was I too concerned about the matter, as I had found that many truths on barracks were exaggerated. But look out if you did something against the grain, either in town, on barracks, or even down the road at Newcastle; for most of the barracks would know of it the following morning – and that was the only truth I was really concerned about.

Locals were soon settled however, when they realised that 90 million dollars was being spent on the Infantry wing of the barracks. The infantry were to remain after all.

Temperatures during winter dropped to below freezing and by summer it was as hot as Townsville. Flies were by far worse than the heat, arriving with the waves of scorching temperatures, laying their eggs in the flesh of dead kangaroos, the larvae soon coming of maturity. One season was as bad as the next.

If you were keen to be in the infantry, then this place was going to be one of the highlights of your career, each day bringing about

Nigel B.J.Clayton

something exciting and new. If your request at Kapooka was to be posted into a non-field force corps, then you were going to have one of the most miserable times possible, knowing in your own mind that living in hell would be a whole lot better.

All-in-all, I personally enjoyed the posting, in particular my second year there. The first year saw me receive, on behalf of my section, the Chief Instructors Trophy for having the champion section; and the third year was simply pitiful, where working under most officers was a pain in the arse, pure and simple.

School of Infantry

Teaching the Basic of Basics
1991-1993

Platoons would vary in size from 30 to 75 men – between 3 and 4 sections per platoon.

Sections normally averaged 14 men at 'week one' of training, but dwindled slightly as the weeks progressed, sometimes to as few as eight, eight being more in tune in regards to that of the size of a section in the rifle battalion.

The first few days of 'week one' always seemed to be the slowest, with an opening address being given by the OC, and a variety of talks by others being met: The PL COMD, PL SGT, MPs, Pay, Movements, Orderly room personnel, Coy CSM, Padre and platoon administration corporal.

Kit checks on equipment issued since the soldiers joining the army took almost an entire afternoon, followed by an introduction to the PTIs at the gymnasium, along with a quick 35-minute circuit of physical training.

This week also saw a trial run of the CFT being undertaken, the real test being conducted sometime in the near future. The PTIs conducted this trial run so that the overall fitness level of the platoon could be engaged, some of the PT lessons conducted during the running of the course then changed to meet the requirements as indicated by the trial. This also gave indication to the PTI as to individual weaknesses, thereafter he would indicate to the instructors the type of punishments which should be issued and when, benefiting the soldier concerned, so that each individual had a better chance of passing the course and marching into a rifle battalion on the conclusion of his training.

The CFT was a simple test and didn't require any brain matter to be employed in its performance. Climb a rope twice, which was between 3 and 4 body lengths in height, with webbing and rifle. Two; run through a small obstacle course in less than 40 seconds, consisted of a small 6 foot wall, negotiating a dodge through 3 fence-like adaptations, jumping a ditch, side step through half a dozen horizontal logs, turning around at a post, and then conduct the same in reverse.

Three; fireman's carry a man 100 metres in 60 seconds, and four; complete the 15 kilometre run under the time limit imposed, a time which has changed several times during the course of its history.

Lessons during the first few days were very basic, (remembering that these soldiers were only trained to the level in which all soldiers must endure as a basic recruit, in order for them to be further trained as a private in (hopefully) the corps of their choice (or that to which best suited their individuality and demeanour)): Lessons such as the organisation of an infantry BN, PL, SECT, and battalion histories.

Wednesday would see them venture to the field for three days and two nights. Here they would be taught the most rudimentary of infantry skills: Living in the field, how to conduct a double staggered picket, how to bed down for the night, night routine, day routine, gun pickets, sentry duty, sounds by day and night, erecting hutchies, establishing a section post, track plans, target indications, fire control orders, judging distance, personal hygiene, target detection, range cards, and the list goes on and on; just the basics.

Along with this short bush phase, a dramatized night move was conducted after enemy mortar simulation was directed onto each 'section post' position. The move from the area was to be quick and swift, to teach discipline in regards to moving by night, having minimum gear out at any one time, and the keeping of noise down to a minimum; all in the pitch of darkness. The following morning they would be returned to the section post and see exactly what had been left behind in the rush to scramble to safety. All were shocked at the amount of equipment left by them to be employed by the enemy as he saw fit.

The final morning brought about a short walk to coaches and then their return to barracks. Here they would clean their weapons under the watchful eye of the instructors, themselves giving advice as necessary.

All of the soldiers were looking forward to a restful weekend, after this, their first week in training.

First Week in the Field

1991-1993

A soldier confronted me, just hours after he'd been placed on the ground and issued his arcs of fire, his position within the 'gun pit': This was to be his position within the platoon harbour and would eventually be turned into a fighting bay with OHP. The soldier insisted I 'come-see'.

I approached the gun position to see three faces staring at me, and all appeared rather concerned. It was soon pointed out to me the reason for their dismay; there was a huge bull ant nest just two metres from where they sat... inch long, red ants, with nippers as large as anyone would care to imagine.

The issue was this; the soldiers felt that they should be provided with another position, as their current one was simply not suited to them. Fair enough, too; after all, what would the platoon commander know about 'defence' and 'lines of fire'? Now how was I to approach the platoon commander and advise him that the gun position 'stank' and that it just wasn't good enough to have the soldiers sleeping so close to such a menace? Wasn't it enough that they had to spend four days in the field without a shower?

So with a gentle touch and a soft approach I explained to the three soldiers, and in a manner – to be accepted by the fraternity – that I didn't give a rats bleeping bleep about the bleep, bleep bleeping with such a bleeping bleeps bleeper bleeps and furthermore, you bleepers bleeping can all go and get bleeped.

The soldiers well understood the position I was faced with and saw fit to drop the subject; but still one thing concerned them; what if the ants came sniffing around looking for food.

I turned around with eyeballs clicking and smiled at all three, explaining further, and quite calmly, that they should try feeding the ants a small portion of food from their ration packs, preferably the luncheon meat, last thing at night; this would sooth the ants so that they would sleep blissfully throughout the night.

Two months later, before filling in pits and marching back to the barracks in full kit, I questioned one of the soldiers about the ants and

as to whether or not anyone had been bitten.
   'No, Corporal; we fed them just like you said and they never came near us.'

Shooting Skills

1991-1993

There was one course of action a corporal could take with his soldiers, which would endeavour to teach the soldier in question what he had failed to assimilate during the practical phases of the course. This course of action was a removal of the individual from the platoon he was in, and then placing him into another that was further behind in training, therefore, re-teaching and re emphasising to the student what was required. Of course, these measures weren't implemented straight away, although most instructors could usually predict who was going to be a prime candidate for such a move.

I now stood behind such a soldier, but due to the perseverance of that individual, he got to remain with the platoon through the entire running of the course. The following explains why.

One of the main aspects of an infantry soldier was his ability to kill the enemy. How could one do this if he was unable to hit a target with the very basic of weapons such as the SLR or Steyr? Allowing him to march into a battalion would be like allowing a blind man to become a taxi driver, which I guess has been known to occur from time to time.

The soldier wore a patch over his left eye. The reason for it, he says, was that his eye was lazy and that a pogo instructor from Kapooka had told him to wear the thing, telling him that there wouldn't be a problem when he marched into the School of Infantry. That instructor definitely made the matter worse.

How were infantry instructors expected to train a soldier to kill, if when confronted by the enemy his first requirement was to cease all actions until he had a patch placed over his eye? Quite ridiculous from anyone's point of view. You certainly couldn't expect him to patrol through the bush with the eye patch on his face.

The soldier had the weapon pulled into his right shoulder. He was asked, 'are you left or right handed?' 'Right handed.' 'Which is your master eye?' 'My left.'

Further examination; on requesting him to; first close his left eye and then his right, proved that his right eye was incapable of remaining steady or fully open. Basically, he was incapable of taking a sight picture when trying to close his left eye; but on closing his right, his left would remain perfectly steady and fully open.

He was then informed that he was no longer to operate the weapon right handed, for he was now a left-hander. Within six weeks he was shooting as well as any of the others in the platoon and was never required to be put back in training.

Very few of the instructors' problems at Singleton arose from minor incompetence displayed by individuals at Kapooka, namely those instructors from a non-field force environment; for most of those at Kapooka did an overwhelmingly exceptional job.

Allowing non-field force personnel to instruct also allowed for a fuller understanding of how the military functioned, but, let's face it... some instructors just required a good kick in the arse.

Weapons Training

1991-1993

A bulk of the weapons and navigation training was to be taught early on in the course, but revision upon revision was an on-going occurrence, never enough being seen.

A soldier was always taught in the most logical of sequences, and when this came to the teaching of weapons, then the foremost aspect must surely be description, characteristics, tabulated data, and then the carrying out of the safety precautions; taught to be carried out as an individual, and as a group.

Once the basics were taught the men could then get on the ground and get dirty, working the weapon, with their hands and minds, simultaneously, being shown first hand all of the drills to be taught during any one lesson prior to the said lesson being talked through and rehearsed. The soldiers would slowly build their knowledge on the weapon taught until each was capable of carrying out each action when given the appropriate word/s of command.

The SFMG MAG58 was only one of the many weapons to be taught. The IAs and stoppages of this weapon seemed to be the most demanding and hardest to learn.

Weapon fires, weapon stops. Cock the working parts to the rear, lower the butt, lift up the feed cover and clear the feed plate. Lower the feed cover, fire the action, lower the butt and open the feed cover. Place on some link, close the feed cover, cock the weapon, push the cocking handle forward and continue firing.

Then the operation becomes slightly more controlled by the soldiers, emphasis being played out on all commands. IAs and stoppages were then pieced together, to create the logical sequence that was required to remedy the weapons stoppages.

Time and time again the actions were rehearsed until all soldiers had carried all actions out to a satisfactory standard. In a few weeks' time they would be tested on the fundamentals of all weapons. The SLR or Steyr (dependent on the year of training), the M16, the MAG58, the Minimi, the M203, M79, 66mm SRAAW, grenades, claymores and trip flare. Besides these came other pieces of equipment. Patrol ambush light, radio, night sight and compass. Then knowledge; weapon pit construction, ambush drills, fire and movement, searching POWs, range card construction, standard operational procedures, types of patrols, section formations, field signals and cook a meal whilst in the field. The list goes on forever, and even after sixteen years, one still learnt and continually revised, the built up of knowledge never ceasing for a moment during a soldier's career.

The above was a minute speck compared to what the instructors taught during the conduct of the training course at Singleton – a grain of sand upon a vast beach of many grains.

A Week at the Range

1991-1993

An entire week was spent at the range qualifying students in all of the small arms weapons.

Weapons that created shrapnel were fired and thrown on other purpose built ranges.

Although a soldier was not actually tested on his operational skills of the weapons during this week – which apparently changed in 1994 – he did risk being thrown off of the range, and put back in training, if he proved himself to be unsafe whilst on the range and/or behind a weapon under his control. There was no room for unsafe persons, or those incapable of conducting themselves in a safe manner. The soldiers were, however, required to qualify in some aspects of the shoots that they were about to encounter.

A grouping and zeroing practice took the bulk of a day to complete. This was a crucial part of the week for the soldiers, for without a weapon being zeroed to the individual, how was he to hit the target. Most were too inexperienced to 'aim off'. All the soldier had to do was to create a line of sight from the eye, through the aperture, to the tip of the foresight (or through optic sights) and then, of course, the target. To some it seemed an impossible task.

Shooting was conducted from the 100m mound, the 200 and 300. The instructors were there too, coaching the firers through each of the shots where required, even where the shoot conducted was a terminal test. Re-shoots were a 25% occurrence.

Most of the problems arose from soldiers not listening to simple suggestions; suggestions that if not carried out, would do nothing but impede the final shooting result.

How many times do you tell a soldier to squeeze the trigger and not to pull it? How many times do you tell him not to jerk the weapon? And advise on how to hold the weapon off of the ground to aid in breathing (for the SLR and M16) and support. It was no wonder instructors were all stressed and growing grey hairs.

By the end of the week, all had passed, usually by way of threats of kicks to the groin.

Field Punishment

1991-1993

Time for the field again, the infantryman's bread-and-butter. Before now the soldier had learnt just the basics of skills that would get him through the process of a day and a night; building blocks of knowledge were still to be placed however, an endless placement, one upon the other.

Their skills with the weapons they used in the field were in some cases atrocious and hard to maintain a watch on. With anywhere up to 14 guys to report on in a week it wasn't easy to catch guys out when one made an error; and it 'was' a matter of catching them out.

If ever they made a mistake, or were unsure of what to do, they would always go to their mates first. There they would be given advice, but not advice that was always stable. If he made a big blunder, he was more apt to think to himself, 'you-beauty, I got away with it.'

They failed to see that if the same mistake was to occur during the final testing phase, that they could very well end up being back-squat, to be taken from the platoon they were in and placed into the one which, in most cases, was 2 to 5 weeks behind in training. Here he would be retaught everything he'd already learnt, so that the instructors could be happy in the fact that when the student marched into the battalion they would be of a standard acceptable to the unit.

It came to pass during one of my earlier platoons that a particular soldier I was training was far below the acceptable standard. I tried emphatically to have him placed back in training on three different occasions, my final attempt being accompanied by written statements, and have the soldier confront, a face-to-face interview, with the platoon commander, who's most emphasised words during his first meeting with the instructors were: 'I want to pass all of the soldiers that we train.' It turns out that this officer had a brother in the army, and that brother had been my platoon commander for around twelve months back in 1983 – but at least his brother of years past was competent in his ways. Good officers were always hard to come by in Singleton; don't ask me why. When I found myself in 2/4RAR in 1994, I was approached by a section commander who asked if I was the same instructor that had sent him a soldier some years before. I tried to explain to him what the situation was at the time, but I don't think it was accepted. Thanks to a platoon commander whose only thought was for himself, I was now suffering sly remarks unfitting to be worn; but then again, some of the discipline encountered in Townsville was woeful.

During the first night of this bush week I had spent several hours in the administration tent some five hundred metres from where the soldiers conducted their night routine. Here I wrote notes on soldiers, good and bad; this was done daily. On completion I took off into the night and headed for the section post. On coming up to the gun I saw a dull glow, and there in the bottom of the gun-pit were three soldiers smoking cigarettes. In most cases it's hard not to lose one's temper at times like this, but boys will be boys, and solutions to problems had to be thought out the best as possible. For simple problem solving the cigarettes were confiscated for a minimum of 24 hours.

The following morning I awoke to see another soldier urinating on the spoil of his pit just two feet from where he slept, ate, and basically lived. From here on, anytime he felt like urinating, he was to inform me directly. He would then be issued a tree some four hundred metres away, and told to run over and dig a hole in the ground so that he could do his deed.

If he were caught to be urinating in an illogical place again, I would do my best to place him back in training.

All in all the week was going well. This was another learning week, not a testing week. The new platoon commander failed to see it as such. His only comment was 'stuff 'em. They're only IETs.' He was my hero. Unfortunately, as an NCO, I believed that soldiers came first and dickheads last.

Fun at the Grenade Range

1991-1993

Emphasis was placed on the M26, M18A1, 66mm SRAAW and M203 at the beginning of 'week six'.

Tuesday would see the platoon move out to the grenade range where they would spend the following three days and two nights.

This was one of the objectives of the course, but very simple. If you couldn't throw a grenade on a range, you couldn't do so in war. I never saw anyone fail this phase of the course, but a few close calls were met. It was the cause of another handful of grey hairs on head.

M30 grenades were a practice grenade, and two of these were to be thrown in exact similarity to that of the M26 fragmentation grenade. The short exercise with the M30 had to be conducted within 72 hours or less of actually throwing the real McCoy.

M26

A man stands opposite you as required, ready to throw a grenade at a target represented as a bunker. He has sweaty palms and you can see the uneasiness in his eyes and upon his face.

He holds the grenade to his chest and identifies his target; then, placing his finger into the safety pin he pulls. It comes from the grenade and slight force is felt upon the grenade safety lever in the man's palm, the striker pin trying to push its way free so as to strike the primer.

The man holds the grenade at arm's length to ensure that the whole of the safety pin has been extracted, that the hole is free of any obstruction, then back into the chest. Confirm your target and throw the grenade.

The man stands and watches its flight through the air to the target. He knows that the striker has hit the primer, igniting the delay element that gives 4 to 5 seconds of delay. He wants to get down below cover but has to wait for the command.

The grenade hits the ground and commences to roll towards the target, then suddenly swings to the right, coming to rest several metres to the targets right side, and then the command comes. You both duck for cover behind the wall to your front and the grenade explodes. 'Next!'

Each man receives between 2 and 5 grenades, and you have – let's say – 45 in the platoon. After the grenades came the 66mm and the M203 (in the years before end 1992, the grenade on L1A2 launcher used to be fired from the end of the SLR by way of grenade cartridge F2). It all made for a long week. Although injuries were extremely rare, close scrapes were seen on the odd occasion. One such incident saw a guy freeze when the grenade safety lever was flung from the grenade whilst attached to the SLR by way of the L1A2. He now had a maximum of four seconds to fire the weapon so that cover behind the wall could be sought – slightly different to taking time out to aim the weapon at a target and grasping the SLR correctly with butt held against the hip (which would have been the case if the safety lever had remained in place). He fired the SLR on being told, 'Fire the weapon NOW!' No problem, but his hip never forgave him. Two days later he was still bruised from the kick of the weapon. He was lucky not to have had his thumb behind the grip of the weapon when it was fired, otherwise he would have discovered a broken thumb also. Another consideration has to be thought of here. If the soldier failed to comply with what was ordered, then the rifle, along with the attached grenade, would have to have been thrown over the wall of the pit, by the instructor. The weapon would have been destroyed.

Thank God for discipline and soldiers who obeyed orders. Another lucky scrape, and another grey hair.

Unauthorised Discharge of Weapon

1991-1993

A further five days in the field towards the latter portion of the course started to see skills come together with less and less occurrences of stupidity arising from thoughtless minds acting irrationally.

Patrolling was the essence of the week's training; fighting patrols, patrolling techniques, minefield incident drills, immediate ambush, ambush drill, counter ambush drill, reconnaissance patrol, standing patrol, clearing patrol, clearing defiles, and obstacle crossings – both major and minor, both as a section and as a platoon. All made up a small

part of the job.

When the above wasn't being pursued then day routine would be in full swing.

Digging to stage three was required to be completed as soon as possible so that during 'week nine' more patrols and defensive routine could take full effect. Stage three for the soldiers didn't entail riveting the fighting bays, but did include the digging of sleeping bays, and erection of overhead protection. The sleeping bays were dug as an extension to the existing 'fighting bay'. Sleeping in such a hole in the ground with a roof was quite cool by summer and warm by winter. Not good for the claustrophobic of mind.

Digging usually finished at 0100hrs each morning, four hours sleep a night being the norm.

Operating the radio was also important. During the running of the course the soldiers had heard of the Artillery's Initiation Program, where a few of the Arty Corps members had problems facing up to expectations, and were obviously troubled with sexual fantasies. It was here that sick individuals gave the army a bad name and reputation. Due to these stories of pathetic proportion, the infantry soldiers, whilst on course, came up with some rather strange code words and passwords – but all in the name of good fun, poked in the direction of the Artillery. Some of the more profound were 'sausage sizzler', 'humming lips', and 'tight ring'. According to what all had heard, or had been told, the artillery initiator of this ritual was imprisoned for six months; sorry, no room for sick bastards in the military. To 'say' something was one thing, but to 'act it out' was simply sick.

Another occasion for laughter during the week was when the platoon commander had an unauthorised discharge (firing his weapon without authority or reason to do so).... A soldier had reported to the administration tent in readiness for removal from the platoon, as he was not meeting with the standards required – but neither was the PL COMD. The soldier was quite distraught, and when told to unload his SLR, was not quite quick enough for the PL COMD. The PL COMD in turn grabbed the soldier's weapon, commenced to clear it, failing to cock the weapon fully to the rear, and fired the action. A shot rang out for all to hear – lucky the weapon wasn't pointed at anyone, because even firing blank ammunition can have dangerous ramifications.

The PL COMD never said a word about this on return to the barracks and kept it from the OC's ears, even though it was an officer's duty to 'charge' himself when required.

This poor excuse for an officer obviously didn't have the nerve to admit when he was wrong or made a mistake.

Many soldiers during the conduct of teaching a platoon had UDs, and after the incident in Somalia, the punishment for such rose to 14 days confined to barracks, and a fine of $400.

A few weeks after this saw the 14 days dropped. Further into the year still and it came to reign that a soldier should not be charged with a UD if he wasn't qualified to use the weapon in question. Now, none of the instructors were qualified in the weapon, so how were they to teach it. This was remedied by placing all instructors on a Steyr Conversion
Course.

After this, qualifying a soldier still did not occur until he had passed his test. The test was then quite rapidly brought forward from 'week four' to 'week three', remembering that it'd already been brought forward from 'week eight' to 'week four' earlier on in the year (a few days before moving to the range for a week at Stockton). So according to the law of qualifications, if a soldier failed his weapon handling at the range, he should be retested or put back in training. It was one headache after the next, all brought on by a few high-ranking officers of that year, who liked nothing more than to ignore any idea an instructor had in respect to training.

Now, if a soldier hadn't been qualified in the weapon he was using, or similarly, was taught by an instructor who wasn't qualified, how on earth could he be fined $400 for such a thing as a UD? It came to play that not a single soldier received the money back as an error on behalf of the School of Infantry; prejudice beyond the standards befitting for a so-called society where all were treated fairly and the same.

The army was quite pathetic at times, and as for the officer with the UD, the less said about him the better. Thank God they weren't all like him, and thank God that being in the army, in its majority, was a fantastic place to be.

Close Terrain

1991-1993

Training in close terrain was always give-and-take. Most enjoyed operating in close country, but as an instructor, it was a shambles.

The soldiers to date had only learnt how to move through open country, and although movement through thick brush and vines, across creeks and around boulders, was no challenge for the IET, it came a fact of nature that the instructor could not evaluate the students correctly, because in most cases a single file method of movement had to be conducted. This saw the section spread out over more than sixty metres, and in an area that had a visual distance of just twenty – larger sections were spread even further afield.

Attacks on small groups of enemy were sometimes a cluster, with individuals disappearing from view, due to the extended line of assault being far too long to control, yelling time and time again, 'I can't hear you, Corporal'. No instructor could bring himself to believe that.

Injuries of a varied description were also numerous, and the time taken to travel to such a field environment took far too long. This denied the soldiers the time needed to practise the skills taught, and in the case where injuries were sustained, the taking of that individual from the 'field' environment and into the 'hospital' environment.

Re-org was called and the soldiers commenced to move as indicated by the section commander, into a position of all round defence.

The No2 on the gun came scrambling out of the bush with his rifle in one hand and his shirt in the other.

'What the hell are you doing?'

'I landed in a nest of inch ants,' and was indeed covered in bites.

'Well I didn't think you were sun-baking. You allergic? You want anything from the med kit?'

'No, Corporal.'

'Then put your shirt on and go help man the gun.' If you were in the field with the battalion for four weeks, you weren't going to get any sympathy, so why start here. He had to learn to treat his own wounds. He would be checked again later in any case, and the section medical kit was always available.

In most cases, the close country environment required that each individual cleaned his weapon three times a day. If this didn't occur, in particular with concern to the SLR, then rust soon started to appear.

One morning, after morning routine had been conducted – in this particular case 'it' being cut short due to orders for a patrol the evening before – the soldiers were called into the section commander's pit for a brief on performances and debriefing of the nights activities, a quick five minute pet-talk – if you'd like to call it that.

'Okay, men. Put your hand up if you had a brew this morning.'

Six of the nine placed their hand in the air, each not sure why they were asked such a stupid question, but others believing that the NCO was trying to find out who'd organised themselves in such a way that it was possible for them to grab a quick morning coffee, 'hot or cold'. Those that had a brew then had their weapons inspected for cleanliness and compared to those who 'hadn't' had a brew. A lesson was learnt, some punishments issued, and similar mistakes made the following morning. The lesson was this: Meals always came second to weapons: you would have had trouble killing the enemy with an empty tin can, but a weapon that functioned well performed much better.

Constant fault checking was the key to success.

Officers, Not Men

1991-1993

Some stories now, of officers, not men, at the School of Infantry.

As mentioned previously, a BFT was one of the benchmarks for an infantry soldier; so too should it be for the instructors... fair enough.

I recall quite adamantly how an officer in 1993 took it upon himself to order his NCOs up-and-down a vertical rope, in order that each of the men – myself included – could pass the BFT, along with the soldiers of the company. I see nothing wrong in this; I believe in fair treatment and that none should be given favouritism over another.

Over the Run, Jump, Dodge course we went, one after the other, the fireman's carry, and then the ropes:

'Are you not joining us, sir?'

'No... I hurt my finger.'

And yet another, believe it or not, down at the ropes... hanging there, soldiers waiting, innocent to the goings-on around them. The company had just completed the BFT and were forming up in three files, ready for the march back to the barracks. Our Platoon Commander, of Army-Reserve status, saw the local – unauthorised – mascot walking over; Deputy the Dog.

The officer bent over and picked up a few stones, pelting them with vicious demeanour at the innocent animal. On the third stone I just couldn't help myself; and being right or wrong, said the following:

'Hey, sir; that's pretty manly of you; throwing stones at an innocent dog.'

'What was that, Corporal Clayton?'

He must have assumed I hadn't the guts to repeat myself, in particular in front of the soldiers... damn him. 'I said, it's not nice, a man throwing stones at a dog.'

The officer in question called me over, out of earshot. 'Just because you've done 13 years' service, Corporal Clayton, doesn't mean anything to me.' Didn't mean much to me either... 'I'll put you on a charge if you're not careful.'

But do you think it would stand; Dickhead?

Period of Transition

1993-1994

It soon came to pass that my posting at the School of Infantry was over and the time to move on had arrived, I unfortunately had no say in my destination, although this was one particular aspect of my life which didn't affect my personal outlook on career progression. My only aspiration now was to complete my 20 years of service in order to receive a lump sum payment and small pension on retirement from the forces.

When the posting order finally arrived it was accompanied with a little relief. I was being posted to 2/4RAR; a by far better predicament than that of any of the Sydney based battalions – or so I thought (personal preference).

The first twelve months experienced in the battalion were similar in respect to training and teachings as those of other battalions, but the professional standard and attitudes of all soldiers were very slightly below that anticipated. My thoughts on this also happen to coincide with the views of 13 sergeants in which I'd had something to do with, during my posting at both Singleton and Brisbane. They, too, agreed that the 8/9th battalion was better in all respects and that the soldiers of Townsville were somewhat like a Neanderthal with concern to brains, temperament, and attitude. How hard it is, not to exaggerate; because when all is considered they are mostly genuine, friendly, and easy to get along with… humph, did I just say that?

This became more than evident when I received a posting to B Coy for a trip to New Zealand for a period of five weeks. It was here that I received strong suggestions from particular elements of the company (being of higher rank than me) that I not change my attitude, or my personality, as most members to whom I was going to become familiar were undisciplined and insubordinate. Never in my fourteen years had I met with such insolent soldiers who claimed to be men of great stature.

We were several weeks into the trip when one of the other NCOs of the company confronted the platoon sergeant with complaints from the soldiers that I was being somewhat unfair in my treatment of them.

The NCO was then informed to leave the subject be, and that I was doing okay. At least now some of the more aggressive and argumentative members of the platoon started to get the message that they needed to grow up a little and stop being somewhat, fool-hardy.

How was it that men like these could think themselves as the best in the regiment when they hadn't even seen how other battalions operated. The 8/9th battalion, back in 1990, was by far better than this unit. So it came to pass that I didn't change my ways, and kept myself and my hierarchy under the terms of agreement as to the 'way I was'. Some of the soldiers started to show signs of change in some form of discipline. It was certainly nothing less than disgraceful to see one individual in particular, stand to the rear of a group of men that were all receiving a brief by the platoon sergeant, merrily talking away to a friend. I'm sure that if the shoe was on the other foot that the individual would have been more than displeased to have been rudely interrupted – I heard, many years later, that he'd received a promotion to sergeant himself: Pte Casuallybad. The soldier in question was also known – on quite a few occasions – to say, 'I'm one of the best soldiers in this unit', and when he said it, he meant it.

I'll never understand where he got the idea that he should have been promoted. The man was always complaining about not getting to do real infantry tasks, but anytime he went bush, or was seen to be taking part in other aspects of infantry training, would be one of the first to say, 'why do we have to do this shit for?'. Never did a day go by where he wouldn't complain about something. But then again he didn't have red hair, as some of the soldiers I had experiences with, who had, just had to prove how ill-disciplined and insubordinate they really were. There was even another known to have cursed the platoon commander behind his back during his handling of the massacre at Kibeho, and the comments made were entirely undeserved; but of course, I can't give you his name, such a 'worm-of-a-man' he was. But I'm pleased to say that not all soldiers encountered were as bad as these examples; these few guys were nothing less than rotten apples that deserved nothing less than to be thrown away by a group of starving kids residing in Ethiopia, whether such soldiers had white hair or red; whether feeling 'well' of themselves or 'worn numb' in the head.

Ideology was a bad thing, in particular when things didn't prove themselves to be, as they should. The only reason, as far as I could understand, as to why discipline was the way it was, may have been the idea that this was a 'Deployment Force' available for deployment, at a moment's notice. Such labelling made big heads bigger and loud mouths 'dribblers'.

A small percent of the NCOs were no different, disobeying orders and blatantly disregarding New Zealand's standing orders (when posted there for four weeks in 1994 with B Coy, 2/4RAR), by walking between boozer and lines with a can of beer in hand, abusing other NCOs who tried effortlessly to remind them that they shouldn't be doing such; and all in front of soldiers who wore the rank of private. There was even a period where groups of Private soldiers had plans to gang up on individual NCOs, to purposely beat them senseless, simply because they were doing what they were asked, doing nothing less than their job in most cases.

I could only give praise to soldiers of the platoon to which I was attached, that although they were displeased with the change in their routine of being ill-mannered and continuously disobedient, that they stood up for their NCOs by threatening to beat up on any other soldier within the company, if they as much as put a finger on their section commanders. Was discipline changing for the better, was it all a fluke, and were the threats to corporals going to cease?

This act turned all of the tables around, and as such brought to light some of the more outstanding qualities of the men in this group of thirty odd soldiers, in particular when the platoon were informed – along with the remainder of the company – that they were to be deployed to Rwanda. Guys like myself felt as though we could be very comfortable in carrying out such a task with those that we now worked with. The soldiers that worked below me were definitely reliable.

They weren't that bad after all, although I did escape a midnight bashing by a tattooed freak one night, in Queenstown, on the southern island of NZ, for as soon as he saw I was awake, awaiting him to make the first move, his attitude changed and he cowardly crawled off to bed.

It seemed to me that I had been much mistaken, and that my displeasure in individuals ability to disrupt the workings of a 'finely tuned machine', had grown out of control for a few simple reasons: I was stagnating, and basically tired of training for something which didn't appear to be forth-coming. It would seem that my piss-poor attitude towards others was due, not only for their lack in discipline, but my festering itch to get something done in the 'real world' –

something we were training for, but never carried out.

It seemed obvious to me that others were simply showing the same attitude that I had locked away inside of me for years and years and years – or was I mistaken?

I do now apologise to those individuals and groups for what I have written, but it must be recorded; after all, why should I hide behind a shield and a lie.

Rwanda

Rwandan history, for a vast majority of the world, started on 6 April 1994, when anti-aircraft fire brought down a passenger plane in Kigali. Two presidents died on that flight, they were Rwanda's, President Juvenal Habyarimana, and Burundi's, President Cyprien Ntaryarima. It triggered an explosion from the air; and from the ground... a massacre that had never been seen before in the history of African affairs; it was sheer genocide.

It seems too much of a coincidence to think that the plane was shot down by accident, or even that those responsible didn't know who was on board at the time... ludicrous. The following day, several murders took stage; the Prime Minister of Rwanda, Agathe Uwilingiyimana and family; peacekeepers also came under this hammer of murderous content, for ten Belgians were killed, soldiers doing their duty in trying maintain order in a city on the verge of crisis; petty crisis no more, for there was no turning back the heinous tide which had now been unleashed.

The Tutsi population were of the country's minority, and the elimination of this race was the answer to the Hutu's forage for victory; for class and status.

Rwanda boasted the highest population density of human beings in one single African country, where eucalyptus trees were as common as people. It was a framework of fertile hills surrounded by land, locked in, no access to the ocean: Other than Lake Kivu to the West. In fact, four other countries bordered Rwanda: Zaire to the West, Uganda to the North, to the Tanzania East, and Burundi to the South.

It was a country administered by other powers, the Germans for quite some time – and we know what happened to that power-hungry nation of Jew-haters. Power switched to the Belgians who, for fear of the struggles and shifts in power between Tutsi and Hutu, turned favouritism from one to the other within the space of a few years.

Civil war came to the country in 1959, where the Hutu majority took swift action and reprisal against their brothers of colour and kin. Many Tutsi extremists, power brokers, and innocents alike, fled the country they had loved for so long, their seat of power and status changed for the worst. Hutu men and women, children too, enjoyed their newfound existence of majority rule, which they had always been in possession of, but never employed. Independence in 1962 brought about the end of the change that had started just 3 years before.

But like the IRA of Ireland, and terrorists of Iraq and Afghanistan, the Tutsi saw to it that revenge attacks into their once-homeland were attended to. The Tutsi weren't welcome in any land, and so say all they encountered, 'return to your land, for we have no space for you here'. So in 1990 an invasion was attempted by the exiles in Uganda, 7,000 strong and after a return to their original status. The Rwandan Patriotic Front (RPF) was hence born and forced a peace agreement to take form in 1993, whereby the UN was asked for aid... UNAMIR was formed (United Nations Assistance Mission in Rwanda – assistance in the implementation of a peace agreement where both parties, the Hutu and Tutsi, could live in peace).

Fingers started pointing, the Hutu displeased with the way in which things in general were proceeding. The UN was favouring the Tutsi: This was the claim and accusation. Hutu death squads walked the streets at night, cowering in corners as they did their deeds, killing innocents, the Tutsi, who for a better word, had forced the UN to take the side of the enemy – but I am no history-buff and limited in my education.

The shooting down of the aircraft on the 6th April was blamed squarely on the Belgians, and I guess they would try to insist that the radio broadcast, condemning the Tutsi and labelling them all as enemies of the state, was the fault of the Belgians as well. The RPF couldn't resist the opportunity provided to them and invaded Rwanda, developing a rapid advance onto the capital, Kigali. The Hutu majority shook in their boots and the murders of hundreds of individuals took a turn for the worst, and the Hutu unleashed their hatred for the Tutsi, upon women and children, the young and the old, and they fled like the cowards that they had shown themselves to be. In the villages from all around, thousands of Tutsi were massacred. The Tutsi (RPF) soldiers advanced upon the withdrawing Hutu, advancing upon empty lands filled with displaced persons, the Hutu withdrawing, leaving a carpet of blood to fill the void between the two factions.

France entered the picture and placed a Humanitarian Protection Zone, dividing the country into three main areas; one controlled by the RPF, one by the Hutu, and the other, France. But life was short-lived and the HPZ was soon lost, and UN soldiers deployed to the country were forced, for Rules of Engagement reasons, to sit back and watch as the murders and humanitarian crisis continued, and the RPF took control of Rwanda.

Australia now enters the scene and the first deployment of Australian troops to enter the country step from a plane in Kigali, once a city of 300,000 souls, now and a city of 5,000 men, women, and children (these are documented figures I heard about and more-than-likely not representative of the actual number).

The peace process for the Australians had commenced.

Point of View

During the deployment of Australian Infantry troops to Rwanda, many a variety of task was met: Carrying stretchers through the AUSMED hospital; escorting dental technicians, medics and other specialised personnel through the winding hills of this land-locked country; and conducting security pickets on key installations to which were our sole responsibility – namely the hospital and our barracks in Rwanda's capital of Kigali.

And although any inspiring infantryman was prepared more for a situation as likely to be found during the war in Vietnam or the Falkland Islands not all criteria to his forte were to be encountered during his deployment to Rwanda. Although many would argue the sanity of such prose, I could possibly substantiate such by saying that we

were all regulars, and only the keen were to be given a ticket for the task ahead, and that the task given to the Infantry soldiers during this deployment could only be expressed as static and mobile security.

Many disciplinary upsets were met by the keen eye of the infantry soldier in this segment of his life which was far different to that for which he had trained so hard. He wasn't fighting a war, but war was evident; he didn't get to fire his steyr or pistol, but weapons from all around lashed out their evil; and he never killed, but bodies were all around. All he could do was report an incident, only permitted to deploy preventative measures if human rights were being violated and only under specific situations (our Rules Of Engagement), but basically, not permitted to fire any weapon unless under dire circumstances (literally, self-defence); you might imagine the disgust felt by us all. But initiative and common sense were to be the main weapons of this deployment.

Departure and Arrival

19-20th February 1995

The departure from Townsville was originally set for 2145hrs on the 18th, though due to problems with the aircraft in which was to take the contingent to Rwanda, the timings were changed. The Boeing 747 of Tower Air had been grounded and parts now had to be flown in from Singapore, in order for repairs to take place.

Much apprehension was met over the next fourteen hours, as all could only wonder as to whether the aircraft was going to make it to the small African country, for stories started to flow in from all sources. All odds stood in favour of the aircraft plummeting into the ocean, killing us all instantly. It reminded me of an incident some nine years before when a company exercise saw us airlifted out by Chinook. We'd just passed over some ranges when there was some engine trouble. We made a hard landing on a pasture, the approach being at an almost completely devastating angle, and after being asked to step from the aircraft were asked for our service flannelette, the same we used when cleaning our rifles.

The aircrew took these simple pieces of cloth and then went about cleaning the engine and after 90 minutes of laying around, playing cards, we were ushered back on board and once again took to the air.

By 1200hrs on 19th all had commenced to move onto the aircraft, this was followed by an uncomfortable airborne time of sixteen hours, with two stops being met – Singapore and Nairobi.

Touch down in Kigali was much to the relief of the 300 odd members of the contingent, a contingent that was to primarily provide medical support to the forces of the United Nations. The company of infantry soldiers provided for the security of the Australian contingent as a whole.

As we moved into the main building of Kigali airport, the first effects of the civil war were seen. Glass shattered windows, bullet holes and even evidence of RPG rounds having been fired; the scars of war were everywhere. Craters created by 60mm mortars or grenades also covered the floor of what once must have been a very handsome building. RPA soldiers also made themselves present in what must have been their effort to show some type of authority by force, a stand that only brought an unkind stare of an aggressive nature from some of the Australian infantry soldiers.

The move through customs was surprisingly quick, and as members of UNAMIR II, soon found ourselves loaded onto transport and ready for the short half hour trip to the barracks in which we were to spend a majority of our six month stay, a period of time that passed with the blink of an eye.

The barracks came to view at 0430hrs and were moved into, UNAMIR I members moving out, the rotation being completed by 1100hrs. The first contingent was more than happy to see the end of their six-month tour.

The accommodation was divided according to numbers, task, rank and gender. The rifle company building was cramped to say the least, with 18 persons per room. This was sorted within several weeks, allowing for a section of ten men to have a room to themselves.

Although privacy was a problem, there was no other better way of getting to know each other. I was quite sure that we would be sick of the sight of each other by the time we returned home.

The routine of the Rifle Company took a while to get off of the ground, but once each of the rifle sections had rotated once through each of the main tasks, all was 'sweet potato'. There were three tasks; barracks security, hospital security, and rest. Rest week was not what it implied. It wasn't spent on backs reading books, but gave the sections responsibilities of providing security to varying groups venturing outside of the barracks, conducting a variety of tasks.

The contingent was in full swing by the end of the first month, and most aspects of the stay soon became second nature.

The Hospital

Late February

As each section took on the responsibilities of security for the hospital, a tour was met with in order to introduce all to their new surroundings. The main complex of the hospital was a well-organised structure. All of the basic necessities for which it required to run were to be found in the one wing. A laundry was also established next door and there was a morgue no more than 100 metres from the hospital's back door.

One platoon would spend a week here, rotating its sections through the three main tasks that were to be maintained during the six-month period. Security for the front and rear gate was priority. On several occasions members of the RPA found themselves disarmed and escorted into the grounds of the hospital when visiting friends of theirs, patients of the UN; it was one of the many needs of the trip, the Australians being required to treat soldiers and civilians alike, where there was the 'order' and 'moral obligation' for such to take place.

The UN was trying to establish a relationship that would be beneficial to UNAMIR II during the duration of its stay and a worldwide friendship that could help to ease the suffering of the people.

Some civilian patients were in the direct threat of being executed by the RPA, so whilst any RPA soldier was being escorted through the main complex, to the ward which housed the RPA patient, the RPA soldier – or suspect spy – would be prevented from venturing into rooms to which he had no business. Hence, he was being restricted to the floor space in accordance to the looming threats, refusing the RPA from freely gaining information that could disclose to him whether or not the hospital held the man or woman that they were after. In one such case a little boy was given aid by the hospital, and then finally a job within its walls, as the RPA would have executed him if he so much as stepped outside of its walls; and when I say 'little boy', I mean just that.

Here too, was a couple of Rwandans who worked as interpreters for the Australians (being given the position via the UN). Each spoke between three and five languages, most of which were on the verge of fluency. I was at one stage advised that they were also at risk if they chose to walk freely outside of the protection offered by the walls of the hospital. On more than one occasion these two were offered threats of death by the RPA. Towards the end of the tour it was announced via different means that certain persons were making arrangements for these two, to be allowed into Australia, under legislation of status as a permanent residence, for to stay in Rwanda would have meant certain death. This was the type of reception one got for working with the UN.

The front gate security also required members of the section on this post to escort medics, and other persons between the hospital and front gate of the barracks. The distance between the two was a good 300 metres, a right angle bend in the road making it impossible to see one complex from the other. On some occasions medics went against the imposed standing orders, and travelled the road without escort, literally taking their safety into their own hands.

Due to the system used, those travelling from the barracks to the hospital would be provided escorts from the guardroom, on the front gate of the main compound. Due to other tasks, and vehicle escort requirements between UN headquarters and UNAMIR's location, it was an inconvenience for the medics to wait for an available escort on some occasions. I never heard of anyone waiting more than 15 minutes for an escort. Emergencies were provided for immediately, even if it meant calling the hospital up via landline and requesting an escort from them, due primarily to numbers depletion and other tasks having to be met by

the section in the guardroom.

The third task to be provided for within the hospital was the 'rest section'. This section provided men for stretcher parties and assisted the medics when patients were dropped off for treatment: Car accidents, landmine blasts, burns victims, broken bones etc.

The rifleman's simple task was to cut the patient's clothes with scissors, removing them from the body in preparation for medical aid to be administered. The only bright side to the task – if such a word could be used – was the experience of seeing first hand a medical team going to work on patients, and the effects of injuries such as a missing foot caused by antipersonnel landmines.

On many occasions soldiers were able to witness the complete operation, as there was always the space available for soldiers to stand in the back of the operating theatre and watch the surgical team go to work; scrubbing open wounds, scraping tissue from bone, or simply cutting legs off from above or below the knee.

The NGO wards were to the rear of the hospital. This was where Rwandans were treated on a large scale. Australian nurses aided by giving first hand instruction, assistance and advice, to the workers and nurses here – those of Rwandan heritage. The entire place stunk like nothing I'd smelt before, patients lying in their own excrements; the simple overcrowding of such a place. It was disgusting. It was filthy. It was unbelievably unhygienic.

Minor Incidents

Bodies

The atrocities created by the hand of this civil war were clear from the very start, and just down from the hospital was a large depression in the ground. This particular depression was an excavation of sorts said to have housed some 4,000 victims of the war (though 10,000 may have been a more correct figure), a mass grave of discarded flesh.

For days on end a mass of black smoke could be seen to rise over the tops of trees as bodies were burnt. Bodies were also evident along the roads; rows and rows of them, all covered in plastic sheeting; hundreds upon hundreds. These stunk even more so than the NGO wards at the hospital. Now we knew what the smell of death smelt like.

Guys from the Infantry Company would point to black birds that flew around the masses, saying how the food it carried in its beak wasn't a worm, but more than likely the flesh from a corpse. One man reported how he saw a dump truck drive past the front of the hospital, stockpiled with bodies, arms and legs visible around the lip of the dumpster. The morgue was another experience, where a body was seen to have no face, its eyes literally hanging from the sockets. Living shells of life also came in the form of children, dozens upon dozens visiting the soldiers at the rear gate of the hospital, all with limbs missing. And then another blast was heard in the distance, another landmine putting claim to a few more limbs of children; and that was another thing playing on the minds of some individuals, the actual threat of mines being trodden on.

Going for a run around the immediate area, as a section, brought light to bear upon more reality as hundreds upon hundreds of bodies would be run past, all lined out in rows and decaying, most (if not all) beneath some form of covering and out of view.

A man was herding his small band of 20 odd sheep along the roadside, himself at the rear of the sheep. He was the one to step on a hidden mine; no more leg. A six-year-old boy was playing with some friends when he saw a grenade. He kicked it and lost his foot, his face was also buried under fragments caused by the weapon – just 100 metres from our barracks.

It was reported that the Interahamwe (Hutu militiamen) were coming into Kigali by night, burying mines for more victims. It was also reported that they might try and plant some near the contingent's barracks, to force some type of action between the UN and RPA.

It was nice to know that the Australian presence was acknowledged.

The Padlock

One night whilst on the front gate at the hospital, I sat with another. It had just turned 2100hrs and all was quiet. Not even the RPA were out tonight. Normally they patrolled Kigali from dawn till dusk in section and platoon lots, establishing ambushes or simply forcing their way into homes. Three out of every seven days you could see tracer ammunition flickering through the night sky, two to three round bursts being fired as another human life was put to waste by the RPA. It all took a week or more to get used to.

An RPA ute with six persons in the rear passed between me, and the RPA opposite the hospital – the reciprocate guard box which had been placed shortly after the Australians had erected theirs. He looked up briefly and then stared out down the road. An RPA officer was approaching. His rank was confirmed as he approached the gate... he didn't hug and kiss the guard; he must have been an officer.

A minute later and the medic came running up from behind: 'Who's this?'

'Corporal Clayton, sir. Why, what's up?'

'Someone's just fired a weapon at us.'

'I don't think so, sir. If someone had fired a weapon, we would have heard it.'

'I'm telling you, someone has fired a shot at us. If you were with us when the round came through the glass window, you wouldn't be saying that.'

The officer wasn't convinced, but had taken to panic, as did the others in his midst.

They were all quick to hit the floor.

The infantry platoon commander was called up and the story explained to him. The medical officer was still unconvinced however; no matter how much I and the other guard on duty swore that we'd heard no rifle being fired.

An inspection of the said window revealed a large hole. A search for the bullet by the half dozen officers present turned up nothing. I soon found the article responsible for the hole. A tiny padlock. Obviously thrown by either the occupants of the vehicle that had passed earlier, or the officer who was seen to approach the RPA compound front gate.

All things soon settled down again, and normal routine was once more adjusted to.

The padlock that obviously had a muzzle velocity as that of a round of ammunition was discarded.

This put an end to the medic's mad minute of panic, although justly so. It could quite easily have been a hand grenade. All were vulnerable and no chicken wire was available for the screening of windows or guard box. Wire was however put on order; just never issued. Ground floor hospital rooms were blacked out though, screening the occupants from view, in particular protecting those who were wanted by the RPA.

More than once the RPA did make the threat to attack the hospital and barracks.

Luckily for them it didn't result, or there would have been a hell of a lot of dead RPA. No foe was going to take out the Infantry Company, not alive in any case, not after what had happened to the Belgiums prior to our being committed.

15th April

It was said that the padlock affair was the RPA's method of payback for an incident that should never have occurred. One of the Australian soldiers had fired a sling shot at the RPA guard box opposite the hospital. This act of stupidity could have quite easily have caused a major incident and triggered an eventual clash of forces.

The said soldier remained in the country however, against the option of shipping him back to Australia, and he was posted to the SASR the following year.

If the SAS were allowing such soldiers into their midst, then there was room for any fool with a body which acted before the brain. The SAS must have been desperate and without the knowledge that I possessed. It was also another understanding that at any time the SASR numbers saw depletion in their ranks, due to aircraft accident, etc; that the following years course was somewhat 'less picky' in the

221

soldiers they passed and welcomed into their ranks.

In fact, I can honestly say that I know of several SAS soldiers of whom should not be there, due to incompetence, and hope I never have to see them again.

RPA Lust

A nurse was running towards the rear bunker of the hospital, quite shaky from an experience that she wasn't going to forget for quite a while. There was also a lesson to be learnt here.

Whilst assisting a patient outside of the hospital grounds – within the designated NGO ward area – the nurse was approached by four members of the RPA, grabbed and pushed backwards towards one of the beds. Whatever happened next was very vague, but she escaped unharmed – the RPA lust for rape was very evident.

From that day forth she would always insist on having someone with her; and who could blame her.

In situations like this the rules and regulations of the area were somewhat of a contradiction by terms; one for us, and one for them.

Not far up from the bunker and hidden by the shade of several trees almost a hundred metres away, was an RPA sentry post that was seldom seen. These soldiers, as for all of the RPA seen (the NGO ward area being their responsibility), moved around with their weapons slung or held in hand. The Australians were restricted in the fact that no weapon on their part was permitted past the rear bunker and into the NGO ward boundaries. The best the Australian could do in respect to this was to restrict all personnel of movement into this area during times considered to be unnecessarily violent.

And as for the bunker; it wasn't uncommon to have rocks thrown at us during the night from within the dark of the shadows. This was just one of the small evils that the rear security element had to put up with.

Hygiene

Some of the sights seen from the rear gate were funny but filthy. Women from within the ward closest to the security here would squat just 20 metres from the boys and urinate. Each night was the same.

It came as a surprise to see that the grass in that area wasn't affected in any way and grew just as green as in other areas.

Theft

Our relationship with those in this country was practically none existent. The RPA were getting, and we weren't receiving; our tokens of good gesture were seemingly taken but never returned.

It was at one stage during the second half of the tour, and passed down from headquarters itself, that the relationship with the RPA was in some cases quite good. The only advantage to this may have been that the contingent wouldn't be wiped out by the thousands of AK47 and machete-wielding murderers. Their aggression for such was known, and there were more than several instances where somewhat of a Mexican stand-off was met, except that the Australians didn't return the RPA's verbal threats of death.

As the relationship was supposedly improved (through the eyes of those on high horses), RPA officers with motorolas were given a fair go, for they found that they had no means for which to recharge their batteries, but were now provided an open door. The batteries were now brought to the front bunker of the hospital where the RPA soldier waited whilst an Australian digger ventured into the hospital orderly room, exchanging it for a fresh one.

After several days of this, minor vengeance was sought by soldiers returning from the orderly room with either; a battery which had been reported as being faulty, or an explanation expressing deep regret that no recharged battery was available, and that they should 'come back later, mate'.

Where the RPA came into contact with motorolas in the first place was a concern in itself, let alone the fact that they now wanted us to supply them with recharged batteries for their stolen merchandise.

It was during this same period that some drivers for the UN had been given permission to park their minibuses out in front of the hospital for security reasons, parking it in front of the bunker. The drivers simply handed their keys over to the guys on duty in exchange for a receipt. The guard on duty maintained a half portion of this receipt. As all drivers were Rwandan, it was hard to extinguish one from the other – not meaning any prejudice, but they mostly looked the same, as I'm sure we mostly looked the same to them, which was good for some of us as it meant that when we accidently gave the 'finger' as opposed to scratching our faces that they would have no idea who was responsible when confronting us the following morning.

Due to complications met by one of the infantry minor call signs of another section, keys to one of the vehicles were handed over quite willingly to an RPA thief in civilian clothing. From that day on all drivers were required to sign in and out, as well as to be wearing their personal UN ID card. If on picking up a vehicle the following morning, the driver failed to fulfil these requirements, then the member of the contingent to which saw the driver sign in, was sought and asked for confirmation as to whether or not he was the 'right guy'. This act had its effect on the RPA trying their hand at theft, and enforced the rule for the need of drivers to bring in UN ID, for most disliked being kept waiting when they had a timed schedule to maintain. It also brought confusion to bear upon the shoulders of diggers who would look at the driver and mutter something along the lines of, 'yeah, that's looks like the guy who gave me the keys', when in fact he had no idea, because even if the driver had flashed us a 'brown eye' he would have still had a familiar look about him.

The theft of vehicles from the Australian side of the fence was from that day maintained at one, far from the numbers reported by other UN forces and NGOs in the country. It was a disappointing reality to see first-hand that some of the UN's funding was being flushed down the toilet through such losses. Numerous UN utes were stolen by the RPA. These vehicles were given a facelift by way of camouflage paint, and the only way of knowing that they were stolen from the UN was the fact that they were running very well and didn't have any dents in them for the first few days of their stolen existence.

Nothing, however, could be done in terms of requisition.

Kibeho I

Even before the massacre on 22nd April, 1995, Kibeho was not a very nice place; that description being very placid indeed. Hardliners of the former government were swaying judgement upon the innocents, employing every strategy to keep them in place, within the cordon of the IDP camp. The RPA (Rwandan Patriotic Army, renamed shorter after the

French evacuated the country) were ever concerned with the goings-on for it was their accusation that the camp was being used as a base from which the hardliners could conduct their raids in and around Butare. The RPA commenced to filter the IDPs out of Kibeho and back to their home communes, something that the IDPs would feel comfort in, however, with the pressing accusations and search for evidence, that individuals had any connection, whatsoever, with the former government, or somehow related to raids in the area (related to an Hutu, or having committed crimes against the former RPF in general, or a Tutsi) forced the IDPs to destroy their identification cards, and anything else that might associate them with the Hutu... and who could blame them?

On the 18th of April the RPA made a move and two battalions were sent into Kibeho, surrounding the camp so that there was no way in, and no way out. Some of the soldiers were between 7 and 12 years of age. Firing shots from rifles to force the throngs together, to be more easily controlled, burning their small adobes as they marched the IDPs to their fate.

Every single individual would be interrogated in some way in order to evaluate whether they were Hutu or Tutsi. The 120,000 or so IDPs were now congregated on the high ground of Kibeho, forced to live in conditions that were constantly stirring for the worst. For those that passed scrutiny, they were given the go ahead to find their way back to their home communes, for those that wore accusation of being associated, in any way, with Hutu hardliners; they were executed or thrown into jail, jails which were 'standing room' only:

The prisons were atrocious.

The UN pressed an ultimatum on the 19th and the RPA seemed to settle, a team of 32 Australians were prepared and deployed to Kibeho, setting up a site whereby the injured could start to receive medical aid and 'hopefully', by our advertised presence, prevent further atrocity. IDPs were cleared from the camp, Zambian forces, and Australian, helping people onto UN trucks so that they could be ferried away from hell.

On the 20th the RPA were seen quite clearly, beating men women and children with sticks and clubs, forcing them into imaginary corals, and some time after this IDPs commenced to grow more weary, deciding to take action, by picking up stones and pelting them at the RPA.

Machine gun and rifle fire was the answer, the RPA letting loose with retribution, refusing to submit to the stone-throwing innocents – although we must remember that there were hardliners here too, and it was quite realistically them that had started the commotion, and why not, for they had the protection of 120,000 IDPs.

In the night there was the constant firing of weapons, just as we had witnessed in Kigali, from the safety of our barracks, but the vicious assaults of Kibeho were much worse and would soon escalate out of control.

On the 21st the wounded were cared for, under the watchful eye of the RPA, who insisted that no person receive more than 5 minutes of care, moving the wounded through as quickly as they could, those with gunshots, broken bones, and machete wounds.

Kibeho II

18th-21st April 1995

On the 18th, the legal officer for the contingent was to make a personal visit to Butare, a population of 29,000 – 45 minutes from Kibeho. His prime task was to visit the prison there.

Permission was also sought for entrance into Kibeho whilst in Butare, for this was on the agenda for the legal officer's 'finding of facts'.

As the truck entered the camp, all could see the direct effect of the RPA's call to force between 70,000 and 120,000 refugees onto a prominent spur to the centre of the camp, this being encircled by a small valley. Blue and green plastic sheeting could be seen everywhere, this was the roofing for the IDPs' stick and mud huts – it was no wonder that the refugees had to walk a minimum of two kilometres to get firewood for the much needed fuel for fires and cooking.

Everywhere one looked was dead of activity, except the spur-line that sounded like a million geese chattering away to their heart's content.

The RPA had said that the herding of the IDPs was required if they were to be shuttled off back to their communes. The RPA were sick to death of the crowd, and knew full well that there was a hell of a lot of Hutu extremists amongst these people. It was these Hutu militia of old which had supposedly caused the problems of the 22nd April 1995.

There were many ramifications behind the legal officer's visit, not all of which were disclosed to the infantry soldiers. Although my section and I were to spend several days with him, he was conversed with only when he handed out his directions for the smooth running of his task at hand. One such task was to gather information on the overcrowding of prisoners, and their standards of living in such overcramped places, that there wasn't even room to lay down or sleep; and even if the prisoners did, it would have been in their own excrements. None of those imprisoned saw any legal process prior to conviction, and many were innocent.

Very few IDPs were leaving via the erected boom gate entrance, to

depart the swamped crowd of 100,000 in Kibeho. A vast majority were forced to leave, their water containers punctured with knives by the RPA, and personal belongings thrown to the ground and kicked; many were brutally pushed under the temporary gate, forced to be on their way
 to Butare. Some were fortunate enough to be allowed their possessions. Another man was being escorted by three RPA. He had his hands held high and didn't want to go. No shots were heard, but he was taken away and executed by machete.

The truck loaded with the security section was just twenty metres from the boom gate, the sights and smells hitting our nostrils. One of the guys pointed out a running figure in the distance. He was being chased and shot at by two RPA. The man ran into a mud hut on the hillside opposite. The RPA followed and two shots were heard. The RPA exited and walked off. This act was followed 30 minutes later by another RPA firing a burst of 20 rounds into a smaller group of some 70 odd IDPs 50 metres down the slope from the main crowd. Closer inspection proved that no one had been hit – either that or any dead/wounded had been carried away before a group of medics could push their way through the crowd and to the area of concern.

During the next two hours the legal officer was off with his interpreter and two security, talking with different members of representation from CARE Australia, other NGOs, and members of the Zambian security force posted there, whilst around us, from time to time, individuals were manhandled and 'taken-care-of' RPA style.

At the conclusion of a day's negotiation, the section of security under my command, along with the legal officer, would withdraw before dark to the safety of a Zambian compound in Butare.

By late afternoon on the 21st we were on our way back to Butare, taking time out to visit one of the prisons and another refugee camp on return. We were stopped by two RPA who stood their ground at the entrance of the small commune, and reported that the refugees there had been removed and sent on their way back to their own communes. The RPA soldier laughed whilst conversing with the interpreter who knew full well that the IDPs were still in place just beyond view, hidden by a few trees, rising ground, and the large centre commune building of the province which sat at our side. The truth was found on reaching Butare. The IDPs of that particular camp were still in place, so it stood to reason that the RPA didn't want IDPs returned as gravely

The Long Road to Rwanda

as they made out. Each camp was being systematically sifted through for members of the former government, be they of a political or military importance mattered little, for they would all meet with imprisonment or death.

Whilst at this commune a report was heard as it was sent from Kibeho to Kigali, via another group of soldiers who had arrived in Kibeho on our mission being granted a minor victory by a higher authority, a direct response to the information gathered by the legal officer. A group of 17 odd IDPs had just been massacred by AK47 and machete. Later still and a further 200 had been said to have met their death, by which time the legal officers group of 12 had returned to the barracks in Kigali.

We were to hear later of two reports. The first explained 11 dead children aged between two and thirteen, the second was of 20 dead, 16 shot, two trampled (one of which was six months old) and two killed by machete attack. Both reports were the result of incidents caused on the afternoon/evening of 21st April 1995. The worst was yet to come.

Massacre

22nd April 1995

On that fatal day of 1995, at 0650hrs, a small group of 32 of the Australian contingent, along with a few members of the Zambian security force, became involved in what would never be forgotten. They became a part of the mix and threatened all alike by the Interahamwe, a crowd of over 100,000 IDPs and 2,500 RPA – some of whom were as young as 7 years old.

There have been two books written on the massacre. One is titled 'Combat Medic', by Terry Pickard, and the other 'Pure Massacre', by Kevin O'Halloran; both are invaluable and provide much detail in regards to incidents and timings. These two books should be read for a larger, overall understanding of the events, and for an insight into the thoughts of soldiers on the ground at the time. Another called 'The Kibeho Massacre: As it Happened' was written by me some years later; it is also worth reading, but I suggest the previous two as mentioned above. However, if you like poetry then I suggest 'Kibeho: An Epic Poem'.

From within the crowd the hardliners emerged, thrashing out with their machete, killing all they came across: Babies, women, and the old and frail.

The Zambian compound, upon the spur and high ground, received pot shots, being fired upon from somewhere within the crowd; a hardliner perhaps, or a RPA soldier hoping to force the UN to retaliate, or trying to kill a member of the Interahamwe; and another storm was also brewing, a tropical upheaval of torrential rain, and the crowd commenced to move.

The RPA considered their position, and deemed the wavering crowd as an attempt to break the human cordon around them.

The RPA opened fire with their automatic weapons, rocket propelled grenades and other arms of destruction; sniper fire and fire from Ak47s and machine guns; machete attacks continued unrelenting in their ferocity, even 60mm mortars were seen to have been used, but it was hard to see or hear amongst the mayhem and cries of horror. Interahamwe within the crowd were taking to refugees with machete and the RPA were applying force from the cordon. The IDPs couldn't win. They stampeded, many children and babies being trampled to death during the torment.

There were continuous attempts to force the UN to offer some form of protection to the IDPs by opening fire themselves – the Zambians, however, stood strong. It was quite evident, in all respects, that the RPA wished for some reason to kill every UN peacekeeper and NGO in the area. But how can we be so sure? RPA soldiers were executing men and women in front of the Australian and Zambian soldiers, teasing them to take action, but the only action implemented was to stretcher the wounded to the medical station for aid, and as the wounded were carried, weapons slung over shoulders, the RPA continued with their atrocities by chasing IDPs and shooting them in the back as they made a run for it.

The Australians did as ordered and stood fast, witnessing first-hand the atrocities of that day; RPA continuing unabated, murdering innocent IDPs in front of them, seemingly hoping, praying to God, that the Australians would intervene in some way so that they could then dispose of us as well.

The Australian medics and ground troops sealed a bond, working together like no other. One by one the injured IDPs were brought on stretchers by the infantry to be given medical assistance by medical staff, and on the 23rd April, the true nature of all came to be seen as more of the contingent was deployed to the area.

We [and let's make this clear: myself not included] now numbered 14 doctors and nurses, 30 infantry and six logistics personnel.

Then a Casualty clearing Post [or 'Point' as some might prefer] was established, and further horrendous work continued over the coming days of offering aid to these poor people, the worst situation, for all it was worth, since the most evil days imaginable from both World Wars.

More than 4,050 IDPs had met with death that fatal day. The number was higher but the RPA had taken to evacuating the bodies on trucks to lighten the threat against them regards accusations of genocide; as the sun went down the RPA task had changed, from mass murder, to the clearing away of evidence.

During the body count, one man came across more than 20 dead babies, all hidden from view under the heaps of rubbish that was caused by the massacre. Much of the devastation was hidden from view. Was it possible that individuals thought that if they were hidden that they might forego execution by the hand of the RPA? Many an execution was seen by the Australian contingent, some carried out as the RPA laughed, watching the Australian troops as they carried out their cold blooded murder; shooting another individual in the head, the body falling heavily to the ground. It didn't give you a nice feeling to see a helpless victim being run down and murdered, and I can speak from experience.

650 IDPs were found wounded, piles of dead being stepped over as the infantry stretcher-carried wounded to the Australian Casualty Clearing Post.

It was reported later that the RPA came very near to firing their antitank weapon on buildings that supposedly hid 1,700 hardliners. This action – if carried out – would have been catastrophic. The only deterrent was the very presence of Australian and Zambian forces, but not deterrent enough; and it was to the Australians and Zambians that the very blame for atrocities went.

But where did the blame really lie? I heard, quite convincingly, that a report put some of the blame upon the soldiers of UNAMIR II for not preventing the massacre: 32 Australian soldiers against two battalions in open warfare.

And yes, propaganda was also in full swing. According to the inhabitants of Rwanda and neighbouring countries, the RPA were the lifesavers, aiding the IDPs against the Interahamwe and Former Rwandan Government Forces, whilst the Australians did nothing to assist. This was brought to light on the 30th April when the RPA drove around on the backs of utes denouncing UNAMIR, claiming themselves as stoppers of the genocide, saying how they shed their own blood to save the lives of the Rwandan people and troops of UNAMIR. The people quite believed the RPA, but to what degree and by what numbers, no one really knew.

But this day was soon to pass and the memories left to live on.

From 23rd April 1995, to 9th May 1995, 1,500 IDPs had to be evacuated from the confines of the few buildings of Kibeho. These few had found sanction in a cordon of walls and would budge for no man. This was the compound next door to where the Zambian peacekeepers maintained their headquarters.

Many poor souls lived a life of hell during that 16 day period, bringing corn to the boil which had just moments before been picked from their faeces, deposited on the ground by all of the people combined. All excretion was sifted through for the undigested kernels.

Water was also rare. The RPA wanted these people out of Kibeho as soon as possible, and had punctured the IDPs' water containers. Most of the IDPs were forced to drink their own urine: but one thing baffled me. The urine they were drinking was, for the most part, yellowish in colour. I had always assumed that the yellow tinge seen in urine was an indicator of excess vitamins and minerals – but I could quite easily have been wrong. But if I was correct, then where was the nourishment coming from. Were these few, members of the Interahamwe, and somehow being provided aid; or was there more nourishment in maggots and recycled corn than I knew?

Another woman was approached, to be convinced by me that she would be evacuated to a place where she'd be given food and shelter, but only if she left with me then and there.

She looked sick and moved slightly from where she sat, maggots and blood dribbling from her anus as she moved. I'd heard that maggots cleaned the flesh, helping persons to heal, and how true this was I had no way of knowing, but you could see in this woman's face that there was no chance of survival, there was absolutely no way in which she could live through this ordeal that she was suffering so badly, yet so heroically. She would be dead soon, and someone else would pick up the maggots to be eaten later, to have them put in with the corn, and other scraps, such as cut up portions of animal skin from leather shoes.

This place was beyond explanation, beyond sordid, the most disgusting place on earth that I could possibly imagine.

There was one thing for sure, all of the soldiers here, who had been protected by a technologically sound society all of their life, had never seen things like this before.

There are mothers back home who want Australians to remember their sons who served in Afghanistan and Iraq, and deservedly so, but I wonder how many remember all of the above.

We all remember ANZAC day, and so we should, but who of us remembers the massacre at Kibeho, which occurred just three days before the commemorated date?

Injured

The clearance of IDPs from Kibeho, continued. We had departed

Butare in a truck with rover support, medics, infantry, and communications. We knew well that the IDPs had to be evacuated from Kibeho, and as soon as possible.

None of the Australian contingent were permitted to remain in Kibeho overnight, due to the seriousness of the problems that had unfolded over the past few days, so a camp at be set up not far from that hell hole, where bodies had been picked up and thrown into mass graves, the wounded and sick given medical aid. To prevent further death the IDPs simply had to be moved back to their communes.

It was during one of these trips (by road) that the movement of the truck commenced to aggravate my back injury... it had been a nun that had set the pain in motion. No blame will ever go to her, but she was a little overweight; with only two men to stretcher-carry her, myself and one other, and the effects of the continued work that we had been performing in the country, were taking its toll. The nun on the stretcher was the straw that broke the camel's back – literally.

Shortly after initially receiving the injury, the savage beatings-of-pain had been administered first aid, all seemed to go well... and then weeks later, this; the damn trucks and poor conditions of the road system within this country were seeing the end of my career draw closer; and the pain mounted as we continued, with this, another visit to Kibeho.

By the time the truck had been parked next to the old Zambian compound, all on board had accepted another eye-full of desertion; the entire landscape around was void of people; not even the RPA could be seen, but I knew there must be some around here somewhere. It was like a giant tip had centred itself on a lone spur between two valleys.

Sticks and branches made up the skeleton city of broken down adobes, where blue plastic sheeting, given by CARE, flapped in the little breeze that blew from the valleys below.

The truck had been parked; I was seated in the front seat. I sat motionless, the pain unbearable – and few of you, reading this, will understand how I could possibly continue how I did, in respect to the amount of pain I am telling you I was in? I can only defend myself by offering my military record as an itinerary of the things I had attempted over the years, and those that I had passed. The things I had achieved during the past 15 years cannot be attributed to a bludger and that when I say I was in pain, that is exactly what I mean. I always pushed myself beyond the pain, always doing more than what I knew

The Long Road to Rwanda

others would do in the same situation. This was not a civilian job, you don't just phone in and say you're not showing, simply because you feel under the weather; this was the infantry.

The platoon sergeant came to the door after the driver had made his exit, and opened it as though a chauffeur. 'You coming, Nigel?' and on giving my reply was provided with a few painkillers... although these had little effect.

It took me ten minutes to get into the Zambian compound, an area of ground surrounded by buildings, a giant open area where thousands of Rwandan IDPs had congregated. I could only remain for 30 minutes, for the pain was getting too much. I returned to the truck. A medic arrived later on in the day, just prior to our trip back to our campsite, and prescribed a pill which – for its size – had powers that I cannot explain... damn, I was hoping for a cuddle and a kiss. Within ten minutes I was feeling light headed and the road trip out-of-there was like a dream.

Aftermath

9th May 1995

I returned again to Kibeho, even with my injury, but after it had settled down a bit, and continued to do what I could to help with the evacuation process.

The CCP remained in situ until all remaining IDPs had been evacuated back to Butare and from there back to their home communes. It was another sad thing to see that a lot of these people were shunned by their own kind because of the weight of propaganda that was floating on every breath of wind. No one in Butare wanted to be seen conversing with, or harbouring someone from Kibeho.

The final days saw two men from my section in particular giving their helping hand to the contingent's commitments. Against the wishes of Non-Government Organisations (similar to CARE and World Vision), these two soldiers lead the path to success by learning some of the local language Kinyarwanda. Applying this to logic they commenced to collect the hundreds upon hundreds of machetes in the area, confiscated them. This prevented the IDPs from cutting wood for fires from banisters, railings and other wooden objects; preventing them from cooking; from cutting up their leather goods for food; taking from them their only means of support. This was accompanied with harsh words and forcefulness. The IDPs had no choice but to leave. Was this what the RPA had initially tried to do? The Australians, in a strange way, had reverted to the tactics of the RPA.

All of the NGOs in the area appeared to be sour at this apparent act of cruelty, for the taking of the IDPs' means of creating fire and food. But at least they now stood a better chance of survival. Anything was better than eating corn from faeces and drinking urine. On more than one occasion were Australians asked for saviour, IDPs coming up to them and saying, 'kill me. Kill me. Shoot me please', not all spoken in English, but some by means of sign language, pointing to the weapons we carried and then to their heads, nodding 'yes, do it'. I could see the anguish in their faces as they did this.

Rubbish was moved around with applied aggression by several Australian Infantry, and when a grenade was found hidden under an old and worn mattress, their voices rose a little more. Windows were smashed (but I can't substantiate by whom), and belongings of the IDPs were grabbed and then carried to the main entrance of the IDP sanctuary. Some would follow, some would not.

Then, as though by a miracle granted us all, the last few hundred got up and departed.

No one was sorry to see this place emptied or disappear behind them, and the Australians loaded themselves onto the trucks and departed for Kigali.

On return to the barracks all equipment was deloused and a few months further into the trip, all equipment of a canvas and cloth type, which had seen wear and tear in Kibeho, was purified by flame.

So now the worst of the tour was behind us all.

Many thoughts linger on a person's mind after such things as Kibeho.

This entire country had a share in this war of machete against flesh and bone, against degradation of the body, mind and soul.

When you've seen such things, nothing else matters, nothing can really be more important. Therefore, to go on, would be a waste. Nothing can compare to that already said.

What else can I tell you, the reader?

But I shall continue with my story.

PTSD

After the massacre, the job continued; after all, we were to be here for a further four months.

It was upsetting to see that not all persons involved with Kibeho received some form of counselling; sure, some were offered the service and either accepted or declined, others were 'advised' that they needed to attend; those who were supposedly 'more of a concern' than others, for they had been on-the-ground at Kibeho, at the time of the massacre, had no choice but to attend.

A story reached my ear of how one of the counsellors had entered a congregation of soldiers, where, after introduction, advised all that he understood what the soldiers were feeling, for he too had witnessed some horrible scenes, where bodies lay dead and mangled due to a coach having crashed – back in Australia. Many soldiers – if not all – were insulted by this, and if you have taken stock of what has previously been written then you might understand why; but no true appreciation can be attained without having been there at the time of the massacre, or for those more fortunate, to have simply aided with the IDPs return to their communes (but different things, affect different people, and in different ways).

I recall two incidents in particular – not being able to mention others, due to legal reasons – after having received my discharge from the military:

I was on a train, heading for the city. A 13-year yells out to his mates: 'There it is!'

They pointed and laughed; carrying on like fools, receiving silent stares from all around... all I could do was turn my head, disgusted at their attempts to humour one another. And what was it they had been pointing at? That morning trains had been delayed, for an elderly person had been hit by a train, the body still on the 'out-going' track, covered in a blanket and surrounded by police – no, I didn't look; it was on the news that night. Their parents must have been proud – but what did they know about death?

There was another incident, which matters little; really. I was working 'casual' at the Rye RSL, a customer came to the counter, arm in a sling, metal pins visible. He was one of the survivors of the Port

The Long Road to Rwanda

Arthur Massacre – and without sounding rude: A picnic compared to Kibeho. He had a few family members along, all with smiles. Pats on the back came in thick and fast, drinks here and there; yes indeed, sympathy was flowing well; and I continued with my work in silence, thinking to myself; how many lives had he saved to deserve such congratulations? Was he congratulated for being a survivor? Was he congratulated for escaping death? Or was he being congratulated for the pain he had suffered, a minute speck of suffering when compared to some of the injuries inflicted upon the IDPs of Kibeho, as illustrated without restraint in 'Combat Medic' and 'Pure Massacre'?

I felt as though the contingent was being insulted.

I had read somewhere, that within ten years of the massacre at Kibeho, around 50% of those men and women of Australia, sent to do their duty, had received treatment for PTSD at some time between 1995 and 2005. I guess they call it 'post traumatic' because it's triggered by an event/occurrence after the actual event, something that the memory regards as being similar. But truly, what treatment was there? You can't exactly get a scalpel and cut someone's memory from his or her brain, and I am no damn psychologist. We must all presume, therefore, that PTSD cannot be cured. I guess those affected by PTSD need to be considered, and above all, remembered; I for one won't forget them.

Recovery

Around 4 weeks (give or take) after I suffered the inconvenience of an injury to my back, I was confronted with the fact that it was now time to take nine days leave.

Leave was taken by a small percentage of soldiers at a time, spread out over the tour; everyone received this gift of gifts, and the world was at our fingertips. We had soldiers going to the UK, South Africa, Thailand, and you guessed it, back to OZ; just to name a few. What was I to do? My injury was still in its infancy, it needed rest prior to returning to duty, or I would be sent back to Australia before having served my time in this country. I decided to spend my leave in Kenya, most of my time flat on my back, going for short walks, sitting around and hoping for my injury to heal enough for me to continue with my work.

Nine days was a long time, even longer when you are bored out of your brain, and when it comes down to it, this entire idea was conjured up simply for me to get well enough to continue in Rwanda, to witness more pain and killing. My injury had improved but the pain would never go away again, not like it had all of those times over the past 7-8 years of my infantry career where pain had been experienced.

Effort, in some cases, gets you nowhere; it provides you with nothing more than self satisfaction, that you did your best to achieve your goal… even if you fail.

The Flag

What was discipline and when was it prone to being employed? Does discipline take on more emphasis at one time over another, or was it equally distributed? It was always hard to answer when taking into consideration the diggers. It seems to me that it was always an essential part of discipline to stand fast for the flag: Flag-goes-up, stand at attention; flag comes- down, stand at attention. It's not that damn hard to misinterpret or easy to make a mistake; it happens at the same time every day and there was a whistle blast that lets everyone in hearing distance know that the flag was about to be hoisted or lowered. I would say that the blood spilt for the flag and country was enough in itself to give good reason for 'standing fast', so why was it so hard for the soldiers to carry out the simple task? You'd see the soldiers marching around or doing some physical activity, then just before the whistle blast was due the area around would be vacated… soon after, of course, the soldiers would come out of their hide-holes.

We were entering Ruhengeri at one time, escorting a few medics into the town; in order for them to get a tour into the hills to see the gorillas in their natural surrounds; when all of a sudden the local populace, thousands of them, stopped what they were doing and stood fast: I was acting as security for the truck drive into the mountains, not partaking in the intrusion of the gorilla's natural habitat.

The Rwandan flag; it was being hoisted. It then suddenly appeared to me that these people had more national spirit than we did, but I soon realised too, that anyone who didn't stand fast would be proving allegiance to the former government and would be tempting the very fury of a machete-wielding RPA soldier.

Life certainly stank in this land-locked country; for danger lurked around every corner.

Convoy RTU

My section had been called to duty. We had to provide infantry support to a medical team visiting another medical facility-come-orphanage; they were gravely in need of medical assistance due to there always being a long line of patients: The amount of children present at the centre, and the influx of returning IDPs since UNAMIR's presence in the country, coming in from all quarters of Rwanda.

Several rovers and our infantry truck where winding through the hills of this – sometimes – beautiful country, and when you've seen some of the horrors of this country you can't help but to look out for something more appealing to the eye, even if momentarily, but you also need to watch the road....

We came to a halt. The rovers have pulled over to an accident on the side of the road.

A UN rover had driven over the edge of the winding road and plummeted about 40 metres down a steep embankment. Trees in the hills side prevented the rover from travelling too far down the slope and it would seem that no deaths had occurred. Some members of our infantry element hopped off the truck to provide assistance where required, others maintained vigil on the area surrounding us. Several medics clambered down the 45-degree slope, our doctor – a Major – insisting on having a closer look. She stumbled... snap.

She had fractured her wrist and needed medical attention herself – lucky we were UNAMIR. A few other medical personnel seemed overly concerned, and obviously knew more than me. I failed to see the problem when I received further pieces of information to be added to the puzzle. She had a fracture, was in pain, and had to be attended to back at Kigali.

I continued to look the Captain in the eye. She said to me: 'You're in command of the convoy, Corporal.'

It wasn't a passing-of-command, it was reminding me of my status. Certainly, this was a medical mission, and for all intents and purposes we – the infantry – were here to provide aid to the medical team. All of this said, due to the situation in the country, section commands were the overall commanders of a convoy when one departed Kigali due to the importance of applying 'Infantry Minor Tactics,' to any number of

The Long Road to Rwanda

probable scenarios, amidst this civil war.

This was a medical mission with a need to provide the much-needed assistance to the Rwandan community. I was not a medic and failed to acknowledge the amount of pain the Major was in, and considered briefly that we had the medical supplies with us to treat her for her pain; but take into consideration the roads surface, the amount of time to simply turn around and go back, or to continue with the task and then return to Kigali later, was too much for me to consider when an observer of someone hurt so badly... hadn't we all seen enough pain to last us. I asked the Major a simple and straightforward question: 'I have no idea how much pain you're in, or if you're even able to continue on this road. If you can't do your job then to continue with the task would be a waste. Would you like to turn back?

The mission was cancelled, we returned to barracks; the children would have to wait until another day; after all, it's no good going on safari to kill a rhino, armed with a peashooter.

Snake Bite

It was around 2130hrs and my shift on the front security post of the hospital was to commence in 30 minutes. Even now my attention was easily drawn to the sights and sounds around: The machine gun fire, the Ak47s, and the tracer flying through the night air as RPA set upon more unsuspecting hardliners. The RPA barracks entrance was also opposite the hospital, our sentry post opposite the RPA; only 20 metres separated the two. Another two RPA soldiers were entering, escorting an elderly man, he being supported between them. They continued on into the fading light, towards one of the barracks buildings in the distance. Ten minutes later, BANG! Another dead civilian. The death was never-ending.

The 2IC of another section then saw me moving in the security bunker and asked me over, which I happy did. As I approached I could see two locals, a mother and a father; the mother held a child.

I looked into her arms and saw what was thought to be a boy of three, and looked Lance Corporal Lane in the eye.

'They don't speak English but I think they're saying that the child's been bitten by a snake. What do you think we should do?' he asked of me.

The child seemed to stare at me with fear, and I could understand why – or so I thought. We had been advised that parents in this country told their children that they should never go too far when playing, and always beware of white men, because white men liked to eat small children.

'Let's take them into the RAP; we might be able to get someone to have a look,' which was a dangerous call, for the hospital was there for the UN. The Rwandan people had their own medical facilities, and if we started to help one or two then the following day might see hundreds queuing up for treatment. The medics helped individuals where possible,

and I was certainly aware of this; they were forever providing medical aid to car crash victims, mine victims, to people with gunshot wounds, amputations, broken bones....

The couple with the child followed as we led them into the RAP where one of the SAS guys was seen maintaining some of the stock upon the shelves; the child probably thought we were looking for the salt and pepper, knife and fork....

'Jock.'

'Yeah.'

'We got this child here; think it's a snake bite, didn't know if you could help-out or not.'

The SAS soldier walked towards the patient, had a quick look, and gave indication that he was happy to assist.

The 2IC and myself departed the RAP; the 2IC back to his post and me to mine.

The next morning we heard that the child had survived his snake bite; it was little mercies like this that made the trip to Africa worthwhile: I'm sorry I couldn't say the same for the old man who'd been escorted into the RPA barracks.

Pain

My injury was getting worse. I took the opportunity to attend the RAP as often as I could, which usually amounted to at least three times a week, and if stationed at the hospital, whenever I could; other times it simply wasn't available to me… I still had a job to do. I couldn't understand the situation. Here I was, in terrible pain, getting assistance from the RAP – sometimes on a daily basis – and I was still in Rwanda. Sure I wanted to be here, but that wasn't the question… should I be here?

What aid did I receive? Painkillers were provided to me, eight a day from the medics, as this was all 'anyone' was supposed to have; I was known on occasion to slip into the section medical kit on barracks and help myself to pills. I also received stretching exercises and time on an exercise bike.

At one stage we had to conduct the military fitness test and sit-ups, push-ups, and a 5km run. One of the soldiers in my section was sent to retrieve painkillers from the medical kit… I would have to take double ration to get myself through this test. Unfortunately I never achieved a pass and from that day forth was given a permanent 'chit' from conducting physical activity, but I was still in Rwanda doing my duty. Anytime we conducted patrols, escorts, or rove-n-picket, section webbing had to be worn; however, I made a few changes. I emptied my water bottles, all but a few mouthfuls; and I only ever carried a single magazine of live ammunition, as opposed to a full quota. Rove-n-picket duty for me now involved taking a rest every 20 minutes, whereby I would sit down for 5-10, and this was permitted – several officers knew I was doing this.

Road Block

July

RPA roadblocks were something that was seen every day. Most of these were permanent, in particular at the major arterials that flowed in and out of towns.

The roadblocks weren't something that you'd expect to find in a normal society.

Here in Rwanda a roadblock was distinguished by a piece of string that was pulled taunt across any road. In some cases this was accompanied by a witch's hat, a box, or even large rock, placed to the middle (possibly to symbolise the segregation of the two way traffic; who knows). Needless to say that the roadblocks were always monitored by a section to platoon strength RPA unit, depending on its importance, the threat, and locality.

One such permanent roadblock was erected at the South East entrance into Ruhengeri, a population of a said 30,000 people. In late June this roadblock was the scene of some concern as a Zambian working with the UN had shot an RPA soldier. Before this incident occurred, all UN traffic was permitted immediate passage through such a roadblock.

Some changes were now going to take place.

During the contingents stay in Rwanda, most took the advantage of invading the natural habitat of the gorillas to the North West of the country, in the region where volcanoes were numerous and according to all statistics, ready to blow at any time in the near future.

Each visit to see the gorillas by a group of Australians required a section of infantry for security, and a rover with radio mounted for communications with Kigali and any military observers, who were situated in any of the towns of this small land-locked country.

The rifle section was in the lead truck and approached the roadblock, and via an RPA soldier's uncertainty, the vehicle was permitted to pass through the roadblock; but he quite quickly stopped the two vehicles following behind us.

The guys on the rear of this vehicle soon informed the driver and me that those behind had been stopped. The convoy now found itself separated by fifty metres of road, the RPA between both parties. Our section of security was now separated from its main task, the protection of the rear two vehicles and their occupants.

I set about to reverse back but was prevented from doing so by an RPA officer. He wanted all Australians off vehicles, to use this opportunity to search the cabins etc. But contingent orders didn't allow for this to happen. So the officer was denied his request.

Ten minutes of harassment and apprehension dominated our two groups; the RPA officer was seemingly nervous as to the aggressive nature of those on board, and then myself worried over the fact that the RPA officer's weapon had a round up the spout and his finger was on the trigger, ready to fire. Any second now and all could turn to mayhem, and I could be the owner of a large gaping hole in my gut.

I approached the sig to try and establish communications with the military observers in Ruhengeri. If anyone could get us out of this predicament, they could.

The RPA officer deployed his men and all manner of things weren't looking good, when luck suddenly fell our way; MIL OBS hadn't received our call, but just as I peered up I saw their rover driving past. The RPA officer also saw this and within seconds the convoy was permitted to proceed.

A lesson was learnt. A finer distance between each vehicle was going to be required, and speed reduced, when approaching roadblocks. I couldn't tell whether the members of the section were relieved or disappointed, as during the entire exchange of differences, they had hands on weapons, ready to go into action, to take out as many RPA as they could before they in turn met with death.... More than luck was with us that day.

Emergency

When working in the hospital, it was an everyday occurrence, for someone to be expected to work in the emergency ward. The 'rest' section of the platoon normally filled this duty, although, due to the restriction of 'space and time', and the number of doctors required to be
working on the injured person, it was normal for only one, or possibly two, to be asked to assist.

Two soldiers were carrying the stretcher and I followed. We were being led into the emergency ward where several doctors were waiting for their patient.

We turned into a corridor and could see a few figures dressed in gowns entering an open door to the ward. We followed the lead of our escort and turned into the room, the stretcher being placed upon the table, the unconscious form of a Rwandan national lying there, his clothing not having seen a washing tub for what appeared to be a month. All of the buttons were done up, his belt was tight around his middle to hold up his jeans and the jeans themselves, filthy; then his shoes came into view... one was attached, the other was half missing. It was hard to see at this stage what was 'shoe' and what was 'flesh', for the land mine he had trodden on had done its job well.

Everyone went about their task; I took up a pair of scissors and cut away the jeans, from the wound itself and up to the groin, across, and down the other leg; his shoes were removed with care, in particular where the foot wound existed.

Once the offending footwear was removed it was a little easier to see the damage that the mine's blast had caused. Half of his foot was missing... draw an imaginary line from the fourth toe (in from the left) and down to the beginning of the outside of his heel; that was the damage inflicted, half his foot cut away by an explosion.

The wound was cleaned and they prepared him for surgery... there was a hell of a lot of dirt in amongst the flesh.

I looked over my shoulder and another 5 doctors and nurses could be seen hard at work, a nurse half on top of another patient, half straddled as though trying to mount a horse, forcing pressure down upon his chest in the hope of getting him breathing... you could see from where I stood that the chest bones were displaced a good 8-10 centimetres every time she attempted to revive him; but he died.

The man with the missing foot was treated accordingly and would live to see another day, and what was experienced in the emergency ward during that 20-minute period was part-n-parcel of an everyday occurrence, but in all reality this sequence of two short events were NOTHING when compared to the horrors of Kibeho: it was like comparing a grain of sand to a basketball.

The populace of this country were operated upon, where the contingent had the ability to act, but priority always went to the UN... it just happened to turn out that very few UN personnel needed the services that we provided, so our attention and assistance could be redirected elsewhere.

To Kigali Airport

The six-month tour went by very quickly, and for me personally, the four few months were spent in constant pain. Why had I endured? Why didn't I opt to return home? Why were those with a rank higher than mine willing to keep me in the country?

All of those directly responsible for me knew of my injuries, but still I remained. I can only draw a single conclusion from this; my overall performance was of a standard accepted as appropriate or higher – why else? I could therefore go home, knowing that I had achieved a little, but the idea that we had 'not' been entrusted with better Rules Of Engagement, was disappointing to say the least; but then again, if we carried out actions in accordance with less stringent Rules Of Engagement… we could all be dead right now. It might be that death – for some of those that had toured in Rwanda – would have been preferred.

The sites drifted past us now, as the final leg to the airport was made on the back of trucks, no weapon in hand, dressed in uniform only. This country was still a mess, and would be for a long bloody time. The orphans in the orphanages might get to grow to adulthood, but squaller was their life, now and forever into the future. If the RPA didn't get
them, then the volcanoes that loomed in the distance would.

I couldn't help but feel I was doing a disservice to this country. I would have loved to stay for another twelve months or more, regardless of the pain in my lower back; but then there were so many others who just wanted to get home… so few of them wanted to remain behind.

And even as the plane took off from the ground I peered out of the window and hoped that I could one day forgive myself for not doing more. I had nothing to go home to, no wife and kids… just a room on the barracks. Being in Rwanda was as comfortable for me as being back in Townsville.

Home

It was fairly easy to get back into the swing of things back on barracks, but the memories of the stay overseas haunted most of us at night – some more than others. I could understand why it was that we had it so good in Australia, whilst in Rwanda they had it so hard. Politics, resources, and the neighbours that surrounded your part of the world: that was the answer; not guts, pride, spirit, or the colour of your skin.

Back in Australia there were a few promotions to be seen, postings to be requested, accepted, and turned down. For me, I had the RAP to attend on a regular basis, even though the easy-going life back on barracks provided me with a better opportunity to rest my injury. It was, however, too late for recovery and I was soon provided with a medical downgrade to P3L7, which basically made me unfit for the infantry. I was to be posted to 1RAR, Mortar Platoon – of all the platoons to send me, they wished me there; those bastards. But none of it eventuated. The posting was cancelled, my promotion to sergeant revoked, and a new position was provided me… down to Holsworthy barracks, sitting on my ass for the remainder of my career, being screwed around by the RSM of a battalion – and others like him – who had 'little' idea or understanding of my career as a whole.

I was swung like a pendulum from task to task… I had no real job. I requested a corps transfer; to Clerical, to MPs, to the Q-stream, the bloody post office. Nothing was accepted. It was then that it hit me; after 16 years' service I was no longer viable. If they truly wished, so much, to keep me in an office environment, why the hell wasn't I being provided with a corps transfer to Clerical? Simple; they wanted to abuse me, not use me.

I was downgraded and the new rules underlining employment within the army were changing, in particular, for the infantry.

My time was up.

Final Curtain

I was medically discharged from the army on 24th September 1996, after 16 years' service, my back finally giving way to constant pain during the final months of my stay in Rwanda, a stay supported by the overdose of pain-killers that I took from day by day. I accepted the discharge, as this meant no more physical activity accompanied with pain, and although I had problems since 1987, the injury had always come good after several weeks of treatment and rest; but not this time around. My knees were also no better off as I had good reason to report these to the RAP on two separate occasions when posted to Singleton in the early 90's, and both ankles were showing severe signs of wear-n-tear, only one of which received recognition from the RAP, as it was always hard to report on injuries when in the field. But in the past, as read by you, the reader, I continued with my job and tried to look after myself as best I could, weathering the storm, suffering the pain, and getting on with the job I loved so dearly.

The army was developing a new rule of thumb; by the end of 1997, all those that were below medical standard for their specific corps, were to be discharged. A clipping found in the newspaper of November 1997, and various news reports, put testimony to this.

I never would get to receive my lump sum and pension after 20 years' service, but I did get to do a few worthwhile things whilst in the army.

These things will never be forgotten and the memories will live with me forever.

As for personal achievements:

I was the only 'A' grade shot in my platoon at Kapooka.

I was the best shot at Kapooka.

I qualified as 'marksman' many years running, and proudly wore my 'crossed rifles'.

I was a member of the guard during the Commonwealth Games in Brisbane.

I conducted 3 recon courses.

I was an instructor on 4 recon courses.

I am qualified as an airborne rappel instructor and in suspended extraction.

Nigel B.J. Clayton

I was on the Duke of Gloucester 5 times running and reserve for another.
I received 'student of merit' for my efforts on a recon course.
I received a 'best soldier' award in 8/9RAR.
I received recognition for having the best section in Singleton.
I instructed at the School of Infantry for three years.
I was given the opportunity to train for the SASR.
I served in Malaysia.
I served in PNG as a member of the AATPT.
I served in Rwanda.
I am a trained signaller: blah.
I am trained with mortars, both basic and officer/NCO: yuk.
I served with Mortar Platoon: double blah.
I am fully qualified as Sergeant.

Maybe it is clear, and maybe it is not, but I do honestly value my service in PNG higher than that in Rwanda, though Rwanda is more memorable. I value it more… maybe because we achieved a goal. In Rwanda we had our hands tied and failed to help those most in need.

Does this make sense?

Upgrade

In late 2005 I received information that the service in Rwanda had been upgraded to warlike.

It seems that everyone, especially the politicians and the UN, had underestimated 'everything'. It also helped bring to light what I read in 'Pure Massacre', how several soldiers compared the tour of Rwanda with that of East Timor. East Timor was nothing more than a holiday compared to Rwanda, they agreed; and yet it took so long for the authorities to realise this. And although I can't speak for what service in Rwanda was like when compared to Iraq or Afghanistan, I'm guessing there was a visual gap of difference; just compare Kibeho with Bergen-Belsen; peacetime service with war; and there you might find an answer; but it's not for me to draw any conclusion, but maybe I would like people to understand the truth and reality behind service in Rwanda, and that it was not 'a-piece-of-cake' as everyone back home assumed it to be.

In 2019 we received the Meritorious Unit Citation

Maybe less stringent Rules Of Engagement should have been put in place.

And a last word regards the Returned from Active Service Badge [RASB]. Most guys in the infantry will receive an 'Infantry Combat Badge' [ICB] just for being in a war zone, whether having come under fire or not. I hear someone say, 'so what', and another comment, 'he's only jealous'. This is all beside the point. The point is that I am in the infantry and being so, with a record I consider rather accomplished, it's embarrassing to be considered as non-field force, or anything other than infantry, even for a second. Everyone has a job to fill and all are proud of their corps, as I am of mine. There are guys out there wearing an ICB for being in a war zone but were never fired upon, or never fired a shot in anger; just like me and the others of UNAMIR II. But did we experience combat? But even then, some of the guys did have shots falling all around them as in the book 'The Kibeho Massacre' proves. Believe it or not we are not looked upon as having accomplished anything substantial as it is, and having nothing whatsoever against Vietnam Veterans I hate to say that there are a few there that have even turned their noses up at us for wearing a blue

Nigel B.J. Clayton

beret and RASB. It's as though they don't know the reality of the tour; it's as though we are inferior. I've even heard others comment on veterans of Rwanda as bludgers due to individuals going PTSD, but can you see now why PTSD is so rampant with those of UNAMIR II. Maybe they should do away with a badge completely and award something extra for those that have actually come under fire and did their duty in the face of evil; but as we have seen, evil comes in many different forms.

A Final Word

Cooks always turned out a good meal, and any fun poked in their direction is just that, fun.

I have as much appreciation for the American soldiers as I do any other, but those who have served in a 'combat' zone are the most looked-up-to.

Grunts are not stupid but very smart; otherwise we'd all be led by fools and end up dying for the wrong cause; and rank, in the long-and-short of it all, has little to do with intelligence or common sense.

Women of all calibre are to be looked up to and for the most part, those associated with infantry soldiers in particular are the pillars of men's dreams.

I was extremely fortunate not to have been in Kibeho on 22nd April, as to have been there would have been a great injustice to what I had been taught over the years, and I don't know anyone who was thankful for being there on the 22nd: to have 'wanted' to be there on the day would illustrate just how little you really cared for the people of Rwanda; needless to say that it would have been better if it had never eventuated. I can't imagine what it would feel like to witness so many being massacred before my eyes and then turn my back upon it all, being able to do absolutely nothing about it. It was bad enough witnessing just a few executions, let alone thousands, so I considered myself rather fortunate in regards to that; as for my other experiences... they were to be expected, I suppose. No wonder those poor bastards who witnessed the massacre of over 4,000 IDPs suffer PTSD.

I salute you all; but who am I really to give you such a well-earned compliment, but a broken down machine of little worth.

But something more should be taken away here. If I was on the ground at the time of the main massacre, would I have refrained from opening fire upon the RPA? I don't know if I could have restrained myself, and thankful, I am, not to have been tested in such a way: but would the RPA deserve such bad treatment. There is also one last thing to say. Do I blame the RPA for the massacre at Kibeho? Look at it this way, for just a second; the Hutu killed over a million Tutsi, is it not fair that revenge be performed? If a murderer comes into your home and kills your wife and two kids, will you see him arrested to spend the rest of his life in prison, or would you tie the bastard up and torture him to death? Maybe you believe in 'turning the other cheek' and would allow him to flee, in order to commit such a crime again.

I have nothing more to say.

Glossary

WEAPONS:
Claymore – Anti-personnel mine
M16 – Semi-automatic rifle
M18A1 – see Claymore
M203 – M40 style grenade launcher attached to the undercarriage of the M16
M26 – HE fragmentation grenade
M30 – practise grenade
M60 – GPMG: General Purpose Machine Gun
M79 – grenade launcher (ammo as per M203)
MAG58 – Machine gun
SFMG – Sustain Fire Machine Gun
SLR – Self-Loading Rifle
SRAAW – Short Range Anti Armour Weapon
Minimi – 5.56mm machine gun

RANK:
Boss – Platoon Commander
CO – Commanding Officer
CPL – Corporal
CQ – Company Quartermaster
CSM – Company Sergeant Major
LCPL – Lance Corporal
NCO – Non Commissioned Officer
OC – Officer Commanding
PL COMD – Platoon Commander
RSM – Regimental Sergeant Major
SGT – Sergeant
SSGT – Staff Sergeant
2IC – Second in command

OTHER:
Admin COY – TPT, Medical, Cooks, Q-store…
AJ – Army Jerk
AO – Area of Operations
APC – Armoured Personnel Carrier
AWOL – Absent Without Leave
BFA – Blank Firing Attachment
BFT – Battle Fitness Test
BHQ – Battalion Headquarters
BN – Battalion (consists of 3-4 rifle companies, HQ element, Administration Coy, Spt Coy)
BRA – Bougainville Republican Army
BRL – Battalion Recreational Leave
CCP – Casualty Clearing Post
CES – Complete Equipment Schedule
CFT – Combat Fitness Test – the old BFT
Coy – Company (3 platoons + HQ element)
CP – Command Post
DIV – Division
DS – Directing Staff
ERT – Extra Regimental training
FSB – Fire Support Base
FUP – Forming up place
HE – High explosive
HQ – Headquarters
IA – Immediate Action
ID – Identification
IDP – Internally Displaced Persons
IET – Initial Employment Training
INT – Intelligence
JNCO – Junior Non Commissioned Officer Training
LUP – Lying Up Place (for admin/sleep)
MIL OBS – Military Observer
MP – Military Police
NGO – Non-Government Organisations
ODF – Operational Deployment Force

OP – Observation Post
OR – Other ranks (PTE, CPL and below)
PL – Platoon (3 sections and HQ element)
Pogo – Non field-force
POW – Prisoner of War
PT – Physical training
PTI – Physical Training Instructor
QRF – Quick Reaction Force
RAAF – Royal Australian Air Force
RAP – Regimental Aid Post (medical)
RAR – Royal Australian Regiment
Rascals – Group of criminals
RMO – Regimental Medical Officer
RPA – Rwandan Patriotic Army
SAS/R – Special Air Service Regiment
Scheds – Scheduled communications via radio
SECT – (approx 9-10 men)
SIB – Special Investigation Branch
SOP – Standard Operational Procedure
SPT Coy – supports the battalion to which it is attached (consists of Hvy Wpns Pl,
Recon Pl, Pioneer Pl, Mortar Pl,
Signals Pl)
SRT – Scout Regiment Telescope
SWBTA – Shoalwater Bay Training Area
TOET – Test of Elementary Training
TPT PL – Transport Platoon providing direct assistance to the Battalion attached to
UD – Unauthorised Discharge – of weapon
UH1H – Helicopter
Wantok – Friend/Comrade

www.ingramcontent.com/pod-product-compliance
Lightning Source LLC
Chambersburg PA
CBHW032031290426
44110CB00012B/762